The
Illustrated History
of IRELAND

The
Illustrated History
of IRELAND

✤

SEÁN DUFFY

Contemporary Books

Chicago   New York   San Francisco   Lisbon   London   Madrid   Mexico City
Milan   New Delhi   San Juan   Seoul   Singapore   Sydney   Toronto

Library of Congress Cataloging-in-Publication Data

Duffy, Seán.
   [Concise history of Ireland] The illustrated history of Ireland / Seán Duffy.
      p.   cm.
   Originally published as "The concise history of Ireland". Derbyshire, England:
Arcadia Editions Limited, 2000.
   Includes index.
   ISBN 0-8092-2437-2
   1. Ireland—History.   I. Title.

DA911.D77   2000
941.5—dc21   00-34552

Contemporary Books
A Division of The McGraw-Hill Companies

First published as *The Concise History of Ireland* in the United Kingdom and Ireland by
Gill & Macmillan Ltd., Hume Avenue, Park West, Dublin 12, Ireland.

The moral right of the author has been asserted.

1 2 3 4 5 6 7 8 9 0   0 9 8 7 6 5 4 3 2 1

ISBN 0-8092-2437-2

This book was set in Sabon and Trajan by Arcadia Editions Limited
Printed and bound by Bath Press Colourbooks, Great Britain

Jacket design by Monica Baziuk
Front-jacket photograph by Fiona Gunn
Navan Fort burial mound photo by Dept. of the Environment, Northern Ireland
Portal tomb at Kernanstown photo from the National Museum of Ireland
Sackville Street, Dublin, photo from the National Gallery of Ireland
Broighter collar photo by the National Museum of Ireland
Design, cartography, and picture research by Arcadia Editions Limited.
The picture credits on page 256 constitute an extension of this copyright page.

McGraw-Hill books are available at special quantity discounts to use as premiums and
sales promotions, or for use in corporate training programs. For more information, please
write to the Director of Special Sales, Professional Publishing, McGraw-Hill, Two Penn
Plaza, New York, NY 10121-2298. Or contact your local bookstore.

This book is printed on acid-free paper.

CONTENTS

INTRODUCTION
IRELAND AND THE IRISH

Let Erin remember the days of old,
Ere her faithless sons betray'd her;
When Malachy wore the collar of gold,
Which he won from her proud invader,
When her kings, with standards of green unfurl'd,
Led the Red Branch Knights to danger;
Ere the emerald gem of the Western World
Was set in the crown of a stranger.

The above oft-quoted lines from Ireland's greatest (and nowadays, sadly, all too neglected) romantic lyricist, Thomas Moore (1779–1852), splendidly capture the urge of the Irish to remember their past however rose- (or green-) tinted the glasses, to celebrate a supposed lost Golden Age, and to lament the many years of presumed subjection to foreign tyranny. The people of Ireland are indeed very conscious of (perhaps, some would say, obsessed by) their history. Go into almost any book shop in Ireland and you will find that the Irish history section has some of the most cluttered shelves in the store. Read the weekly bestseller lists for Ireland and you will find a goodly number of the top ten non-fiction works are books on the history of this little country called Ireland.

Yet, it might be an interesting experiment to stop, let us say, one hundred Irish people in the street and, employing the methods of the modern opinion pollster or market researcher, ask them how their country got its name, where this name 'Ireland' comes from. Most would perhaps know that it has something to do with the Irish name for the island, *Éire*, and some that it is simply a compound of Éire and the Old Norse or Old English word *land*: Éire+land = Éireland, and hence Ireland.

But where does *Éire* come from? One of the ancient peoples of Ireland, dominant in the period from which no contemporary written records survive, were the Érainn who lived in what is now Munster. The first trace of them we have is the mention of a people called the *Iverni* in the very first detailed account of Ireland ever written, that by Ptolemy of Alexandria, the famous Greek geographer, compiled soon after AD 100. It is this tribe that seems to have given its name to the whole island and which in Old Irish (say, in the period AD 650–900) was spelt *Ériu* and, as we have seen, is now spelt *Éire*.

This word, like the Irish language itself, is Indo-European in origin, and it has been speculated that it may mean 'fertile country'. *Ériu* is the nominative case of a noun whose dative and genitive forms are *Éirinn* and *Éireann* respectively, and these have given us the Anglicised and romantic name Erin, as appears in Thomas Moore's lovely song and in so many others, but they probably also explain why classical Greek writers referred to the island as *Ierne*, which in turn may have become corrupted to provide the Romans with the name *Hibernia*, usually translated as 'land of winter'.

As to the inhabitants of this 'land of winter', many people would perhaps be surprised to hear that in medieval times they had no concept of themselves as 'Celts', although many of them were undoubtedly of Celtic origin. We do, however, know from the voluminous writings which they began to leave behind them, following the introduction of the written word which came in the wake of Christianity in the fifth century, that the Irish had a strong sense of belonging to one nation. But they didn't call themselves 'the Irish', the inhabitants of Ireland, they called themselves the *Goídil* (or

Scotti in Latin), which gives us the modern Anglicised forms Gaels and Scots. And the thing that helped to intensify their sense of nationhood more so than anything else was the fact that they all spoke a common language, *Goídelg*, which in Modern Irish is spelt *Gaeilge*.

This latter point is of crucial importance. The Goídil were not the inhabitants of Ireland *per se*, but rather the speakers of the Irish language. And, since the early centuries AD, these included a considerable portion of the population of what is now Scotland. The latter were people from Ireland (known as the Dál Riata) who migrated across the North Channel from the Glens of Antrim and settled in Argyll and the Hebrides, and were, understandably, regarded by others as Gaels/Scots. In the course of time, the territory they conquered in northern Britain was given a name derived from them: it became *Scotia*, or Scotland as it now is, but the homeland of the Goídil was, however, the island of Ireland, the Goídil of Scotland being regarded as exiles.

Most nations try to explain, for themselves, for other peoples distinct from them, and for the benefit of future generations, where they think – or would like the world to think – they came from. And we know that by the seventh century the Irish had devised a pre-history of their own nation (culminating in the composition of a set of myths known as the *Lebor Gabála Érenn*, 'The Book of the Taking of Ireland'), in which the various tribes and dynasties of the Gaels were all linked by a common line of descent. The mythical ancestor-figure chosen by them was a man called Míl, or Milesius, of Spain, whose sons first settled in Ireland, and hence the Irish are sometimes euphemistically known as the Milesians. From Míl of Spain they traced themselves back further to Egypt, to the daughter of Pharaoh, a woman called Scota, from whom the Latin name of this people and their new homeland derives – the Scotti and Scotia respectively – whose husband, Gaythelos or Gáedel Glas conveniently gives us the Irish name for them and their language, and, of course, all are then traced back all the way to Noah and Adam!

As origin-legends go, it is a lovely story, but it is no more than that. Nevertheless, it goes to show the emphasis that the early Irish placed on who they were, and how they got to be where they were, and so demonstrates a strong desire to reinforce their separateness, so to speak, from other nations. However, it should be stressed that in spite of this sense of national unity, early medieval Ireland was notoriously divided politically, although the leading dynasty in the country, the Uí Néill, who traced their origin back – rightly or wrongly – to the semi-legendary Niall of the Nine Hostages, were able to exploit this sense of common ancestry. They asserted the existence of a high-kingship which they claimed was rightfully theirs, and which had its symbolic capital at Tara. And their propaganda eventually won out, so that by, let us say, the end of the first millennium AD – and, in truth, the perception has not changed greatly in the course of the second millennium – most people in Ireland believed that Tara was the ancient capital of Ireland: Ireland was one nation, with one ecclesiastical capital at Armagh, within the territory of the Uí Néill, and one political and symbolic capital at Tara. Whether it was true or not is another matter: what mattered is that people believed it.

This Irish awareness of their racial distinctiveness was heightened when, in the ninth century, the island suffered sustained Viking assault, which at times looked likely to overwhelm the country, and which saw the establishment of a number of enclaves and towns, including the eventual capital of the country, Dublin. Although they were gradually integrated into Irish society, becoming Christian, marrying into Irish dynasties, sometimes adopting Gaelic personal names and commissioning Gaelic verse, the Vikings continued to be regarded as *Gaill*, 'foreigners', until, in the late twelfth century, Ireland was again invaded and colonised, this time by people of Anglo-Norman origin. The communities of Viking extraction were absorbed by the new settlers (some of them gaining recognition as Englishmen in the eyes of the law, a law denied for the most part to the native Irish) and, to the Irish, it was the English colonists who were now the *Gaill*.

Society in later medieval Ireland was, therefore, once again dominated as it had been during the Viking Age by two peoples regarding themselves as distinct nations, whose relationship was dogged by racial antagonism. Although in time many of them too were assimilated into Irish life (and, indeed, were dubbed 'the middle nation' by the Irish author of a complaint against their oppression sent to the Pope in 1317), the new colonists never, in the medieval period, came to see themselves as Irish, preferring to call themselves 'the English of the land of Ireland', though they were gradually becoming increasingly similar to the Irish in their daily lives, and foreigners found it hard to distinguish between them.

The English government in later medieval Ireland repeatedly legislated to prevent further acculturation, most infamously in the Statutes of Kilkenny (1366), though this proved largely ineffective. In the late Middle Ages, elements of a separatist tendency began to emerge among the Anglo-Irish, which manifested itself in an irritation at day-to-day interference by the English government, and a feeling that they should be allowed to legislate for their own affairs without having to look to Westminster for approval. But their sense of Englishness nevertheless remained uppermost, and they only began to merge with the native population when, from the mid-sixteenth century onwards, both faced the prospect of dispossession by a new wave of English Protestant plantation.

The divisions that have bedevilled Ireland in the last four centuries are largely a product of this new religious dimension. Earlier generations of settlers in Ireland could, in time, begin to make common cause with those who had been there before them because the divisions of blood could be ended by intermarriage and the divisions of language and culture by mutual assimilation. The Normans, however superior they believed their society and culture to be by comparison with that of the native Irish, understood that one thing would always bring them together, their religion. In an age when there was only one great divide in Christendom, that between East and West, both were firmly and proudly part of the Western Church.

In the aftermath of the Protestant Reformation, however, divisions greater than those between East and West existed within the latter, and those divisions were played out violently and protractedly on the soil of Ireland. The last great struggle waged by the native Irish to try to overturn this new English Protestant domination was the Nine Years' War (1593–1603) but the armies of Hugh O'Neill and Red Hugh O'Donnell, in spite of some spectacular victories, were overthrown at Kinsale in 1601 and when they and their followers left Ireland for good, on 4 September 1607, in what has become known as the Flight of the Earls, the Gaelic order of which they were part ceased to be.

The century that followed was perhaps the bloodiest in Ireland's history and by its end the seeds of future conflicts which have lingered into our own day were yielding forth their bitter fruit. Ulster in particular had been extensively 'planted' with settlers from England and Scotland, the latter predominantly Presbyterian, but a disinherited and resentful native population survived in sufficient numbers to mean that life in the new Ulster was unlikely to remain trouble-free for long. The 1641 rebellion showed quite how violent the reaction could be and though the Cromwellian and Williamite settlements sought to remove the risk to colonial stability by reducing ever further the rights and property-holdings of the majority Catholic population, culminating in the various legislative restraints introduced in the early eighteenth century known as the Penal Laws, that threat never waned.

This was demonstrated most forcibly when the ripple effects of the American and French Revolutions reached Ireland's shores and led to large-scale rebellion in 1798, and Robert Emmet's aborted rising five years later. In the interval, the response of the British government to Irish unrest had been to abolish the Irish Parliament under the Act of Union of 1800. Although it had always been an instrument of colonial policy and a symbol of the power of the colonists, nevertheless the loss of the parliament appeared in time, even to Catholics, as another nail in the coffin of Ireland's independence, and when they secured full rights of citizenship by the enactment of Catholic Emancipation in 1827, under the remarkable leadership of Daniel O'Connell, repeal of the Act of Union became the goal of Nationalist Ireland.

In this, O'Connell failed and, amidst the cataclysm of the Great Famine (1845–49) others, notably the romantic leaders of the Young Ireland movement, began to believe that peaceful agitation would not suffice, though their rebellion in 1848 and that of their successors, the Fenians, in 1867 secured no practical advance. Ireland's cause later found an unlikely champion in the British Prime Minister himself, W. E. Gladstone, while in Ireland, and on the floor of the British House of Commons, Home Rule as it was now called was energetically fought for by a new Nationalist leader, Charles Stewart Parnell. He joined forces with Michael Davitt's Land League to secure the rights of Irish tenant farmers to better terms, including, ultimately, the right to own their own land, but the attainment of self-government eluded him.

By the time Home Rule was finally and grudgingly conceded on the eve of the First World War it was too late for another generation of idealistic young men and women, who believed that the establishment of a Republic was the only answer to Ireland's problems, and a protest in arms the only way to achieve it. Their Rising in 1916 may have failed in the short term but it led to a bloody Anglo-Irish war (1919–21) and eventually to the concession of an Irish Free State, admittedly one whose powers were circumscribed, at least to begin with. The Anglo-Irish Treaty signed on 6 December 1921 appeared to give the Irish that which they had sought since they became subject to English rule in the late twelfth century, but the settlement fell far short of the independent Republic which had become the ideal for many and a tragic, if short-lived, Civil War (1922–23) followed its ratification.

But more damaging in the long run than the Civil War was the decision to exclude from the Free State six of Ireland's 32 counties – those in the north-east which had the most substantial Protestant populations and where opposition to independence was strongest, largely out of fear of domination by the Catholic majority. The problem with this attempted solution was that the great majority of people in the other 26 counties were unwilling to accept the partition of their country for long, while even within the boundaries of the six-county statelet that became known as Northern Ireland a very considerable minority felt likewise. The only way that the northern state could survive was by keeping the southern government at arm's length and the Catholic minority underfoot, and this it managed to do, with only limited violent or public protest, for over forty years.

It may not be true to say that an outburst of such protest was inevitable, and given a more tolerant regime in the North it is impossible to say what accommodation might have been reached. But the regime that ruled from Stormont, until it was prorogued by the British government in 1972, was anything but tolerant. It was brought to an end because of its inability to reform itself and its unwillingness to grant full Civil Rights and a proportionate share of power to the Catholic nationalist minority.

If, however, anything is inevitable it is that the failure to satisfy a modest request will stimulate more radical demands, and a deaf ear turned to peaceful protests will encourage a resort to other methods. For most of the last third of the twentieth century, therefore, the streets and country roads, housing estates and farmyard ditches of the six partitioned counties of Ulster have been the scene of a lamentable and tragic little war which nobody could ever hope to win. The twenty-first century, however, looks brighter – we can but look on in hope. The words of another rather less well-known song of Thomas Moore spring to mind:

Erin, thy silent tear never shall cease,
Erin, thy languid smile ne'er shall increase,
Till, like the rainbow's light,
Thy various tints unite,
And form in heaven's sight
One arch of peace!

Seán Duffy
Author

N

0   20 km
0   20 miles

Malin Head

Rathlin I.

North Channel

55°

Loch
Swilly

Lough
Foyle

U l s t e r

Rossan Point

Belfast Lough

Donegal Bay

Lough
Erne

Lough
Neagh

Erris Head

Sligo Bay

Upper
Lough
Erne

54°

Achill Head

Dundalk Bay

Clew Bay

*Irish
Sea*

Lough
Mask

C o n n a c h t

Shannon

M e a t h

Slyne Head

Lough
Corrib

Lough
Ree

Galway Bay

Liffey

Dublin Bay

Aran Is.

53°

Lough
Derg

*A T L A N T I C
O C E A N*

Shannon

Barrow

L e i n s t e r

Shannon

Nore

Suir

M u n s t e r

Carnsore Point

Dingle Bay

Blackwater

52°

Lee

Youghal Bay

St George's Channel

Bantry Bay

Mizen Head

Stone Age Ireland

• Early Mesolithic sites

• Later Mesolithic sites

CHAPTER I

BEFORE HISTORY

For all the richness and variety of its prehistoric remains, Ireland is a country still quite new to man. Although there has been a human presence on this planet for perhaps as much as 1.7 million years (at the latest estimate), only within the last 9,000 years or so has man made his way to Ireland. While civilisations flourished in Africa, and mankind spread northwards through Iberia, eastwards along the Danube valley, and to the eastern shores of the Mediterranean and beyond, none thought to venture as far as Ireland. Even after the mammoth-hunters of the Eurasian landmass had traversed the Bering Strait into the Americas and journeyed another ten thousand miles to the plains of Patagonia, Ireland went untouched.

This is all the more remarkable in view of the fact that there may have been near-neighbours inhabiting what is now the south of England a quarter (if not a half) million years ago. The latter were able to do so for one simple reason: this area was not covered by ice, whereas much of Ireland was for long in the grip of a perennial frost and shrouded in an extensive ice-cover. At the peaks of cold it could harbour very little life and would have resembled a sparse treeless tundra, though there were warmer interludes with sufficient vegetation to support reindeer and woolly mammoths, and, as the ice-retreat finally got underway perhaps 13,000 years ago, it provided a salubrious habitat for that magnificent animal, the great Irish deer.

It must have been the fluctuating 'thaw–freeze–thaw' conditions towards the end of the last Ice Age that brought about the extinction of the great deer, but in compensation the warm conditions which stabilised about 10,000 years ago and in which we still live witnessed a massive immigration of new plants and animals into Ireland, carried perhaps by sea or wind or birds, or across a now submerged land-bridge. In the post-glacial millennia Ireland provided a home for juniper and willow which could tolerate its poor soil conditions but, as the latter improved with the benefit of centuries of organic decomposition, birch and hazel woodland began to prosper; these in turn competed for primacy with the Scots pine, the elm, and the oak, and alder and ash too made their appearance in what was, by say 5000 BC, a dense primeval forest cover.

The variety of flora available enhanced the faunal environment

The Irish Giant Deer (Megaloceros giganteus) reached the zenith of its success perhaps some 12,000 years ago, but was struck down in its prime by a dramatic climatic deterioration which destroyed the grasslands upon which it depended. It stood about 2m high at the shoulder, or over 3m in the case of the male whose magnificent antlers, spanning almost another 3m, were frail and more for show than combat.

by providing fodder for herbivores and cover for predators and their prey, so that in time Ireland's grasslands and forest sustained for several millennia the now extinct brown bear and wolf, wild boar and wild cat, as well as the badger, fox, hare, otter, pine marten, pigmy shrew, red squirrel, stoat, wild pig and humble woodmouse.

The First Irishmen

It was, of course, this variety of fauna, together with the birds of the air and the fish in her rivers and around her coasts, that finally made Ireland attractive to humans. Where these first people came from, and when precisely they came, we can but guess at. If they arrived initially as hunters in pursuit of Ireland's hitherto unexploited animal-life and gatherers of the fruit of her trees, they are not likely to have travelled far, and were probably mere wanderers from what is now Britain. If their tools, containers, clothing and sleeping-quarters were made of wood or any form of plant-life or animal skins, they will long since have disintegrated, and even their very bones may have been dissolved by Ireland's often acidic soil. So it is quite possible that we will never find traces of the earliest bands of hunters and foragers to visit Ireland's shores.

Only those who left something indestructible behind can be traced, and since there are few things more durable than stone, the earliest known occupants of Ireland are those whose stone tools have since been found. Flint, a type of quartz that occurs in chalk, can be chipped to produce a very simple tool with a blade-like edge, excellent for chopping plants, scraping the hides from animals, and dismembering their carcasses, or it can be attached to wood to give an axe or arrow head, or a knife, or set as barbs into the shaft of a harpoon. Vast numbers of these flint tools and weapons have been discovered in Ireland over the years, often by amateur collectors in newly-ploughed fields or by the banks of rivers, and as such they cannot tell us much about their original owners. But when a number of them are found together they can help pinpoint the location of an early flint-using community or even, if there are quantities of discarded flint nearby, a Stone Age craftsman at work!

Mount Sandel, Co. Derry, has been helping to throw light on the lifestyle of Ireland's earliest known Mesolithic hunters and foragers for more than a century, partly as a result of the discovery of vast numbers of flint tools, including microliths, used for hunting and skinning of prey.

Mesolithic Hunters

This particular period of the Stone Age is known as the Mesolithic, from the

Greek words *mesos* meaning 'middle' and *lithos* meaning 'stone', and many of the earliest mesolithic sites in Ireland are found in the north-eastern corner of the country, around Lough Neagh and northwards along the Lower Bann, as well as elsewhere in Antrim and Down, especially the Strangford Lough area. This might at first suggest that the earliest settlers in Ireland were based here, but it is not quite as simple as that: flint, as we have seen, is found in chalk, and the best chalk deposits in Ireland are located in this area, where, millions of years ago, they were trapped beneath basalt, the solidified volcanic lava which has given the area its greatest natural wonder, the Giant's Causeway. If many mesolithic sites have been discovered in this corner of Ireland it is partly because a piece of worked flint is readily recognisable as such. Elsewhere in the country, where flint was harder to come by, mesolithic tools and weapons were often made from other less easily-recognised materials: the mesolithic hunter was there alright, he's simply harder to track down.

The most famous of these mesolithic sites in the north-east is Mount Sandel, near Coleraine, Co. Derry, where archaeological excavations in the 1970s yielded important evidence of early human settlement, in fact, the earliest man-made structures hitherto known in Ireland. Radiocarbon tests have shown that they belong to the period from *c.* 7010–6490 BC. They would have been no more than huts and the only traces to survive were the hearth near their centre and a ring of holes in the ground where posts and stakes had been driven in and then perhaps curved over to produce a circular tent, possibly roofed with animal hides. The remains of up to ten huts in all were found, including four of these little dome-shaped ones, each about 6m (20ft) across, while the burnt remains of the hearth, around which the occupants would have gathered for warmth or perhaps to cook, were about 1m across. But what is most interesting about them is that the four huts were built on top of one another, and so were not in use at the same time. The implications of this are significant: it means that these early mesolithic people did not simply wander aimlessly around; they returned to Mount Sandel and rebuilt their huts in the same location over a number of seasons. There was therefore a pattern to their lives, dictated no doubt by the seasons and by the availability of food.

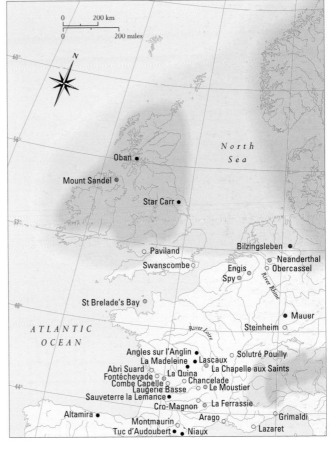

Earliest People and Settlement

ice cover

         c. 300000–200000 BC

         c. 110000–15000 BC

sites

●   Australopithecus advanced

◉   classical Neanderthal man

○   modern man of the late Upper Pleistocene

●   site important both before and after the climatic change of *c.* 10000 BC

●   important early Irish site

As it happens, we know what the Mount Sandel community ate because many pits were found on their camp-site which might have originally been dug to store food (some had traces of burnt hazel-nut shells), but later became filled with the site's rubbish. Burnt mammal bones turned out to be almost exclusively those of wild pig and the occasional hare, testimony to the community's hunting skills, while the bones of wood pigeon, mallard, snipe, thrush, grouse, and even eagle and goshawk, indicate that they were well equipped to trap birds. But on a site overlooking the River Bann and just a few miles upstream from the sea, it is not surprising to find that the plentiful seasonal supplies of salmon, trout, eel and sea bass were heavily exploited. In fact, analysis suggests that eighty-one per cent of the identifiable bone remains at Mount Sandel were those of fish, fifteen per cent of mammal, and four per cent birds. The array of food supplies available was such that this may well have been an all-year-round settlement: the salmon-remains indicate that the Mount Sandel people fished there in spring and summer, whereas eels run downstream in the autumn; at this point the hazel nuts would have been ripening, and could have been stored for winter, during which the pigs, which appear to have been young when slaughtered, would have sustained the inhabitants through the lean season.

Because flint is scarce in the Irish midlands, the tools found at a similar camp-site discovered beneath the bog at Lough Boora, near Kilcormac, Co. Offaly, were made of a darker kind of quartz called chert found in the local limestone. However, they are very much like the worked flints from Mount Sandel and to other similar stone blades or 'microliths' which have been found, for example, along the banks of the River Blackwater, near Cappoquin, Co. Waterford. These are characteristic of the early-mesolithic period, approximately 7000–5500 BC, and prove that Ireland's earliest mesolithic families were not confined to the north-east but dispersed about the island.

The Later Mesolithic Period

The reason that prehistorians distinguish between the early and the later mesolithic is because after about the year 5500 BC a noticeable change takes place in the type of stone tools and weapons being used by Ireland's inhabitants, and also in the technique that was employed to make them. Small and narrow blades, which would have been made using quite a sophisticated hammer-and-chisel device, were abandoned, and – in what would appear to be a backward step – replaced with larger and heavier flint flakes produced by simply hitting a block of flint directly with a hard stone such as quartzite. Likewise, small flint axes were replaced by a larger type of axe, not necessarily made of flint but of schist or mudstone perhaps, and sometimes polished.

In many respects we know more about the early than the later mesolithic in Ireland, partly because no site as exciting as Mount Sandel has thus far been excavated. Perhaps the most revealing is Newferry, again on the Bann, to the south of Portglenone, Co. Antrim. It has produced radiocarbon dates from its various layers stretching from 5500 to 3500 BC; in other words, there was human settlement here (though perhaps intermittently) throughout all of the later mesolithic, covering a period of 2,000 years. Newferry is most important for the range of stone implements it has revealed, from the occasional narrow microlith at its lowest levels, showing the continuity from the early mesolithic, to the broader type of tool associated with the later period, especially the classic 'Bann flake', a leaf-shaped instrument similar to a spearhead, many thousands of which have been found in Antrim and scattered throughout Ireland.

However, given that Newferry was occupied for at least two thousand years, perhaps one of the most surprising features is just how little change occurred on the site, at least in terms of technology as reflected in the range of stone implements employed by its inhabitants, and their method of manufacture. It suggests a community which lived for two or more millennia having little contact with the outside world. But a discovery among the silt and gravel at the uppermost layer of the Newferry site indicates that a massive change was by then underway: sherds of clay pottery point to a new dawn, the beginning of the neolithic period.

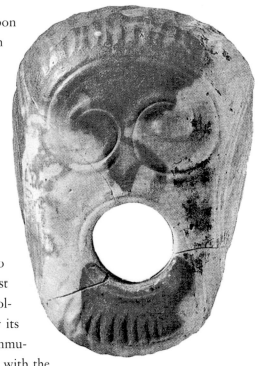

This ceremonial macehead is made from flint and highly polished. It was found in the eastern tomb of the massive Neolithic tumulus at Knowth, Co. Meath. It is one of the most impressive objects to survive from prehistoric Ireland and may well have been imported from Britain or further afield.

Neolithic Newcomers

Some time around 4000 BC a dramatic change took effect in Ireland. In place of the earlier evidence of small bands of animal-hunters and fruit-gatherers, living a necessarily migratory existence, we start to find signs of forest-clearance, the practice of agriculture, and communities living a more sedentary lifestyle, as they chose to live close to crops which they themselves had planted and animals which they themselves had domesticated. One method of detecting this change is pollen-analysis. Trapped in the peat of bogs and the mud of lake-beds are successive generations of pollen-grains which have been accumulating for centuries, and scientists can arrive at a very clear picture of vegetational change at such locations by taking a vertical series of samples of these grains from the top to the very bottom of the deposit, and identifying and counting each type, which can then be submitted to radiocarbon analysis for dating purposes.

For instance, an analysis of pollen from a site at Ballynagilly, near Cookstown, Co. Tyrone, showed that at about 3900 BC there was a noticeable decline in the pollen of elm and pine and an increase in that of grass and the weed ribwort plantain, as well as some cereal: it seems a reasonable conclusion that there was a farming community in this area about 5,900 years ago who were clearing the land of trees, growing some crops in the newly-cleared fields, and most probably grazing stock on newly-created pastures. Not far away at Beaghmore a similar

The first pollen diagram is from Scragh Bog, near Lough Owel, Co. Westmeath. It shows a marked decline in elm coinciding with an increase in the beginnings of arable farming and grazing. The second, from Lough Sheeauns in north-west Connemara, shows a similar growth in grasses and weeds, coinciding with a decline in oak, elm and hazel (after O'Connell).

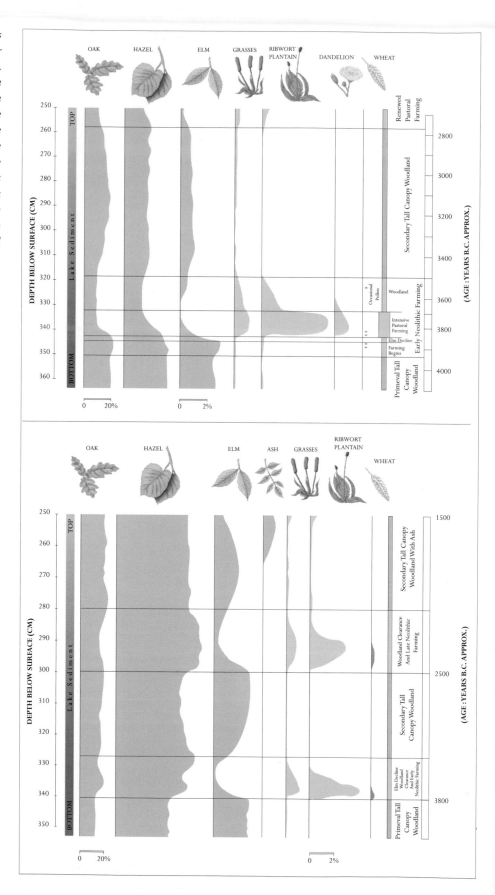

picture emerges. Pollen-analysis indicates that starting at about 3800 BC there was a period of at least a century of clearance of oak, pine and especially elm (though something like the modern Dutch elm disease could account for the huge decrease in the latter at this time both in Ireland and elsewhere). There was also some cereal cultivation over a period of several centuries, more perhaps than the results indicate because its pollen does not disperse very well, an impression reinforced by the presence at this and other sites of pollen from nettle, dock and ribwort, weeds associated with arable farming. At Beaghmore there was also a considerable rise in grass pollen and this suggests that grazing, probably cattle-rearing, was becoming an important part of the economy.

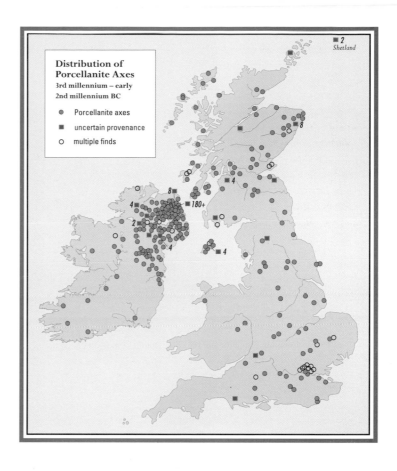

These County Tyrone findings have been replicated throughout the country and the change is so sudden and so consistent that there seems no reason to doubt that we are entering a new phase in Ireland's story – one which prehistorians call the neolithic – very probably brought about by the arrival of a new wave of immigrants. Where they came from is unknown, but since they seem to have brought with them Ireland's first domesticated cattle and sheep or goats, in what were probably very small sailing-craft, it does seem unlikely that they travelled a great distance by sea. They need not necessarily have come as part of a large-scale 'invasion', and perhaps only small groups of people strayed into Ireland over the course of a long period of time, possessing more advanced technology and a quite different lifestyle from that of the mesolithic communities already there. And they need not necessarily have 'conquered' or eliminated the latter, who may simply have adapted themselves to the newcomers' way of life. The truth is that the answers to these and many other questions about Ireland's neolithic are, and are likely to remain, a mystery.

At Tievebulliagh, almost a mile up the side of a mountain near Cushendall, Co. Antrim, outcrops of porcellanite were exploited to produce polished axeheads from which a thriving export trade developed. The map shows their distribution as far south as Kent in England.

Neolithic Homes and Farmsteads

The houses in which Ireland's neolithic people lived are not easy to locate since they were generally made of timber and leave few traces on the surface, but some examples have been found, including one found in the 1960s buried beneath the blanket bog at the Ballynagilly site in Co. Tyrone, which carbon-

Neolithic house foundations at Corbally, Co. Kildare. In the foreground is the smallest of the three houses, the two larger buildings lying alongside each other in the background, both of which have two separate rooms. The walls were made of upright posts set into deep foundation trenches, as shown. (Photo: A. Purcell)

dating techniques show was constructed at about the time that the surrounding forest was being cleared (*c.* 3900 BC). It was roughly square in shape (6m x 6m), the walls being made of oak planks set into a trench, and there were traces of internal holes in the floor surface where posts holding up the roof may have stood. It had an open hearth at its centre, and in a shallow pit elsewhere within the house archaeologists found several well-executed flint arrowheads shaped like a leaf, and fragments of pottery from simple bowls with a round bottom and a curved rim.

By the mid-1980s the foundations of seven such similarly elaborate neolithic houses had been discovered, including one at Tankardstown, near Kilmallock, Co. Limerick, again roughly square in shape (7.4m x 6.4m), and likewise built of split oak planks set into foundation trenches, but with strong corner posts and both internal and external uprights to give the roof and walls added support. This house also seems to have had a central hearth, and once again the finds included pottery sherds, a leaf-shaped flint arrowhead, and, crucially, charred grains of wheat to indicate that its occupants were agriculturists. Radiocarbon tests suggested it was lived in somewhere in the period 3938–3378 BC. When a quite similar house was later excavated at Ballygalley, north of Larne, Co. Antrim, not only were quantities of cereal grain found but at least seven querns (stone hand mills for grinding corn), showing how central grain-production was to the community.

Tools from the latter site were made of pitchstone from the island of Arran off the coast of Scotland and possibly also Cornish greenstone, as well as two stone axes from Cumbria, a strong indicator of what appears to be Ireland's new-found contact with the outside world in this age. The point is well demonstrated from the distribution of Irish polished stone axes, the archetypal tool of the Irish neolithic. Over 18,000 of them have been recovered, more than half of which are made from a blue-grey stone called porcellanite found at Tievebulliagh, near Cushendall, Co. Antrim, and on Rathlin Island: the product of these 'axe factories' is found not only elsewhere in Ireland (though predominantly the north-east) but in the Isle of Man and the Northern and Western Isles of Scotland, in Scotland itself, and scattered all the way to the far south-east coast of England. How they found their way there must forever remain a mystery.

It is a reminder, though, that we should not underestimate the sophistication of what we sometimes pejoratively call Stone Age man. Another insight into that world is provided by the houses at Tankardstown and Ballygalley because in both instances a second house was found nearby, 20m (65ft) and 30m (97ft) away respectively, which is suggestive of communal settlement. Then in 1998, at Corbally, near Kilcullen, Co. Kildare, the sites of three neolithic houses were discovered in close proximity. The smallest, similar in size to others found

The best known of the Irish passage tombs, Newgrange, at the heart of the mythological Brú na Bóinne, has been a source of investigation and wonder since the 17th century, and is the most stunning testament to the sophistication of Ireland's Neolithic architects. The photograph shows the spiral decorations on the passage wall, looking from the central chamber towards the entrance.

elsewhere, is situated 12m apart from the other two, which are very alike and lie precisely end-to-end only 3m apart, for all the world like detached bungalows along a roadside. As usual, all three are made of posts and planks set into deep foundation trenches, with internal and external roof-supports, but both of the larger houses (one 11m x 6m, the other 11m x 5m) are divided into two rooms separated by a deep trench like that along the perimeter walls, and in both instances there are hearths in the larger of the two rooms. Another curious fact is that, in the case of all three houses, the entrances were in the south-eastern end walls, which, coincidentally or otherwise, look towards nearby Silliott Hill, the location of an ancient 'ring-barrow' or burial mound. These are comparatively highly evolved structures, where design is standardised, activities are compartmentalised, and, perhaps, individuals segregated. They were constructed to an advanced formula with a view to longevity (hence the metre-deep foundation trenches at Corbally in which the wall-planks were embedded), and are gauges of a settled and sophisticated community.

Those who, in the Neolithic period, first migrated to locations in Ireland which were blanketed in virgin forest may have started out as just a cluster of individuals, but they came to form a community when together they began to clear the forest and to engage in the cultivation of crops and the breeding of livestock. If the grouping of houses side by side is one indication of communal association, a far more dramatic demonstration of cooperative activity is the massive complex of field-systems stretching over several townlands near Ballycastle, Co. Mayo, known collectively as the Céide Fields. Here, years of painstaking probing have revealed that hidden as much as 4m beneath the modern surface of the bog are lines of roughly parallel stone walls up to 2km (1¼ miles) long and 200m apart, stretching inland from the sea, and joined at intervals by cross walls like the rungs of a ladder, forming in effect rectangular fields of up to 7 hectares (17 acres) in area.

Although it is likely that the field-system was developed for the purposes of stock-raising, pollen analysis suggests that some of the land may have been under crops, and that the Céide Fields area saw an intensive period of farming spanning some 500 years from about 3700 to 3200 BC, but that by the year 2700 the blanket bog had begun to bury the whole complex. Bearing in mind the communal effort that was involved in their construction, the evident need for subdivision of property, and the large-scale and integrated agricultural system to which they testify, the Céide Fields are proof that the farmers of neolithic Ireland were not transient exploiters of hitherto untapped resources, but long-standing communities rooted in their locality.

Megalithic Monuments and Tombs

However impressive the excavated remains of the houses in which Ireland's neolithic people lived, they are as nothing compared with the efforts to which they went to secure the memory of their dead. At least 1,500 of their tombs still survive in Ireland today, and not without reason are they called megaliths (from the Greek *megas*, meaning huge, and *lithos*, a stone). There are four basic types of megalithic monument in Ireland, as well as some variations on the theme: about 230 (15 per cent) are what are termed passage tombs; there are about 400 (26 per cent) court tombs, about 175 (12 per cent) portal tombs, about 500 (33 per cent) wedge tombs, and about 200 (14 per cent) unclassified.

Newgrange and its Rivals

The passage tombs include some of the most spectacular of Ireland's ancient monuments, and those in the Boyne Valley in Co. Meath, Newgrange being the most remarkable, rank among the world's first great architectural masterpieces, being probably several centuries older than the pyramids of Egypt. Like the pyramids, and the ancient Greek tombs at Mycenae, the concept of the Irish passage tomb, as its name suggests, is that one enters through a passage to reach the burial chamber at the core; but in the Irish instances both chamber and passage are covered by a mound or cairn of earth and stone, the closest parallels to which lie not in Greece or Egypt but along the Atlantic seaboard from Iberia to Scandinavia. They are sometimes erected on elevated sites which can be seen for many miles, deliberately chosen, one presumes, so that the memory of the great ones buried within would not be easily forgotten. And they also sometimes come in clusters, so that the main tomb is surrounded by several satellite tombs: in the case of the Boyne Valley group, for instance, although there are three main sites – Newgrange, Knowth and Dowth – the whole complex contains in the region of thirty passage graves in all.

The main mound at Newgrange is about 11m (36ft) high and is not far short of 100m (330ft) in diameter. It is completely surrounded by a total of 97 kerbstones, many of which are decorated, the most ornate being that at the entrance to the passage itself on the south-east of the mound, one of the finest prehistoric carved stones in Europe. The sepulchral chamber is located a good deal short of the centre, so that the corridor leading to it is less than 20m long, lined with massive upright stones and roofed with large slabs, again elaborately decorated, increasingly so as one approaches the sanctum. Soil from the filling between these roof-slabs has provided radiocarbon dates of *c*.3316–2922 BC. Overhead, in the centre of the chamber, is an ingenious 6m (20ft)-high vaulted roof which to this day keeps it thoroughly dry, a remarkable piece of construction-work which has, therefore, been functioning perfectly for a full five millennia! The chamber itself is cross-shaped, with wings to both left and right, but the latter is considerably larger and probably the more important since the great stone which forms a roof over it is by far the most intricately embellished in the tomb. On the floor here, and in the other recesses of the chamber, large decorated stones shaped like a basin were found, perhaps to hold the ashes or bones of the dead, as the excavation which began in the early 1960s found the remains of at least three cremated bodies and the bones of two others.

But by far the most extraordinary discovery made by the excavators of Newgrange is the fact that the passage to the chamber was placed where it is for a special purpose: it is oriented precisely to the point on the horizon where the sun rises on the shortest day of the year, the winter solstice of 21 December. At dawn, for a few days on either side of the solstice, the rays of the rising sun shine

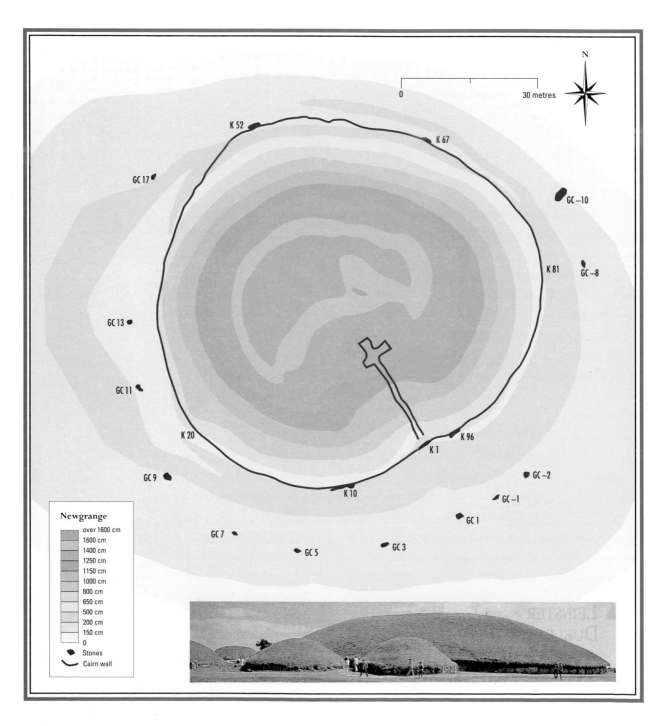

Newgrange

- over 1600 cm
- 1600 cm
- 1400 cm
- 1250 cm
- 1150 cm
- 1000 cm
- 800 cm
- 650 cm
- 500 cm
- 200 cm
- 150 cm
- 0
- Stones
- Cairn wall

through a small opening above the entrance known as the 'roof-box' and briefly illuminate the passageway, but only on the shortest day of the year does the first laser-like beam to peep above the horizon extend all the way to the end of the chamber, and it does so for a mere 17 minutes, from 8.58 to 9.15 am. In fact, it has been calculated that when the tomb was built 5,000 years ago this beam of sunlight the width of a pencil would have precisely bisected the chamber and shone directly on to the triple-spiral design carved on its end wall.

This bizarre solar phenomenon, its purpose accomplished, then vanishes for another year, leaving those fortunate enough to witness it in a state of wonderment, something which is as true today as for those who first experienced it some three thousand years before the birth of Christ. What meaning lies behind this strange occurrence is a matter of conjecture. If the builders of this and other Irish passage tombs worshipped any god, it was surely the sun, and the penetration of the sun's rays into the sanctum may have symbolised the end of mortal life for those buried within, and their translocation to the other world, just as, for those still living, the winter solstice marked the end of nature's annual cycle and the promise of a new beginning.

Hardly less magical than Newgrange are the discoveries at nearby Knowth, which is still producing surprises for its excavators who have been working there since 1962. Like Newgrange, it has one main tumulus but inside there are not one but two great passage tombs, which approach each other from east and west, and this primary mound has been shown to be surrounded by at least 18 smaller satellite mounds with their own tombs at their core. The kerbstones which line the large mound at Knowth, and the uprights and roof-slabs of the passages, contain some remarkable decoration, especially as one approaches the chambers, as at Newgrange. Here again there are decorated stone basins, near which deposits of cremated bone have been found (accounting for perhaps as many as twenty individuals) as well as some unburnt human bones, and carbon-dating of charcoal from the earliest stages of the complex has produced dates of c.3350–2900 BC. Where Newgrange captured the dawn light of the winter solstice, the eastern passage of the Knowth tumulus seems to have been aligned towards the rising sun of the spring and autumn equinox (21 March and 21 September), which perhaps coincided with the beginning of the sowing season and the end of the harvest, while the passage that points west may have captured the setting sun on the same days.

Other passage tombs in Meath include the mound at Dowth which also has two tombs within it, and Fourknocks which produced the bones of over fifty individuals, both adults and children. One of the monuments on the hill of Tara, known as the Mound of the Hostages, has also been shown to be a passage tomb, built around 3000 BC, while further west in Meath, at a place called Loughcrew, is a series of hills where there is an assemblage of at least twenty-five passage tombs, one of which, on the summit of Sliabh na Cailí ('Hag's

Opposite: *An aerial plan of Newgrange, showing the contours of the mound or cairn with the passage and chamber surrounded by a circle of standing kerb-stones, of which K1 is the magnificently decorated entrance stone. K52, directly opposite it, comes closest to it in terms of the quality of its design and the technique of the decoration. The mound is surrounded by an outer series of undecorated standing stones marked 'GC' (after O'Kelly). Inset is the other megalithic masterpiece at Knowth.*

This map shows the distribution of various categories of megalithic tombs. With a half-dozen exceptions, the court tombs lie in the northern third of the country, with strong local concentrations in coastal Mayo, Sligo and Donegal in the north-west, and also around Carlingford Lough in the north-east. Portal tombs also predominate in the northern half of Ireland, but with important concentrations also in Clare and Galway, and in the south-east from Dublin to Waterford. Of the passage tombs, the most impressive examples run in a band from the Dublin–Drogheda area in the east to Sligo in the north-west.

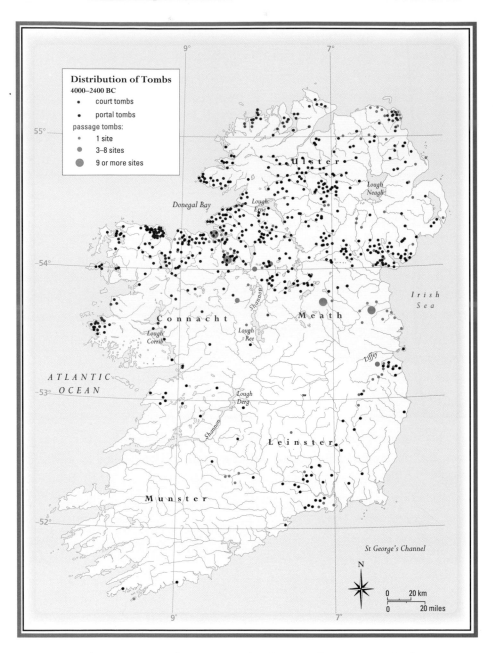

Mountain') has a passage facing east, the decorated stones in which are, as at Knowth, illuminated by the equinoctial sun at dawn. The hills around Loughcrew, spanning some 3km, are like one massive neolithic graveyard, and if one travels westwards into Co. Sligo there are even more impressive examples.

The most impressive is at Carrowmore, not far west of Sligo town, where there is a complex once composed of at least 85 megalithic tombs, one of the largest and oldest anywhere in Europe, though many of them have been shamefully destroyed by gravel-quarrying in recent times. The Carrowmore cemetery is dominated by the 11m (36ft)-high mound on the summit of Knocknarea – a colossal undertaking surely motivated by powerful religious beliefs and immense communal effort. It is traditionally known as Meascán Méabha ('Maeve's

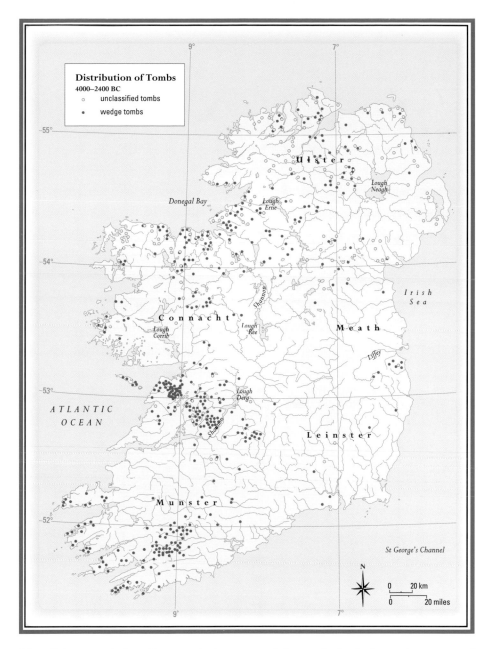

Wedge tombs are the most widespread of the tomb types found in Ireland, the distribution showing a western and southern bias. In Cos. Cork, Kerry, Clare, Limerick and Tipperary alone there are more than 200 examples, half of which are in Co. Clare.

Heap') because it is said to mark the grave of the mythological warrior-queen of Connacht; but it is in fact a passage tomb which has never been opened, and which not only provides an ostentatious and breathtaking panorama over Sligo Bay, but a dominant focal-point for the Stone Age necropolis that stretches out beneath it.

More Megaliths

Passage tombs, as we have seen, are only one of several types of megalithic burial monument found in Ireland. A more common and possibly even older type is the 'court' tomb or cairn, a name which derives from its most distinctive feature: instead of a covered straight passageway leading to the sepulchral chamber, its entrance is by way of a roofless U-shaped courtyard, and, because of their appearance from the air, they have sometimes been dubbed 'lobster-claw' cairns. While passage tombs tend to have a cross-shaped burial vault at the core, court cairns have two, three, or even four separate chambers in a row, the access from one to the next being slightly restricted by upright stone jambs on either side. Presumably, if the chambers within held the remains of the dead, the purpose of the open court in front was for the performance of some ritual associated with the burial. On this point, it may be worth noting that, although cremated remains have been found in court cairns, they may not originally have functioned as tombs. The ubiquitous presence of the forecourt, and the fact that they tend to be located on average about three miles apart, rather than being grouped together like graves, suggests that court cairns may have served initially as temples, not unlike the parish church of Christian times. However, this can only be guesswork.

This wedge tomb is located near Toormore Strand, not far from the most south-westerly point of Ireland. Here there are numerous such tombs especially near the tips of its many peninsulas, often facing a south-westerly direction, presumably deliberately.

Another curious point regarding court cairns is that, with a handful of exceptions, they occur only north of a line from about Galway to Dundalk, with a considerable preponderance in the Sligo–Mayo area. Whatever the explanation for this, they share this latter location with another type of megalith, the wedge tomb, which occurs almost exclusively west of a line from Cork to Larne, being well-represented throughout mid-Ulster, and on either side of the lower reaches of the Shannon, especially in Co. Clare, with another heavy concentration in south-west Co. Cork and, intriguingly, near the tips of each of the south-western peninsulas. They are called wedge tombs, quite simply, because of their shape: inside the tomb, which can range in size from under 2m to more than 10m, the stone roof overhead tends to get lower and the passage narrower the further in one goes.

There are over 500 of them in the country, making them the most numerous of all Irish megalithic tombs, about one third of the overall total. The few that have been excavated have produced human remains, usually cremated, and sometimes pottery of more recent origin than that found in other megaliths, indicating that the wedge tomb may be a later phenomenon. What is most interesting, though, is that they are very consistent in their orientation: it cannot be a coincidence that most point towards the west or south-west, in the direction of the setting sun, which presumably had some religious significance for those who built them.

The final class of megalith, the portal tomb, is usually known as a dolmen or cromlech. This gives the appearance of being the most basic of all since usually all that survives today are several large upright stones upon which one massive lid or 'capstone' rests. Yet the sheer weight of the capstone is such – anything up to 100 tons – that portal-tomb construction, and their enduring stability after perhaps as much as 5,000 years, represents a remarkable feat of engineering. They would originally have been surrounded by a mound, which might have made somewhat easier the colossal task of dragging the capstone into place, but it would still demand a huge cooperative effort. The distribution-pattern of the portal tomb around the country does not lend itself to any easy interpretation, though, interestingly, about another fifty of them are to be found in Wales and Cornwall. One of the most dramatically-sited dolmens in Ireland, that at Poulnabrone in the Burren, Co. Clare, was excavated in the late 1980s, and revealed the bones of at least sixteen adults and six children, placed there at intervals over a 600-year period between *c.* 3800

and 3200 BC. The relatively small number of burials within the tomb, and the lengthy time-span during which it was in use, prompts one to imagine that dolmens may mark the resting places of the chosen few, the aristocratic mausoleums of neolithic Ireland.

Kernanstown, or Browneshill, portal tomb, Co. Carlow, has a massive capstone estimated to weigh about 100 tons and to be the heaviest in Europe. At one end it is embedded into the earth and is supported at the other end by three large upright stones.

From Stone to Metal

The Neolithic period is generally described as lasting from about 4000 BC to about 2400 BC, in other words, sixteen centuries during which fashion and practice, needless to say, did not stand still. Towards the end of this period we certainly notice changes taking place in Ireland. The excavations at Newgrange, for example, revealed that perhaps as much as a thousand years after its original construction a community had settled around the mound, living in houses of wood or wattle, rearing cattle and pigs, growing barley and wheat, and possessing a relative newcomer to Western Europe and certainly to Ireland, the horse. There were other innovations: just as the discovery of any kind of pottery is taken to be a sign of the changeover from the mesolithic to the neolithic in Ireland, the discovery of many fragments of what is called Beaker pottery at Newgrange is taken to mark the end of the latter, and the start of a new age. That age is called the Bronze Age and, sure enough, a bronze axe dating from this precise period was found in the Newgrange excavations.

Beaker pottery has been found throughout Europe and made its first appearance in England, probably by way of the Low Countries, around 2150 BC. It may have been introduced into Britain by new settlers, who perhaps in time made their way to Ireland. But in Britain and Central Europe this type of pottery tends to be associated with burials as opposed to domestic situations, whereas in Ireland (as in the Newgrange houses) the reverse is the case, something it has in common with Brittany and places further south along the Atlantic seaboard. Thus, how Beaker-ware found its way to Ireland remains unexplained, as does the question of whether we should assume that it came in the hands of a new wave of settlers. One thing that does look odd, though, about the Early Bronze Age in Ireland is that there is a shift from the previous communal burial in megalithic tombs to individual burials in single graves: one should not perhaps read too much into this, but large megalithic tombs point to a society that was very regimented and structured and hierarchical, while the burial of individuals in separate graves seems to indicate a less structured, looser form of social organisation.

Be that as it may, the most important indicator of the change ushered in by the Bronze Age is, as its name indicates, the shift from the use of stone to metal. Metal has the obvious advantage over stone that it can be moulded to suit its user's requirements, whether as a weapon of war or as domestic and industrial implements, or as ever more ostentatious jewellery. Metal-using peoples have, therefore, a military, social and economic edge on their rivals: they will inflict greater damage on the field of battle, race ahead in the 'standard-of-living' stakes, and, literally, outshine them in personal adornment. But whether the first users of metal in Ireland were Irish-born or incomers and whether they should be identified with the users of Beaker pottery we will never know for sure.

It is certainly the case that Ireland was well-placed to take advantage of this new technology, as it had abundant supplies of copper, perhaps some tin (though it may mostly have been imported from Cornwall), and its own gold – if one knew where to look. On the slopes of Mount Gabriel, near Schull in Co. Cork, are some of the very few prehistoric copper mines known in Europe, and a network of over thirty mineshafts has been detected, from which radiocarbon dates of *c.* 1500 BC have been obtained. It is difficult to assess how much finished copper the mines produced, but it was quite possibly enough to suggest that there was an export trade in it.

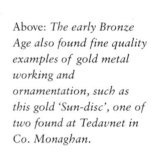

Ironically, the classic object produced in Ireland in the so-called Bronze Age was a large copper axehead, often alloyed with arsenic to make it harder and less likely to fracture. It was only when smiths began to blend the molten copper with about ten per cent tin, that bronze itself made its appearance in Ireland; it is a harder alloy, which can be more easily hammered into shape while still hot to produce tougher implements still. Some of these axes are decorated with, for example, triangular and zigzag motifs and were clearly more than just utilitarian objects, and this kind of geometrical ornamentation occurs on other artifacts dating from the same period, but this time made of gold. These include magnificent gold lunulae, so called because of their half-moon shape, made of a thin hammered sheet of gold and probably worn around the neck, and also another wafer-thin but this time fully circular object, called a 'sun-disc', similarly decorated but sometimes with a cross-shaped design on it; sun-discs have two little holes at their centre, like those on a button, suggesting that they were worn attached to a garment.

Gold objects from later in the Bronze Age tend increasingly to be made, not from these thin sheets of gold, but from thicker bars, used to produce large bracelets and neck ornaments called torcs. This may indicate a greater availability of the metal, which would have been panned from the rivers and streams of Co. Wicklow and elsewhere, if not imported. In any case, by perhaps 1000 BC, spectacularly exhibitionist gold jewellery became the fashion in Ireland, including some strange-looking items which may be dress-fasteners, others which may have adorned the hair, and another peculiarly Irish type of gorget or necklace, the finest examples of which are among the most beautiful *objets d'art* to survive from Late Bronze Age Europe and made by its most skilled goldsmiths.

Above: *The early Bronze Age also found fine quality examples of gold metal working and ornamentation, such as this gold 'Sun-disc', one of two found at Tedavnet in Co. Monaghan.*

Opposite: *Examples of fine quality Bronze Age metalwork, including a copper axehead which would have been cast in an open mould and socketed spearheads cast in complex moulds where a plug was used to form the socket.*

Late Bronze Age Communities

In the early 1990s, at a place called Clonfinlough, just south of Clonmacnoise in Co. Offaly, and on the shore of tiny Fin Lough, mass peat-removal revealed a Late Bronze Age settlement. It had been enclosed by a palisade of between 1m and 1.5m in height, made of ashwood posts which had the cut-marks of bronze axes on them. Inside the enclosure were timber trackways to provide a dry surface, and circular post-and-wattle houses with stone-lined hearths were placed on timber platforms. These were made partly of split oak timbers and dendrochronology (tree-ring dating) proved that the oaks were felled between 917 and 886 BC. Two amber beads were found on the site, which may have originated in the Baltic, and perhaps the closeness of Clonfinlough to the Shannon explains how they got there; the discovery of two wooden boat-paddles indicates that its occupants certainly made use of the river.

Clonfinlough, Co. Offaly, is a fascinating Late Bronze Age site which has revealed evidence of lakeside settlement dating from about 900 BC. It was surrounded by a strong palisade fence and had timber trackways to keep its inhabitants dry under foot. They lived in round post-and-wattle houses, which had their own fireplaces, and the discovery of amber beads may mean that they had contact with places as far afield as the Baltic. (Reconstruction: M. Keane and C. McDermott)

A completely different kind of Late Bronze Age settlement is the hillfort located high up on the Wicklow massif at Rathgall, near the Co. Carlow border. In spite of its inaccessible location, it is protected by four sets of circular ramparts and at its core there was a large circular house, 15m (50ft) in diameter, built of timber posts. Ritual cremations took place on the site; one cremation pit contained a clay pot which had the burnt bones of an adult and child, while another had a hoard of bronze objects, including a chisel, a spearhead and a sword-blade. These may actually have been made at Rathgall since, along with large quantities of pottery itself, the excavators found hundreds of fragments of clay moulds for making weapons like swords, spearheads and axes, as well as lumps of waste pieces of bronze. Items of gold and bronze jewellery, and bracelets of jet and lignite, may also have been manufactured in the workshop, and it is interesting to note the discovery of small pieces of amber and numerous blue and green glass beads, some of which are decorated and may have originated on the European mainland. However inhospitable its location, Rathgall was evidently a place that enjoyed a high status during the Bronze Age.

Iron Age and Celtic Ireland

On the available evidence, it seems that during the late seventh and the sixth centuries BC, bronze began to be replaced by iron in Ireland as a result of contact – either direct or mediated through Britain – with iron-using communities on the European landmass: the Bronze Age was nearing its end, and the Iron Age about to begin. This was a dramatic change and although, of course, the transformation may have taken place over a long period of time, there is always the tendency to associate it with equally dramatic changes in society – in this case, the arrival of the 'Celts'. The truth is, though, that there is no good archaeological evidence to prove a Celtic 'invasion' of Ireland. Celtic-speaking peoples did certainly occupy large areas of Europe in the last centuries before Christ, and few would dispute that Ireland was among them, but whether they were the people who actually introduced iron-working into the country is another matter.

What we can say is that there was a style of art practiced among the Iron Age Celtic peoples of Europe (called La Tène after an important site in what is now Switzerland) and this style somehow became established in Ireland by about 300 BC, though evidence of it, for whatever reason, is limited to the northern half of the country. With the exception of some decorated stones, and even bones, it is 'Celtic' or La Tène metalwork which, for obvious reasons, has tended to survive, though, ironically, since iron tends to corrode badly some of the finest of Ireland's surviving examples of Iron-Age metal-working are in fact made of gold and bronze!

The abiding weapons of this period testify to the importance of close-quarter combat with sword and spear; magnificent bronze trumpets which can measure up to 1.5m (5 ft) from end to end were presumably used for occasional formal purposes; and some dazzling items of gold jewellery and ornaments such as those found in the famous hoard from Broighter in Co. Derry, again appear too awe-inspiring to have seen the light of day on anything other than ceremonial occasions. What seem to be more abundant, and clearly testify to the importance of the horse in La Tène Ireland, are great quantities of bridle-bits and other horse-trappings which have been uncovered over the years, and although we tend to think of the aristocrats of this period riding on chariots, proof of it is wanting.

We do know that wheeled transport of a more basic horse-and-cart kind was used, and miles of wooden trackway have been uncovered beneath the bogs of the midlands; they are made of huge oak planks resembling railway sleepers and the roads themselves are not unlike railway tracks: a 2km (1¼ miles) stretch at Corlea, Co. Longford, has been dated by dendrochronology to 148 BC. It is the largest of its kind in western Europe, and the sheer labour of felling and skill of splitting the oaks must have called for advanced communal effort. The labour involved is not far short of what must have been required to build linear earthworks, the miles of banks and ditches and timber palisades which occur throughout the country but especially in Ulster, such as the Black Pig's Dyke, which has been radiocarbon-dated to 390–370 BC, and the Dorsey in south Armagh, timbers from which have been dated by dendrochronology to 140 BC and 100–90 BC.

The latter date is interesting because not too far north of the Dorsey, also in Co. Armagh, is Navan Fort, the Emain Macha of early Irish history and literature. This massive enclosure, 6 hectares in area, 286m in diameter, has been subject to extensive excavation which has proved that it was in use at various periods throughout Ireland's prehistory, but radiocarbon dates from one of its mounds placed it between the fourth and first centuries BC. However, its excavators also discovered the remains of an extremely large and very strange structure composed almost exclusively of ever-decreasing circles of upright timber posts leading to a massive central mast; but the circles are not quite complete because they are broken by three parallel aisles, again lined with posts, leading to the centre. Such a building, cluttered with a total of 280 upright poles, could hardly have been lived in, and indeed seems to have been promptly covered by a mound and purposely set alight, so that it may have been some kind of temple; but the stump of the huge central pole survived and dendrochronology proved that it was felled in the winter of 95–94 BC.

This discovery may be extraordinary, and very useful in helping to elucidate some of the ritual practices of early Celtic Ireland, as well as providing a chronology in the absence of documentary evidence; but surely the most startling discovery at the Navan complex was the skull of a Barbary ape. This originated in North Africa and was most likely transported up the Atlantic seaways to Ireland. Whether it was imported as an exotic pet or exported as a prestige gift, it is proof of Ireland's far-flung contacts at the dawn of the Celtic Age. If such outlandish items found their way to Ireland, we should not be surprised if the processes of exchange and trade brought considerable quantities of more mundane material. And, no matter how conservative one's interpretation of the business of prehistoric exchange and trade, or of the more elusive means by which new technologies or fashions are absorbed, ultimately all items and all ideas which originated elsewhere but ended up in Ireland were brought into it by individuals – by 'Irishmen' travelling abroad or 'foreigners' travelling to Ireland.

We could, of course, assume that it was the former who brought the Barbary ape to Emain Macha, and that it was also Irish travellers and traders who brought all the other imported Iron Age objects, including La Tène-style Celtic art objects, into Ireland. We could also assume that Irishmen working abroad learned the craft of iron-working and Celtic art techniques, and brought those skills home with them. But we are still left with one thing unaccounted for: when we break through the blurred barrier between prehistory and history – by the fifth century AD – Ireland appears as a country with a single firmly-rooted language. It is a Celtic language and Ireland comes into view as a thoroughly 'Celtic' country.

Navan Fort, the ancient Emain Macha in Co. Armagh, 'capital' of Ulster at the dawn of Irish history. This was the ceremonial headquarters of the Ulaid and plays a central part in the early medieval saga literature of Ireland.

Prehistoric Irish traders may have imported tools and jewels, and, not for the last time, returned Irish emigrants may have introduced the latest international styles to their homeland. But languages, and the whole cultural superstructure which surrounds them, don't really work like that. Strangers to a new land bring their language and culture with them. The all-embracing Celtic environment, which is evident in Ireland once the light of history is shone on it, is so firmly entrenched there that it can only have been the product of a successful population implant and several centuries of growth and stabilisation.

That the Celtic colonisation of Ireland, albeit perhaps a slow and incremental affair rather than a lightning invasion, appears to have left no discernible imprint on the archaeological record is remarkable. It is also unfortunate, since the Celtic contribution to Ireland is still visible (and audible) today; it is arguably the most formative force that went into the making of Ireland, and certainly still represents the most characteristic mark of distinction between the Irish and other non-Celtic nations. Ultimately, of course, we know little about the arrival of the Celts in Ireland because it took place at a time before men kept a contemporaneous written record of their actions – before history.

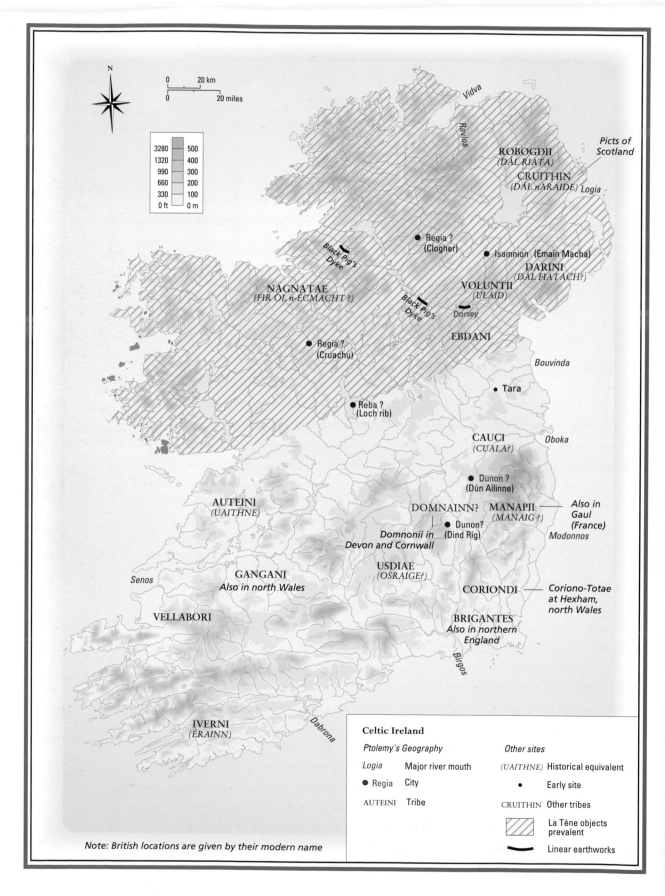

N

| 0 | 20 km |
| 0 | 20 miles |

3280	500
1320	400
990	300
660	200
330	100
0 ft	0 m

Vidva

Ravios

ROBOGDII
(DÁL RIATA)

Picts of
Scotland

CRUITHIN
(DÁL nARAIDE) Logia

● Regia ?
(Clogher)

● Isamnion (Emain Macha)

DARINI
(DÁL FIATACH?)

Black Pig's
Dyke

NAGNATAE
(FIR OL n-ÉCMACHT ?)

Black Pig's
Dyke

VOLUNTII
(ULAID)

Dorsey

EBDANI

● Regia ?
(Cruachu)

Bouvinda

● Reba ?
(Loch rib)

● Tara

CAUCI
(CUALA?)

Oboka

● Dunon ?
(Dún Ailinne)

AUTEINI
(UAITHNE)

DOMNAINN?

MANAPII
(MANAIG ?)

Also in
Gaul
(France)

● Dunon?
(Dind Ríg)

Modonnos

Domnonii in
Devon and Cornwall

USDIAE
(OSRAIGE?)

GANGANI
Also in north Wales

Senos

CORIONDI

Coriono-Totae
at Hexham,
north Wales

VELLABORI

BRIGANTES
Also in northern
England

Birgos

IVERNI
(ÉRAINN)

Dabrona

Celtic Ireland

Ptolemy's Geography

Logia Major river mouth

● Regia City

AUTEINI Tribe

Other sites

(UAITHNE) Historical equivalent

● Early site

CRUITHIN Other tribes

La Tène objects prevalent

Linear earthworks

Note: British locations are given by their modern name

CHAPTER II

THE CHRISTIAN TRANSFORMATION

Although we may not know for certain when the people known to the Greeks as *Keltoi* came to Ireland, their legacy lives on. The Celts spoke an Indo–European language which developed into P-Celtic, the speech of Britain and Gaul, ancestor of Welsh and Breton, and also into Q-Celtic, the language of the Celtic inhabitants of Ireland, ancestor of Gaelic, the Irish language. This is the Celts' most obvious gift, in the sense that its impact still reverberates today: it is a remarkable fact that these people, whose arrival in Ireland seems to have left no discernible trace on the archaeological landscape, nevertheless brought a language which is still the mother tongue or a second language spoken by many Irish people to this day, perhaps two and a half thousand years later. And a language, of course, is not simply a collection of words and a system of grammar: it is a means for the expression of thoughts, feelings, ideas and so forth, and just as it is the overriding distinguishing characteristic between man and other animals, so the development and use by a people of their own language distinguishes them from all other peoples. It makes them a separate people, it gives them a separate identity, it is the core part of the culture-package which is their 'society'.

The problem is that we know very little about the society that developed among these people in Ireland before the dawn of history. There is perhaps a clue to be found in some of the physical objects which, in addition to their language, they left behind. These include, as we have seen, some magnificent examples of artwork in the La Tène style associated with the Celts of central Europe, and among the most elaborate of these are beautifully crafted war-trumpets, golden ceremonial collars or torcs, and decorated bronze scabbards and horse-bits. If one were to extrapolate from these, they would seem to be the relics of a warrior society. There may be something of significance too in the fact of their prevalence in Connacht and Ulster since this part of Ireland is the setting for the famous mythological tale known as *Táin Bó Cuailnge* ('The cattle-raid of Cooley') and other great sagas of the Irish heroic age. These tales, even in their earliest forms, were written several centuries later than the events they purport to recount, and therefore need to be used with considerable caution, but, having said that, their authors had a far better vantage-point than we have today, and they must surely capture *something* of the society that was thought to exist in Ireland in the immediate prehistoric period. And when one examines them, the society that emerges from their pages is one not unlike that portrayed in contemporary descriptions of the Celts elsewhere.

The doorway of one of the early churches at Glendalough, Co. Wicklow, founded by Cóemgen (St Kevin), one of the early Irish saints around whom a cult was later to develop. The cross marking a grave in the foreground may be medieval.

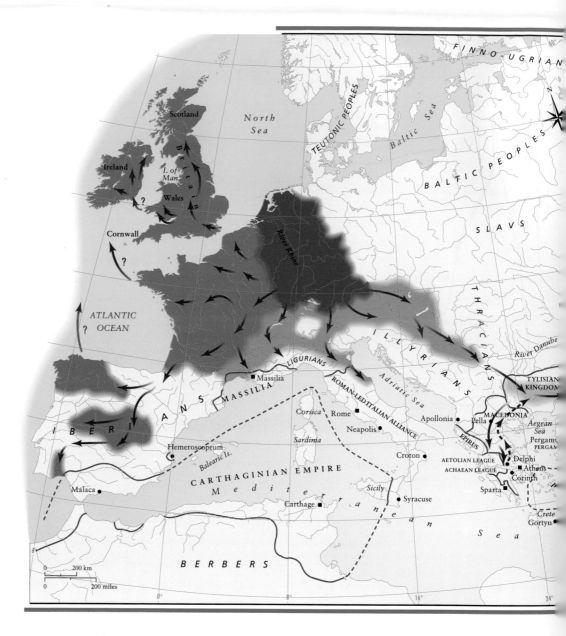

Greek and Roman Observations

Julius Caesar (d. 44 BC) is the most famous early commentator on Ireland but unfortunately he does little more than report the calculation that Ireland was less than half the size of Britain. His Greek contemporary Strabo (d. *c.* AD 21), famous for his *Geographia*, had more to say about Ireland, although contrary to the view of most others of that age who thought it lay somewhere between Britain and Spain, he placed Ireland just north of Britain, but was certain that 'it is there that the limits of the habitable earth should be fixed'. His account is important too because it has some of the earliest in a long queue of disparaging remarks about the Irish, saying that they 'are wholly savage' and 'lead a wretched existence'; Strabo, though, unlike some of his more credulous successors, was careful to point out that he had no trustworthy witnesses for these

The Celts

Celtic territory

7th–8th century BC

6th–5th century BC

4th century BC

3rd century BC

→ direction of expansion

observations, and in fact blamed the 'wretched existence' of the Irish on the coldness of the climate! His bleak view of Ireland was not shared by the great Roman historian Tacitus (d. *c.* AD 120), writing just a couple of generations later, who thought Ireland much like Britain 'in soil, climate, and the character and civilisation of its inhabitants'.

There are contradictions in many of the various scraps of information provided by these and subsequent writers, but in general a picture of Ireland emerges which has three basic components: first, it is situated at the edge of the known world; second, partly as a result, its inhabitants are barbarians given to uncivilised behaviour which at its mildest might include fornication and incest or, at its most extreme, cannibalism; and third, again because of its out-of-the-way location, it was bound to be something of an El Dorado, a land of plenty, rich in resources, and enjoying a healthy climate which made it free of pestilence and bountiful in crops and animals. This is the sort of composite picture which emerges in the famous work of Solinus, who wrote in the middle of the third century AD: while he accuses the Irish of barbarism, he also points out that the country's pastures are so rich that the cattle must be regularly restrained from eating, lest the rich grass cause them to burst. Solinus also, incidentally, alludes to the fact – two centuries before St Patrick's mission! – that there are no snakes in Ireland.

Ptolemy's 'Map'

What all of these accounts lack, however, is hard evidence as to the identity of the peoples inhabiting Ireland in the early centuries AD. We know that the Greeks called the island *Ierne*, and we can hazard a guess as to its derivation, as we shall see. But was the island occupied by one or more 'tribes', and if so, what were their names? Did they live in cities or palaces or fortresses, and again, if so, where were these and what were they called? Some of the answers are provided by the most detailed of the early accounts of Ireland, that by Claudius Ptolemaeus, known to the Romans as Ptolemy, the great Alexandrian Greek geographer and astronomer, writing shortly after AD 100. His information is certainly confused, but there is no reason to doubt it completely, since his Roman contemporary Tacitus, for example, stated that Ireland's 'harbours are reasonably well known from merchants who trade there'. Presumably, therefore, Ptolemy got his information from Roman or British sailors, familiar with the island's east coast and the main rivers, fifteen of which he notes. Of these, it seems that his *Vidva* is the Foyle and his *Logia* the Lagan; *Bouvinda* is certainly the Boyne, and *Birgos* may be the Barrow, while *Senos* is probably the Shannon. Of the peoples whose territories Ptolemy records, he places in the north-east a group called *Robogdii*, whom we can probably identify as the Dál Riata of Antrim (soon to found a powerful kingdom in Argyll). Somewhat further south, where we would expect to find – in the historic era – the Dál Fiatach dynasty of Down, Ptolemy has the *Darini*, who may fit the bill. However, in the immediately prehistoric period (in the early centuries AD), before they got pushed east of the Bann, the Ulaid ruled much of the north from their cult centre at Emain Macha, scene of much of the action of the early saga literature: Ptolemy seems to recognise their importance, and his geography gives a prominent place to both the Ulaid and Emain, if, as seems likely, they can be equated with his *Voluntii* and *Isamnion*.

As Ptolemy moves from the north-east, it becomes harder to match his territories with known dynasties, and it is surprising that he has no mention of the massive Iron-Age earthworks at Tara, Co. Meath, perhaps the most important of the early royal and ritual sites. He does, though, include a place further south called *Dunon*, which may be one of the early-historic royal sites of Leinster, perhaps Dún Ailinne or Dind Ríg. One could suggest that the tribe whom Ptolemy calls the *Usdiae* are the Osraige who are found some centuries later inhabiting the frontier between Leinster and Munster, while his *Auteini* resemble the early dynasty called the Uaithne in what is now Co. Clare. Most interesting of all, perhaps, are the *Iverni*, whom Ptolemy places in the south-west, and who look very much like the Érainn, a dynasty which would have dominated Munster in this very early period: it must surely be from them that the Greek name for Ireland, *Ierne*, derives, which was itself a version of the Irish word for the island, *Ériu* (later, *Éire*).

Ireland and the Empire

If classical writers based far from Ireland's shores had access to such detailed information, it is not unreasonable to suggest that the Roman occupants of Britain were in routine contact with the island. Merchants from the Empire visited Ireland's harbours and the importance placed by Ptolemy on identifying her

Ptolemy's Map
c. AD 100

[promontory icon] promontory

[river mouth icon] river mouth

• city

Iverni tribe

P. of Vennicnion

Argita   *P. of Robogdion*

N

Northern P.

Vennicnii   *Vidva*

Ravios   **Robogdii**

Erpeditani   *Logia*

Nagnata •   **Regia** •   **Darini**

Libnios   **Nagnatae**   *Vinderis*

P. of Isamnion

Voluntii

• **Raeba**

Ausoba   **Auteini**   *Buvinda*

Senos   ○ *Adros*

Eblani

Gangani   **Laberos** •

Regia •   • **Eblana**

Cauci   *Oboca*

Dunon   ○ *Limnos*

Dur   **Macolicon** •   **Manapia**

Manapii   *Modonnos*

Vellabori   • **Ivernis**   **Coriondi**

Iverne

Brigantes

Iverni   **Usdiae**

Sacred P.

Birgos

Southern P.

Dabrona

This map of Ireland is reconstructed from the coordinates supplied by the Alexandrian Greek geographer, Claudius Ptolemaeus (Ptolemy), writing shortly after AD 100. Much of it is no doubt conjecture, but he does seem to have had a fairly reliable source for some of the names which he attempts to reproduce.

rivers suggests that the latter too were regularly plied. It may be that Roman – or, more likely, Romano-British – traffickers established trading stations at convenient coastal locations or at fording points on navigable rivers, in order to facilitate trade and exchange. On Lambay Island, off the coast of Dublin, Roman artefacts have been found at the burial-site of a warrior who probably lived in the first century AD. Just onshore from Lambay is the impressive cliff-surrounded promontory of Drumanagh (near Loughshinny, Co. Dublin) which still has the remains of three earthen ramparts at its landward side, which would have made it a very heavily defended fort. We do not know when or by whom this was done, but Roman pottery has been found there, dating from the first century AD, and Roman coins from the following century have been unearthed nearby. Drumanagh may have been the bridgehead of an intended large-scale Roman incursion into Ireland, or it may have been occupied by Romano-British traders or raiders. On the other hand, it may simply have been a coastal outpost occupied by Irish people who made their living trading with Roman Britain and for whom such a secure base was needed; most probably, we shall never know.

Nonetheless, if we include in our reckoning the amount of Roman material which has turned up at important archaeological sites in Ireland – such as valuable gold objects and coins found at Newgrange which may have been presented by pilgrims as offerings to the gods, or the remnants of wine-flagons from Gaul found at the 'Rath of the Synods' at Tara – and add to these scattered finds and coin-hoards from throughout the country, though mostly along the east coast, then the evidence for contact with the Empire is quite considerable. One can well imagine gold and silver being plundered by Irish raiders from wealthy Roman villas in southern England, and some of the coin and the gold and silver ingots may even have been pay received by Irish mercenaries in the armies of the Empire, but there is no hard evidence that Roman legions ever set foot in Ireland, let alone occupied it. It is true that their general Agricola (d. AD 93) who, as governor of Britain, advanced Roman rule as far north as the Firth of Forth, contemplated the conquest of Ireland, and it is interesting to speculate how the course of Ireland's history might have changed had his ambition been achieved, but it was not. Ireland remained beyond the Empire and remained unconquered. Agricola lay seven centuries in his grave before Ireland became the object of serious assault and this

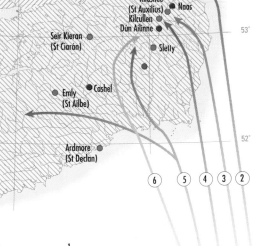

The Arrival of Christianity

- ● Royal sites
- ● Early missionary churches
- ● Sites called *Domnach Pátraic*
- ▨ Main focus of Patrick's mission
- ▨ Main focus of non-Patrician mission

1. St Patrick from Britain, mid-5th century
2. St Secundinus from continent, mid-5th century ?
3. St Auxilius from continent, mid-5th century ?
4. St Iserninus from continent, mid-5th century ?
5. Early Gaulish and British missionary activity, late 4th – early 5th centuries
6. Palladius from Auxerre (?), AD 431

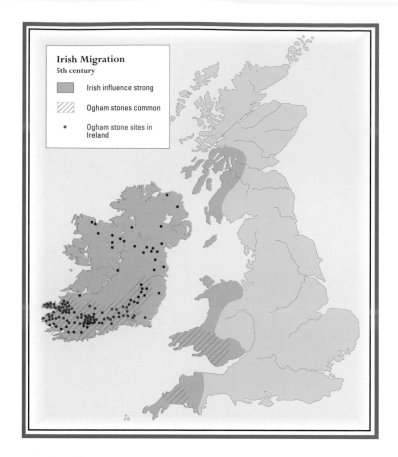

Map showing those parts of Britain which, it seems, the Irish sought to colonise at about the middle of the first millennium AD. The most successful of these movements was from the Antrim area into the western part of what subsequently became Scotland, and the Gaelic language is perhaps its most visible trace today. Further south, in Wales and south-western England, the survival of stones which have Irish 'Ogham' inscriptions on them is a strong pointer to an Irish presence which has left few other traces.

was not from Rome or her former provinces, but from another so-called barbarian outpost, Scandinavia.

Early Irish Colonies in Britain

Although, therefore, Ireland lay outside the Roman Empire, it must surely have been heavily affected by it, and, provided the Romans never got around to putting their invasion plans into practice, there were more than enough advantages to be gained from having such a wealthy next-door neighbour. As Roman power in Britain weakened, by the early fifth century AD, the Irish were not only peddling and plundering there, but settling along its west coast. The most successful of these was the colony which the Dál Riata of the Glens of Antrim established in Argyll and the Hebrides. There can, in fact, be few more successful examples of colonisation than those which involve, not simply the movement of peoples and languages and ways of life, but the actual transference of the name of the homeland to the new colony, and that is what happened in this instance: in this period the Romans called Ireland *Scotia* and its inhabitants *Scoti*, and the Dál Riata colony had such an impact on its new homeland that the name Scotia was actually transferred in time to it, so that what we now call Scotland was born.

Another Irish dynasty, the Déisi from what is now Co. Waterford and south Co. Tipperary, also took advantage of the unrest in Britain to establish a colony there, this time in Dyfed in south Wales, while their neighbours known as Uí Liatháin, from east Cork, also settled in south Wales and in Cornwall and Devon. The Irish province of Leinster takes its name from the powerful dynasty of Laigin, and they established a colony in north Wales, where their name seems to be preserved in the Lleyn peninsula in Gwynedd. One approximate way of tracing Irish settlement in Britain in this period is by plotting the presence of Ogham stones, which tend to occur throughout those parts of the south of Ireland from where the emigrants hailed, and in the areas of Britain where they settled. The Ogham script consists of vertical lines of notches on the edges of upright stones, but it is clearly a product of contact with the Roman world, since it is based on the Latin alphabet. Those Irish who adopted the Latin alphabet and learned to read and write in that language, no doubt encountered by the same means Christianity.

The Coming of Christianity

The first Christian missionaries may have come to Ireland from Gaul, in the late fourth or early fifth century, thus making it the first country outside the Roman world to be converted. But the earliest exact date is 431 – in fact, 431 is the first fixed and reliable date in Irish history – because it is the year in which Palladius, a deacon of Auxerre, was appointed by Pope Celestine I as the first bishop to 'the Irish who believe in Christ'. The information comes from the reliable chronicle compiled by Prosper of Aquitaine, and the way in which he phrases his statement clearly implies that there were already some Christians in Ireland, who now needed a bishop to regulate their affairs. Presumably, therefore, Palladius went to Ireland as instructed, and took charge of his flock there, but the fact is that this first bishop of the Irish disappears without trace; we know nothing further of his efforts, and the voluminous records later compiled in Ireland allegedly detailing the history of the early Irish Church make no reference to him whatever.

Doubtless, though, whatever became of Palladius himself, there were Gaulish missionaries in Ireland in this obscure early phase, but their labours may have been confined largely to the east and south of Ireland, and they were soon superseded by churchmen from Britain, the most famous of whom is the still highly controversial St Patrick. Perhaps the similarity in names between him and Palladius accounts for the peculiar amnesia surrounding the latter, or perhaps Palladius was deliberately erased from the record by Patrick's powerful successors in the Church of Armagh, who were much given to composing what we can only call propaganda intended to assert his and their primacy.

Whatever the reason, Patrick is the person who dominates the story of the early Christian Church in Ireland, although the disparate areas in which he is said to have worked, and the confused chronology of his mission – covering more than the lifetime of any one man – have caused some scholars to speculate that there must have been two or even three Patricks! Nonetheless, he is certainly an historical figure, and an extremely

Termonfeckin, Co. Louth, as its name suggests, was founded by St Fechín of Fore (d. 665) and became the residence of the archbishops of Armagh in the later Middle Ages. Its High Cross is early medieval, made of sandstone with the classic, Irish-style ringed head. On the west face, we see Christ in Glory surrounded by panels covered in interlacing and spiral ornament.

Left: *This stone from Coolmagort, Co. Kerry, displays Ogham inscriptions, the earliest written Irish language.*

important one, not merely in terms of the history of Ireland. To begin with, Patrick himself is the author of the earliest written documents to survive from Ireland, and since history depends on the written word we can say, in effect, that Irish history begins with him. But his texts are more important still. In his writings he describes his famous life-story, so familiar to many to this day, including his capture by raiders, delivery into slavery in Ireland, and eventual escape and return as a missionary to his erstwhile captives. This makes Patrick the only citizen of the western Roman Empire who was captured by barbarians and brought beyond its frontiers, but who survived to write his remarkable adventure: his is therefore an autobiography unique in the history of the early Christian West, and surely therefore he stands out as a person of unique importance in European history.

Opposite: The map seeks to capture the shifting boundaries of Irish provinces and lesser territories in the early medieval period. The former greatness of Ulaid (from which the name Ulster derives) is shown by its confinement to the area east of the Bann, while Laigin (Leinster) stops short at the Liffey although it had earlier extended further north. From the west we see the Uí Néill and their subjects, the Airgialla, expanding across the Shannon into the north-west (the Northern Uí Néill), while the Eóganacht of Cashel expand throughout Munster, their various branches becoming dominant in the south-west.

There are two surviving texts written by Patrick, his well-known *Confession*, and a letter written to the soldiers of a British chieftain named Coroticus. In these he tells us that he was the son of Calpurnius, a member of a town council in Roman Britain who was also a deacon of the Church and in turn the son of a priest. The town in question he calls Bannaven Taberniae, and although it is sometimes assumed to be Carlisle, we may never know its true identity. His family owned a small estate from which Patrick was abducted by Irish raiders in his sixteenth year, and brought to Ireland as a slave, where he remained for six years as a herdsman, eventually making his escape after walking 200 miles to the coast, undergoing a sea-voyage of three days and a further 28-day march before being reunited with his family. Eventually, though, a messenger came to him in a dream bearing a letter containing 'the voice of the Irish', begging him to return to them, which in time he felt compelled to do.

St Patrick was most active, it seems, north of a line from Wexford to Galway, and was particularly successful in the north-east. It was a church in this area, Armagh, because of its alleged association with Patrick, that was later to claim primacy over the rest of the Irish Church. However, the cult which grew up around Patrick should not mislead us into thinking that the conversion of Ireland was quick, and largely the work of one man. As already mentioned, we know nothing of the activities of Palladius, but later accounts give the names of other bishops active at this early period. Auxilius is said to have founded Killashee (*Cill Usailli*, 'the cell of Auxilius') which, interestingly, is near Naas, one of the royal sites associated with the kings of Leinster, while Dunshaughlin, not far from another hugely important site, Tara, is attributed to Secundinus: in Irish, it is *Domnach Sechnaill*, and sites with the element *domnach* (from Latin *dominicum*) are known to be early. Like these other early churches, Armagh is near the revered site at Emain Macha, in each case suggesting a deliberate policy of locating the new Christian churches beside old pre-Christian power-centres.

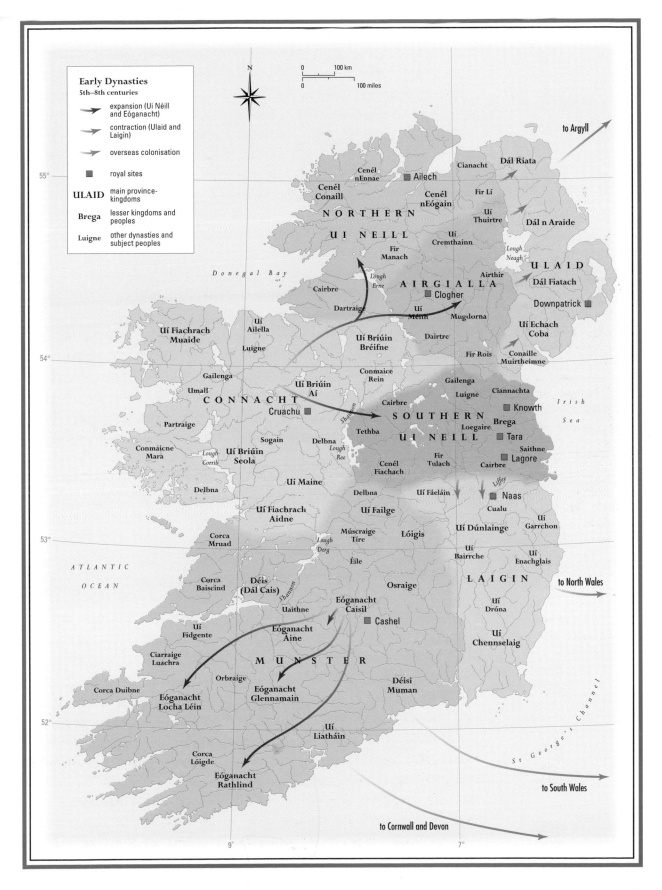

Early Dynasties
5th–8th centuries

→ expansion (Uí Néill and Eóganacht)

→ contraction (Ulaid and Laigin)

→ overseas colonisation

■ royal sites

ULAID main province-kingdoms

Brega lesser kingdoms and peoples

Luigne other dynasties and subject peoples

to Argyll

55°

Cenél nEnnae

■ Ailech

Cianacht

Dál Riata

Cenél Conaill

Cenél nEógain

Fir Lí

Uí Thuirtre

Dál n Araide

NORTHERN

UÍ NEILL

Uí Cremthainn

Lough Neagh

ULAID

Fir Manach

Lough Erne

AIRGIALLA

Airthir

Dál Fiatach

Donegal Bay

Cairbre

■ Clogher

Downpatrick ■

Dartraige

Uí Méith

Mugdorna

Uí Echach Coba

Uí Fiachrach Muaide

Uí Ailella

Uí Briúin Bréifne

Dairtre

Fir Rois

Conaille Muirtheimne

Luigne

54°

Gailenga

Conmaice Rein

Gailenga

Irish

Umall

Uí Briúin Aí

Cairbre

Luigne

Ciannachta

Knowth ■

Sea

CONNACHT

Cruachú ■

Shannon

SOUTHERN

Loegaire

Brega

Partraige

Tethba

UÍ NEILL

Tara ■

Conmáicne Mara

Lough Corrib

Sogain

Delbna

Lough Ree

Cenél Fiachach

Fir Tulach

Cairbre

Saithne

Lagore ■

Uí Briúin Seola

Uí Maine

Uí Fiachrach Aidne

Delbna

Uí Failge

Uí Fáeláin

Naas ■

Corca Mruad

Lough Derg

Múscraige Tíre

Lóigis

Cualu

Uí Garrchon

53°

Uí Dúnlainge

Éile

ATLANTIC

Uí Bairrche

Uí Enachglais

OCEAN

Corca Baiscind

Déis (Dál Cais)

Osraige

LAIGIN

to North Wales

Shannon

Uaithne

Eóganacht Caisil

Uí Dróna

Uí Fidgente

Eóganacht Áine

Cashel ■

Uí Chennselaig

Ciarraige Luachra

Orbraige

MUNSTER

Corca Duibne

Eóganacht Locha Léin

Eóganacht Glennamain

Déisi Muman

52°

Uí Liatháin

St George's Channel

Corca Lóigde

Eóganacht Rathlind

to South Wales

to Cornwall and Devon

9°

7°

0   100 km

0   100 miles

Early Peoples and Provinces

With the introduction of Christianity in the fifth century came the Latin language and, with it, learning and literature, both in Latin and, increasingly, in the vernacular. This material, the most encyclopaedic to survive from any country in 'Dark Age' Europe, enables us to reconstruct the political map of Ireland even at this early period. Using sets of annals which keep a contemporary record of the main events of each year, genealogies which preserve the line of descent of important individuals, king-lists which, as the name suggests, record the sequence of succession to kingship in territories both great and small, along with various other sources, we can assemble the names of the many peoples who together dominated the island, the territories they held, and the rise and fall of the various dynasties.

The first thing that emerges is the extent to which political divisions had changed since Ptolemy's time. Ptolemy, as we have seen, had conferred a certain pride of place on the Érainn peoples in Munster who had given the country its very name, but by the seventh century they had been pushed back from Munster's fertile plains by a federation of dynasties known as the Eóganachta, so called because they traced their descent from their alleged eponymous forefather, Eógan. What is interesting about the Eóganachta is that they may have been Irish colonists who returned from Britain. Their later origin-legend claimed that Eógan spent a prolonged period of exile in Britain before coming home to Ireland and that it was his descendant, Conall Corc, who established their capital at *Caisel* (nowadays Cashel, Co. Tipperary); the legend, of course, may be unreliable, but it is curious that the name of their capital is not in fact originally an Irish word, but rather a borrowing from the Latin *castellum*, meaning a castle or fortress, and the choice of such a Latin term does suggest external influence.

To the east of the Eóganachta lay the over-kingdom of Laigin from which we get the modern province name of Leinster. The Vikings should probably be credited with coining the latter: it seems that they took the name *Laigin*, joined it with the Irish word *tír*, meaning land or country, and produced *Laigin's tír*, and hence Leinster; by the same process *Ulaid's tír* gave us Ulster and *Mumhan's tír* produced Munster. The modern province of Leinster stretches north to include Co. Louth and westwards to take in Offaly, Laois and Kilkenny, but in the early medieval period Laigin went no further west than Co. Carlow, being bounded by the River Barrow, beyond which smaller dynasties acted a buffers between its kings and those of Munster. These buffer-states included the Uí Failge, from which modern Offaly is obtained, though their boundaries bear little resemblance to each other; the Lóigis (which gives us Laois or Leix) and, most importantly perhaps, Osraige (which has given its name to the diocese of Ossory). Although the early province of Laigin never included Co. Louth, it did originally stretch as far north as the Boyne, but it was pushed back to the Liffey after the sixth century, and, with only short-term exceptions, the northern boundary of Leinster remained fixed at the Liffey for the next thousand years. Throughout the early historic period it was dominated by two dynasties, Uí Dúnlainge ('descendants of Dúnlaing'), centred on Kildare, and Uí Chennselaig ('descendants of [Énna] Cennselach'), associated with Ferns.

The Laigin lost their lands in Meath (which comes from the Irish word *Mide*, literally 'middle') to what was to become far and away the most important power in medieval Ireland, the Uí Néill, 'the descendants of Niall'. The Niall in question is Niall Noígiallach ('Niall of the Nine Hostages'), who would have lived in the early fifth century if, in fact, he is an actual historical figure. The origins of the Uí Néill may lie west of the Shannon. Connacht takes its name from a mythical ancestor of Niall called Conn Cétchathach ('Conn of the Hundred Battles'), and was later dominated by the Uí Briúin who, like the Uí Néill and in common with most Irish bloodlines, believed that they all descended from a shared ancestor, in this instance, from Brión, said to have been a brother of Niall of the Nine Hostages.

As the Uí Briúin show, Irish genealogical history is very much like a pyramid with a common ancestor-figure at the apex, whether he be real or imagined. And of course, over the generations, since kings tended to have several wives and perhaps many sons by each, it didn't take long for a royal family to become split into various rival branches, with cousins and second-cousins all trying to push the others out and make their leader king. About the year 700 the Uí Briúin had their headquarters around Carnfree in Co. Roscommon, but we soon find them starting to splinter. Those who managed to hold on to the Roscommon homelands became known as Uí Briúin Aí, while another wing, called Uí Briúin Seola, was pushed south-east to barren lands near Lough Corrib, and a third offshoot of them headed north-east into what are now Cavan and Leitrim, and were known as Uí Briúin Bréifne.

And so it went on over the centuries, one lineage rising in power, another falling, and as families grew they made war on their distant relatives to try to grab the kingship for themselves or they spread out into the lands of other tribes. Nothing stayed constant, the base of the pyramid getting wider and wider with each succeeding generation. In turn, therefore, each of these three offshoots of the Uí Briúin produced their own offshoots! By the time of the English invasion of Ireland in the twelfth century the Uí Briúin Aí were split into several segments, and their leading family were now called the Uí Chonchobair, better known as the O'Connors, taking their name from one of their more successful warrior-kings, a man called Conchobar who died in 973; the Uí Briúin Seola too had their competing lines, the leading one of which were the Uí Flaithbertaig, more familiar as the O'Flahertys, and still numerous in west Connacht to this day; while Uí Briúin Bréifne were led by the Uí Ruairc, the still thriving O'Rourkes.

If it was from Connacht that Niall of the Nine hostages hailed, his reputed descendants had, by the early medieval period, long since abandoned their western homeland and are found occupying an arc of territory running, with interruptions, from Donegal to Meath. Tradition has it that Niall had fourteen sons and it is from these that the various branches of the Uí Néill are supposed to descend. There are two main groups, one of which held power in the north-west of Ireland, and are known as the Northern Uí Néill, with a focal point at Grianán of Ailech near Derry, the other being based in the north midlands, and called the Southern Uí Néill. All are said to descend from various of Niall's sons, one of whom, for instance, Conall, gave his name to a people named Cenél Conaill ('the family of Conall') inhabiting a territory simply called Tír Conaill ('the land of Conall'), which approximates to modern Co. Donegal, while the name of another, Eógan, is preserved in the Inishowen peninsula, and in Tyrone, which in Irish is Tír Eógain, the people of which are therefore termed the Cenél nEógain.

Although Tara was an Iron Age site, it remained important in early medieval times, as we can see from these two linking ring-forts within its main enclosure known as Ráith na Ríg ('The Rath of the Kings'). Here, the Feis Temro ('The Feast of Tara') was held by its kings to celebrate Tara's divine nature and to emphasise its special status in Ireland. The monument in the foreground is thought to be Tech Cormaic, supposed home of the legendary heroic king of Ireland, Cormac mac Airt, while that in the background is traditionally known as the Forad, the platform on which the king of Tara was said to have been inaugurated.

The Southern Uí Néill had their own distinct groupings, and they wrested Tara from the Laigin, so that it became their 'capital', as it were. In spite of severe competition between the Northern and Southern Uí Néill, they rotated the title 'king of Tara' between them, and in time their powerful propaganda-machine was able to convince provincial rulers throughout the country that possession of Tara signified possession of the high-kingship of Ireland. They commissioned propaganda claiming that Tara was the ancient capital of Ireland, and fabricated a pre-history of the country which linked all the dynasties and all the various peoples inhabiting the island by descent from a common set of ancestors, leading ultimately to the mythical Míl, or Milesius, of Spain, and thence to Noah and Adam. This allowed to take hold the belief that the Irish were a separate nation: they were the *Goídil* (or *Scoti* in Latin) and spoke a common language, *Goídelg*, or Gaeilge is it is spelt today. The result was the belief that in the past the Irish had one king, one set of laws, and one capital; and in time the Uí Néill were able to convince most people that that ancient capital was Tara.

As the Uí Néill pushed north, so too did various of their subject-peoples, principally the Airgialla, who established a firm foothold in mid and south Ulster. The result of this was that the great over-kingdom which had dominated Ulster just before the dawn of Irish history in the fifth century, and from whom the province takes its name, the Ulaid, had their power very considerably circumscribed. Once, from their capital at Emain Macha, they had ruled as far south as the Boyne, and they defended the boundaries of their kingdom with massive linear earthworks, like the Black Pig's Dyke and the Dorsey Ramparts, traces of which still survive. We do not know when precisely Emain fell, but for most of the historic period Ulaid's power was confined to the area east of the Bann, and their most important dynasty was Dál ('the share of') Fiatach, who ruled the Mournes from their new capital at Downpatrick.

Homes and Lifestyles

While few traces survive of the lives of ordinary people, the rich and powerful inhabitants of early-medieval Ireland have left behind the remnants of their civilisation. The countryside is dotted with the remains of thousands of ring-forts, the farmsteads of early Ireland. Ring-forts were usually constructed in places where the land was worth farming, often near the top of a hill with a good view of the surrounding countryside. Ringed by as many as three ditches up to two metres deep, with banks made from the earth taken from the ditches, they had a strong defensive capacity. Such an earthen ring-fort is known as a *rath* and the area inside it where the occupants lived is a *lios*. In parts of the country where the land is stony, ring-forts are generally constructed of stone and known as a *caiseal* or *cathair*, the word *dún* usually being reserved for exceptionally large examples. The farm-houses and buildings would have been at the centre, with perhaps a milking-yard outside, a mill for the corn (if the owners were wealthy enough to afford one), and servants' huts, and stretching beyond them would have been the fields of crops and pastures for grazing animals. The lake-dwelling, or *crannóg*, is another form of habitation surviving from early-medieval Ireland, though far less common than the ring-fort. Many of these are man-made islands, and thus more difficult and more expensive to build than a ring-fort, but providing better defense since they were difficult to overrun. Being so costly to build, we can be fairly sure that they were the well-defended homes of powerful people, and some the palaces of kings.

Until the late Viking Age, Ireland was a coinless society where cows were a common medium of exchange, an indication of both their prevalence and their economic importance. Land was measured in terms of the number of cows it could sustain, while fines and rents were also calculated in cows. A well-off farmer was a *bóaire*, a 'lord of cows', and cattle-raiding was an everyday occurrence. Dairy-farming was at the heart of the Irish agricultural system. In summer it was normal to live on milk and dairy products while in autumn some cattle were killed, their beef being salted to eat in winter, though meat from pigs was also quite common. Sheep were kept more for their wool than their mutton, while the native horse was small, and horse-meat, though occasionally consumed, was generally frowned upon.

Some arable farming was done in all parts of Ireland, but it was generally not as important as pastoral farming, and obviously the situation varied from region to region in accordance with landscape and climate. Ploughing was carried out in spring using oxen rather than horses, though the possession of a full plough-team of four to six animals was beyond all but the most prosperous farmers. Harvesting was done, using the sickle, by a team known as a *meitheal*, and, once harvested, kilns were used to dry the newly-threshed grain, which was milled in quite sophisticated water-mills served by an artificially-diverted mill-race, and the mill-wright was a craftsman of some stature in early Irish society. Mills, like kilns also, seem to have been jointly owned and the subject was contentious enough for a law to exist to regulate their shared use. The main crops were oats, barley and wheat, used for making bread, porridge, gruel and, in the case of the barley, for brewing beer.

Social Structures

We are not dependent on archaeologists alone to piece together this picture of early Irish economy and society. The Old Irish law-texts (the Brehon laws as they are often called, from the word *brithemain*, meaning 'judges') give a remarkably detailed picture of Irish society at the time of their composition beginning in the seventh century. The greatest influence on the development of Irish law was the Christian Church. The churchmen who came to Christianise Ireland in the fifth and sixth centuries brought the works of learning produced by the early Church fathers. In the late sixth and the seventh centuries the church-run schools of Ireland became great centres of learning in such Christian literature, and a caste of scholars emerged who were lawyers, canonists, historians, poets, and grammarians, who wrote in Latin and Irish. When these men were drawing up rules for governing society, they looked to the Old Testament and embraced the biblical example as their own, adapting it to suit particular Irish circumstances.

The society that they helped to mould was one that was intensely aristocratic and hierarchical. Status and honour (*enech*, literally 'face') meant everything. To offend against a person of high status, to outrage his honour, incurred a greater penalty than a similar crime against a person of lower status. Status was measured in terms of one's 'honour-price' (*lóg n-enech*), which had to be paid in restitution for major offences against him, being considerably higher for a king than a commoner. The law made a basic distinction between those who were *nemed* ('sacred'), including kings, clerics and poets, and those who were not, and then a further distinction among the latter between those who were *sóer* ('free') and those who were *dóer* ('unfree').

According to the law-tracts, there were three grades of kings. At the bottom of the scale was the king of a small local kingdom or *túath*; then came

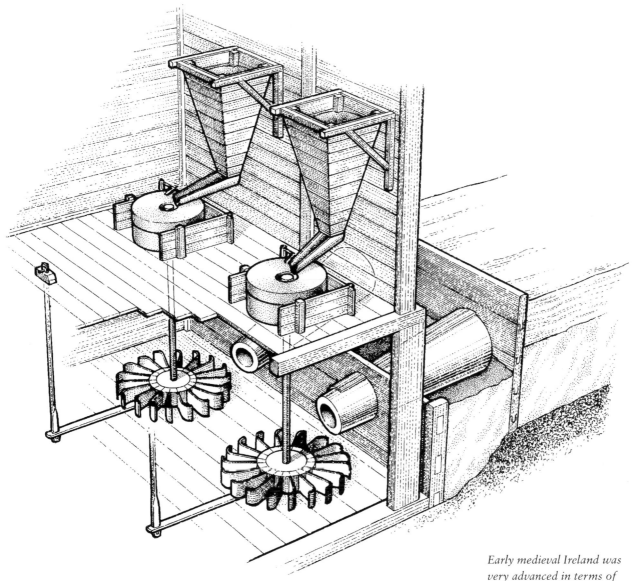

the 'overking' who was king not only over his own *túath* but over several other petty kingdoms; and finally, there was the 'king of overkings' who effectively ruled a whole province, though even his power was rooted in his own core territory. The annals and sagas frequently accord individuals the title 'king of Ireland', but this is extremely rare in the law-tracts. Whatever about the theory, in practice kings lower than the province-king hardly mattered. Irish society revolved around the figure of the king, and great symbolism was attached to his inauguration, his mating with the goddess of the land from which would come fertility to man and beast throughout his reign. Stress was laid on a king's justice, from which flowed peace and prosperity, and from whose injustice sprang famine, plague and infertility.

Below the kings stood the noblemen, and below the nobles the commoners. A nobleman or lord (*flaith*) was obviously distinguishable from a commoner

Early medieval Ireland was very advanced in terms of the development of water-powered mills. Excavations have produced the remains of the earliest examples in Europe of certain types of watermill, while 7th-century laws written in Old Irish preserve the earliest vernacular terms for their principal components. The illustration shows a conjectural reconstruction of a double-flume horizontal watermill excavated at Little Island, Co. Cork, which dated from c. AD 630 (after Rynne).

by virtue of his birth and wealth, but, in early-medieval Ireland, it was the possession of clients (*céili*, literally 'companions') which conferred the status of lordship. Clientship was the institution which bound the lord and his dependant together in a relationship which had mutual benefits, but was, of course, more favourable to the lord. In essence, the lord granted the client a fief of land or stock, and in return the client bound himself to make specific payments to the lord: he might provide a food-rent in the form of part of his produce, or hospitality to the lord during winter. It was part of the duty of the lord to provide physical defense for the client and to protect his rights from outside encroachment.

The early Christian monastery of Nendrum is located on Mahee Island in Strangford Lough, Co. Down, and is only accessible by causeway. It was founded perhaps as early

as the 5th century by St Mochaoi and excavations have shown that its various quarters were divided by a series of three concentric walls, the first wall surrounding the monastery buildings themselves, including a small stone church and the stump of a Round Tower dating from the 10th or 11th century. Within the other walls stood more buildings, including workshops and perhaps a school (after Hamlin).

Although the clients were free men, that is not to say that early Irish society was in any sense egalitarian; quite the reverse. The family, or kin-group (*fine*), rather than the individual was the legal unit recognised under the law. It was the family which owned property, which came into an inheritance, which was held responsible for the misdemeanours of its individual members. If a man was murdered, it was the prerogative of the family to seek revenge or to claim compensation in the form of a 'body-fine' (*éraic*) from the culprit. The family group that mattered most in the early period was the *derbfine* or 'true kin', made up of all those descended from a common great-grandfather in the male line. Today's family would be rather surprised by its medieval equivalent. With few exceptions, women could not buy or sell or make any form of contract or transaction without the consent of those who had authority over her, her father when she was a girl, her husband when she married, her son when she was a widow. Although in the sagas women are frequently very powerful – one only has to think of Queen Medb in *Táin Bó Cuailnge*, who was the real leader of Connacht rather than her weak husband Ailill – in real life the power of women was much more circumscribed. The annals are our primary source for early Irish history, and it is hard to find in them a single example of a female political or military leader. Sexual promiscuity by women was condemned though men fared rather better and among them polygamy seems to have been rife.

The Golden Age

Although the beginnings of a diocesan structure may have been given to the Irish Church by the early missionaries, by the sixth century Ireland's most important churches were ruled by a monastic hierarchy, and certain of its monasteries, which were believed to share a common founder, were grouped together in what is known as a *paruchia*. The largest and most influential of these was Armagh, still today the centre of both the Roman Catholic and Anglican Church in Ireland. Armagh's primacy is the product of its supposed association with St Patrick – indeed, the official title of the archbishop of Armagh in Irish is *Comharba Phádraig*, 'the Successor of Patrick'. But there is no proof of this link, and, in fact, Downpatrick has a stronger claim to being the main focus of Patrick's activities. Patrick *may* have founded the Church of Armagh, but the most important documentary records which assert this are preserved in a manuscript called the *Book of Armagh*, which was compiled there in the first decade of the ninth century, precisely for that purpose: to demonstrate to the rest of the Irish Church that Armagh was entitled to claim primacy because it had been selected for that task by Patrick, and that Patrick was the founder of many other listed churches in Ireland, which, therefore, effectively belonged to Armagh and should pay tax or tribute to it. Having said that, Armagh's special status does seem to have been widely recognised: it is hardly fortuitous that the bishop of Armagh heads the list of Irish Church leaders written to by the pope-elect, John IV, as long ago as 640.

Part of the impetus for the wave of monasticism that had swept over Ireland by the sixth century came from Britain. St Enda, founder of the church on Inis Mór, the largest of the Aran Islands in Galway Bay, studied with St Ninian in Galloway in Scotland. The Welsh saints, David and Cadoc, were the inspiration for St Máedóc of Ferns and St Finnian of Clonard. Finnian then taught men who were important monastic founders in their own right, including Brendan (Clonfert), Ciarán (Clonmacnoise), and Colum Cille (Durrow, Derry and Iona). The monastic centres were not the exclusive preserve of men, the most famous house of nuns being St Brigit's at Kildare, and while some churches were easily accessible and richly endowed, and undoubtedly places of commerce as much

The Book of Kells, preserved in Trinity College, Dublin, is a copy of the Gospels written in Latin, most famous for its lavishly decorated full-page depictions of the Four Evangelists and their symbols, portraits of the Virgin and Child and of Christ, including the depiction of His temptation and arrest, as seen in the accompanying photograph. However, even the text pages are full of life, the initial letters being decorated with often comical human and animal figures. Most scholars now accept that it was compiled in the monastery of Iona off the west coast of Scotland, around the year 800, and that after a Viking attack in 806, it was brought for safekeeping to another of Colm Cille's monasteries at Kells, Co. Meath, from which it takes its name.

as prayer, others, most notably Sceilg Mhicíl off the Kerry coast, were retreats from the world.

It was a hermit's desire to renounce home and family that brought Colum Cille (Columba) to the Hebridean island of Iona in 563, but his efforts were soon channelled into the conversion of the Picts. Later, monks from Iona spread Christianity in the Anglo-Saxon kingdom of Northumbria, and by the end of the sixth century another wave of *peregrini pro Christo* ('pilgrims for Christ'), led by Columbanus of Bangor, had begun missionary activity in France, spreading within a generation to the Low Countries, and the Rhineland, reviving Christianity wherever they went, and leaving monasteries after them to continue their work.

The monastic schools of Ireland had by now attained a high level of scholarship and Irish scholars began to make their imprint on European culture. When a renaissance of learning got underway in the court schools of Charlemagne and his successors, Irishmen were very much to the fore. Dicuil was an Irish monk who taught at the palace school of Charlemagne in the early years of the ninth century and was famous for his study of world geography based on classical authors. Sedulius Scottus taught at the court of Charlemagne's grandson, Charles the Bald, in the middle years of the ninth century, and was one of the most learned men of his time, being a gifted and witty poet, a philosopher, theologian and grammarian. Most important of all, though, was Johannes Scottus Eriugena, the controversial theologian, philosopher, and scholar of Greek, perhaps the most outstandingly gifted man of letters in the Europe of his day.

Increasing secularisation, wealth, and lay patronage enabled the monasteries to make an important contribution too to the visual arts. Much of the finest metalwork of the period, including the famous Ardagh and Derrynaflan chalices, was produced under Church auspices, as were such beautiful objects as precious shrines and covers made for relics and books, though not the elaborate jewellery of which the Tara brooch, which contains an astonishing amount of the most minutely detailed ornament, represents the greatest triumph. The High Crosses still testify to the skill of the church's craftsmen in stone, becoming ever more vivid in terms of the scenes depicted on them, usually Biblical episodes, and ever more complex in design and technical ornament, so that the best are comparable to manuscript art. The latter began simply enough with books such as the '*Cathach* of Colum Cille', a Psalter written in the early seventh century, and displaying few signs of external influence of more recent vintage than La Tène. Then a generation or so later, after contact with Northumbria had been well and truly established, the *Book of Durrow* was compiled, a set of the Gospels still displaying Celtic design but showing new influences too from Anglo-Saxon art, including full pages given over to

The Viking Wars

▢	Dublin Vikings active, 917–1014
▯	Viking settlement
▲	Viking encampment
★	Viking raids and battles, 795–835
★	Viking raids and battles, 836–902
◤	Vikings inward
▸	Vikings outward

1. First Viking raid, 795
2. To York, 920–940
3. To Scotland, 866–870
4. Dublin taken, 841
5. Danes arrive, 851 and 875
6. To Scotland, 918

Dromiskin, Co. Louth, was an important early medieval monastic site whose Round Tower has unusual proportions and may have been truncated at some point. Its doorway is c. 3.75m above present ground level and just below the roof level are four rectangular openings at each point of the compass which are later insertions. In the background are the remnants of a High Cross.

Opposite: The map attempts to reconstruct the military and naval campaigns of Brian Boru as recorded in contemporary annals. This record is undoubtedly incomplete but nevertheless shows something of the energy of the man and the resources which he committed over a period of more than a third of a century to extending his authority throughout the island. His circuits of Ireland must have been extraordinary logistical exercises, while his use of the Shannon to launch raids on his enemies inland shows his application to Irish warfare of tactical and technical skills learned from the Vikings.

elaborate interlaced animal representations. A whole series of such splendid Gospel books followed, culminating in the supreme masterpiece of the art of ecclesiastical manuscript illumination, the *Book of Kells*.

The Viking Wars

Whatever the underlying causes, bands of Scandinavian warriors, manning fleets of technically advanced warships, began raiding western Europe in the dying years of the eighth century. The first recorded Viking attack on Ireland took place in 795 when Norse raiders assaulted several island monasteries off Ireland's coast. Raids tended at first to be confined to the northern and western seaboards, though by 824 even Sceilg in the far south-west fell victim.

In these first four decades of their campaigns the Vikings rarely penetrated

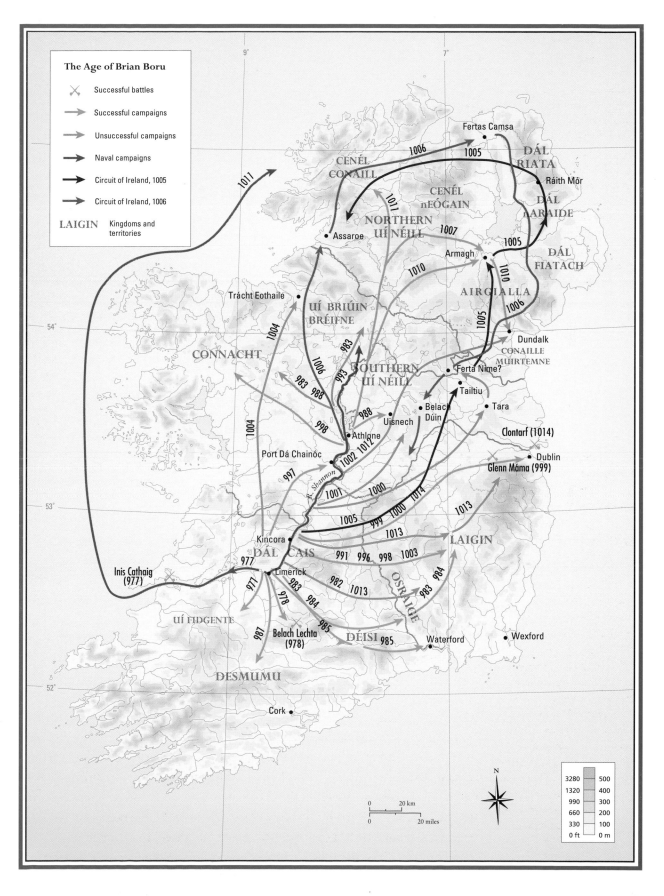

The Age of Brian Boru

✗ Successful battles

→ Successful campaigns

→ Unsuccessful campaigns

➤ Naval campaigns

➤ Circuit of Ireland, 1005

➤ Circuit of Ireland, 1006

LAIGIN Kingdoms and territories

Fertas Camsa

1006 · 1005 · DÁL RIATA

Ráith Mór

CENÉL CONAILL

CENÉL nEÓGAIN

DÁL ARAIDE

1011

NORTHERN UÍ NÉILL

1011

Assaroe

1007

Armagh

1005

DÁL FIATACH

1010

AIRGIALLA

1010

1005

1006

Trácht Eothaile

UÍ BRIÚIN BRÉIFNE

1004

Dundalk

CONAILLE MÚIRTEMNE

983

CONNACHT

1006

983 988

983

Ferta Nime?

SOUTHERN UÍ NÉILL

Tailtiu

988

Belach Dúin

Tara

998

Uisnech

1004

Athlone

Clontarf (1014)

Port Dá Chainóc

1002 1012

Dublin

Glenn Máma (999)

997

R. Shannon

1001

1000

1014

1005 · 999 1000 1000 · 1014

1013

Kincora

977

DÁL CAIS

991 996 998 1003

LAIGIN

Inis Cathaig (977)

✗

Limerick

977

982 1013

1013

UÍ FIDGENTE

983 978

984

985

OSRAIGE

983 984

987

Belach Lechta (978)

DÉISI 985

Waterford

Wexford

DESMUMU

Cork

N

0   20 km

0   20 miles

3280 — 500
1320 — 400
990 — 300
660 — 200
330 — 100
0 ft — 0 m

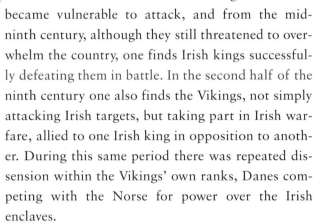

Brian Boru has continued to fascinate the Irish people, perhaps being used as something of a metaphor for Irish success over foreign domination, however anachronistic the assessment. This ludicrously conjectural illustration of him shows the way in which a much later generation of Irish nationalists viewed his supposed stature.

further than twenty miles inland and were still simply sea-borne raiders, based elsewhere. They periodically plundered Irish churches, not simply because Christian targets made suitable pagan prey, but because the monasteries were important focal points of economic activity, and storehouses of moveable goods, inhabited by potential captives. During the next twenty years the raids became more intense, and the Vikings began attacking further inland. In the winter of 840–41 they stayed moored on Lough Neagh and then set up a permanent *longphort* ('ship-camp') at Dublin, which in time became their chief settlement in Ireland, a base from which to launch extensive plunderings in the surrounding territories.

Now that they had permanent bases in Ireland the Vikings themselves became vulnerable to attack, and from the mid-ninth century, although they still threatened to overwhelm the country, one finds Irish kings successfully defeating them in battle. In the second half of the ninth century one also finds the Vikings, not simply attacking Irish targets, but taking part in Irish warfare, allied to one Irish king in opposition to another. During this same period there was repeated dissension within the Vikings' own ranks, Danes competing with the Norse for power over the Irish enclaves.

By the mid-850s the earlier great raids were on the decline, and the Vikings turned their attention further afield, to northern Britain and the settlement of Iceland. Divisions within the Norse communities in Ireland, and more effective Irish opposition, led to their expulsion from Dublin in 902, and no Irish Viking activity is recorded until 914 when Viking fleets reappeared in Waterford harbour, attacking Munster and Leinster, re-occupying Dublin and scoring some notable victories against the Irish kings. For the next two decades the Dublin Vikings were very powerful, and sought to reign over the kingdom of York and over the Norse of Waterford and Limerick. Thereafter, their power declined, the activities of the Dublin Norse being generally confined to the town's hinterland, and by 950 or so this last great phase of Viking warfare was at an end.

The Age of Brian Boru

It would be wrong to exaggerate the ill-effects of Viking attacks on the Irish Church, since the latter was already highly politicised, and monastic centres sometimes suffered as much from the depredations of rival Irish rulers as from Viking assault. The Ostmen (as they called themselves) made, in many respects, a positive contribution to Irish life. They gave the country its first towns, its first coinage, and more advanced shipping and naval capacity. As some of their settlements grew into towns (Dublin becoming one of the wealthiest ports in western Europe), they expanded Ireland's trading contacts, and introduced its artists and craftsmen to new styles and motifs.

The Ostmen generally governed large areas in the hinterland of their towns, and in doing so displaced some minor local kingdoms. Their strength in Munster may also have contributed to the decline of the reigning Eóganachta kings and helped pave the way to power of the rulers of Dál Cais, who controlled the strategic lower Shannon basin.

The first of their kings to attain real power was Cennétig, son of Lorcán, who died as king of Thomond (literally, north Munster) in 951, to be succeeded by his son Mathgamain, who brought east Munster, and the Ostmen of Limerick and Waterford, under his sway, and is described in the annals in 967 as 'king of Cashel', the first member of Dál Cais to win the title, and perhaps the first non-Eóganachta king of the province in five centuries. After Mathgamain's death in 976 his brother Brian Boru succeeded, usually regarded as the greatest of Ireland's high-kings.

Brian was born *c.* 941 and was nicknamed Boru, from the old Irish word *Bóruma*, 'of the cattle-tribute', or perhaps 'of Béal Bóruma', a fort north of Killaloe, Co. Clare. In the course of a military career that spanned five decades, Brian fought quite a few major battles but his first vital encounter was the Battle of Belach Lechta in 978, a contest for the kingship of Munster between Dál Cais and the Eóganachta, from which Brian emerged victorious. He now represented a threat to the other provincial rulers. Not surprisingly, therefore, the Uí Néill high-king, Máel Sechnaill, brought the army of *Leth Cuinn*, the northern half of Ireland, south to Thomond, and broke down the sacred tree of Mag Adair, the Dál Cais royal inauguration site, so as to deny Brian's royal pretensions, but it was entirely without effect. Brian remained in a strong position and came to control most of *Leth Moga*, the southern half of Ireland. Eventually, in 997, Brian sailed to Port Dá Chaineóc, near Clonfert, and there reached a formal agreement with Máel Sechnaill to divide Ireland between them: the latter abandoned the centuries-old Uí Néill claim

The Ardagh Chalice made for dispensing the eucharistic wine at the Mass. One of the finest examples of the metalworkers' craft, dating from the 8th century. It was discovered in the 19th century at, as its name suggests, Ardagh, Co. Limerick, not far from Brian's capital and was probably deliberately buried to preserve it from falling into Viking hands.

to overlordship of the entire country, and became master of Leth Cuinn alone, and Brian was given overlordship of Leth Moga.

This was the highlight of Brian's career to date, but in 1001 he went one step further when he obtained the submission of the Uí Néill high-king, and thereby overturned a convention that was several centuries old, so that he was now entitled, if he could enforce his claim, to call himself high-king of Ireland. Brian set about making a reality of his claim, in a series of major northern campaigns. His 1005 expedition was evidently his most elaborate yet. He came to Armagh, stayed a week, and camped, surely conscious of symbolism, at Emain Macha, Ulster's ancient capital. While at Armagh Brian 'left twenty ounces of gold on Patrick's altar'. The early ninth-century *Book of Armagh*, with its collection of early Patrician texts, was produced for inspection by him, and still contains a note written 'in the presence of Brian, Emperor of the Irish (*Imperator Scotorum*)', a title unique in Irish history.

The Battle of Clontarf

Brian continued to press for dominance throughout the country, but in 1013 the power-structure which he had laboriously built up began to crumble when Dublin and Leinster rebelled. He spent from 9 September until Christmas 1013 trying to force them back into submission, and this culminated in the famous battle fought at Clontarf on Good Friday, 23 April 1014. It was a bloody and lengthy affair, the Dublin and Leinster armies being reinforced by troops from Man and the Western and Northern Isles. The Munster army won the day, although Brian himself was killed. His body was brought ceremoniously to Armagh and there waked for twelve nights, before being buried in a new tomb. Later traditions embellished the account of the battle, especially by casting the affair as a climactic confrontation between the Irish and the Norse, in which the Irish won out, admittedly with the tragic loss of their hero. The trend among modern scholars is to challenge the notion of Clontarf as an epic denouement between the Irish and the Viking invader, and to see the occasion more as an attempt by the king of Munster to gain the submission of the errant king of Leinster, with the Hiberno-Norse of Dublin playing a secondary role.

But the stress laid in contemporary accounts on the foreign composition of Brian's opposition indicates that Clontarf was no run-of-the-mill internal conflict. Brian and the battle are written about extensively by writers in the Scandinavian world, while in Ireland, by the early twelfth century, the battle was portrayed in terms that come close to explicit nationalism, and Brian himself assumed messianic proportions. A poem written soon after the English invasion ends: 'From the time Brian was slain, foreigners did not inhabit Ireland until the present day, with the arrival of the Earl [Strongbow]; from the day the Earl came, a fleet of foreigners comes every year, until, alas, they have taken Ireland in general. When will Brian's like come [again], north or south, east or west, a man to save the Irish from anguish, as he alone saved [them]?'.

Something about the Battle of Clontarf and its hero has never failed to hold the imagination of the Irish nation, and it seems that it will remain an important landmark. With Brian Boru's ultimate victory (however Pyrrhic) over his opponents, his career ended in glory, and he shaped the course of Irish history for the next 150 years. Brian had ended the Uí Néill monopoly of the high-kingship. In a sense, he ended the very concept of the high-kingship as it had evolved under them, since, though Máel Sechnaill recovered it after Brian's death, the title remained in abeyance for a full half-century after the latter's demise in 1022. When attempts were then made to revive the office, what emerged was the quite hollow concept of a 'king of Ireland with opposition'. There seems, therefore, little reason to cast doubt on the generally accepted view that Brian Bóruma has earned himself a truly exceptional place among the ranks of Ireland's kings, and it is little wonder that his descendants should sport with pride the surname Ua Briain (O'Brien).

Brian's campaign which reached its climax at Clontarf was a consequence of a rebellion against him by the Ostmen of Dublin and by the men of Leinster. The photograph shows the arched entrance-way into one of the Leinstermen's most important ecclesiastical centres, that at Glendalough high up in the safety of the Wicklow Mountains.

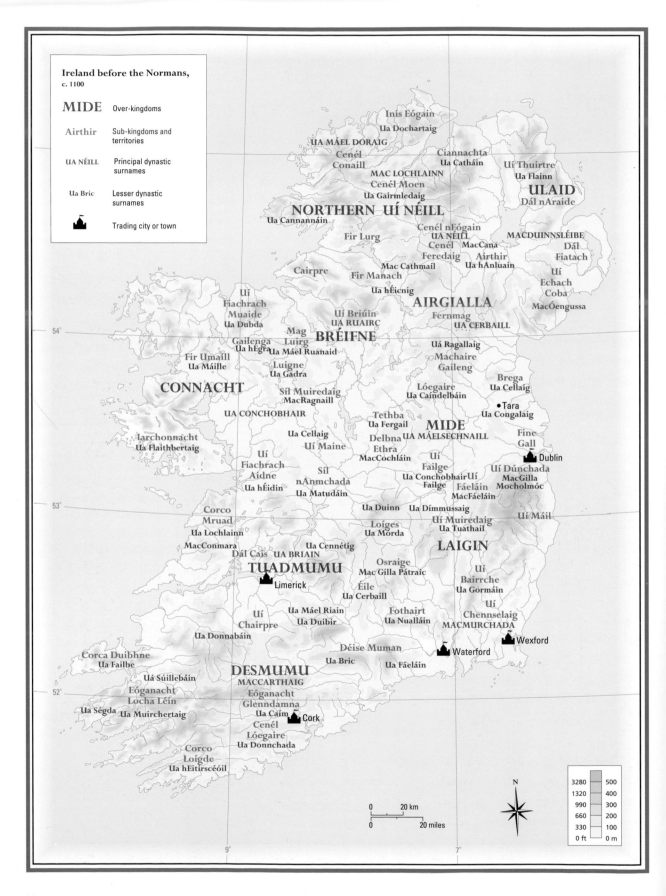

Ireland before the Normans,
c. 1100

MIDE   Over-kingdoms

Airthir   Sub-kingdoms and territories

UA NÉILL   Principal dynastic surnames

Ua Bric   Lesser dynastic surnames

🏰   Trading city or town

Inis Eógain
Ua Dochartaig
UA MÁEL DORAIG
Cenél
Conaill
Ciannachta
Ua Catháin
Uí Thuirtre
Ua Flainn
MAC LOCHLAINN
Cenél Moen
ULAID
Ua Gairmledaig
Dál nAraide
NORTHERN UÍ NÉILL
Ua Cannannáin
Cenél nEógain
UA NÉILL
Cenél
Feredaig
MacCana
MACDUINNSLÉIBE
Dál
Fiatach
Fir Lurg
Airthir
Ua hAnluain
Cairpre
Mac Cathmaíl
Uí
Echach
Coba
Fir Manach
Ua hÉicnig
AIRGIALLA
MacÓengussa
Uí
Fiachrach
Muaide
Ua Dubda
Uí Briúin
UA RUAIRC
Fernmag
UA CERBAILL
Mag
Luirg
BRÉIFNE
Uá Ragallaig
Gailenga
Ua hEgra
Ua Máel Ruanaid
Machaire
Gaileng
Fir Umaill
Ua Máille
Luigne
Ua Gadra
Brega
Ua Cellaig
CONNACHT
Síl Muiredaig
MacRagnaill
Lóegaire
Ua Caindelbáin
•Tara
Ua Congalaig
UA CONCHOBHAIR
Tethba
Ua Fergail
MIDE
Fine
Gall
Iarchonnacht
Ua Flaithbertaig
Ua Cellaig
Uí Maine
Delbna
Ethra
MacCochláin
UA MÁELSECHNAILL
🏰 Dublin
Uí
Fiachrach
Aidne
Ua hÉidin
Síl
nAnmchada
Ua Matudáin
Uí
Failge
Ua Conchobhair Uí
Failge
Uí Dúnchada
MacGilla
Mocholmóc
Fáeláin
MacFáeláin
Corco
Mruad
Ua Duinn
Ua Dímmussaig
Uí Muiredaig
Ua Tuathail
Uí Máil
Ua Lochlainn
Loíges
Ua Mórda
MacConmara
Dál Cais
Ua Cennétig
UA BRIAIN
LAIGIN
TUADMUMU
Osraige
Mac Gilla Pátraic
Uí
Bairrche
Ua Gormáin
🏰 Limerick
Éile
Ua Cerbaill
Uí
Chennselaig
Uí
Chairpre
Ua Máel Riain
Ua Duibir
Fothairt
Ua Nualláin
MACMURCHADA
Ua Donnabáin
🏰 Wexford
Déise Muman
Corca Duibhne
Ua Failbe
Ua Bric
Ua Fáeláin
🏰 Waterford
Uá Súillebáin
DESMUMU
Eóganacht
Locha Léin
MACCARTHAIG
Eóganacht
Glenndamna
Ua Ségda
Ua Muirchertaig
Ua Caím
🏰 Cork
Cenél
Lóegaire
Ua Donnchada
Corco
Loígde
Ua hEitirscéoil

54°
53°
52°
9°
7°

0   20 km
0   20 miles

N

3280   500
1320   400
990   300
660   200
330   100
0 ft   0 m

CHAPTER III

AN ACCIDENT WAITING TO HAPPEN

The real sea-change in Irish politics followed, not the death of Brian Bóruma in 1014, but that of Máel Sechnaill mac Domnaill in 1022, because, for a full half-century thereafter none of the province-kings was dominant enough to impose his rule and there was no recognised high-king of Ireland. For much of the mid-eleventh century the most powerful king was a Leinsterman called Diarmait mac Maíl na mBó, whose dynasty, the Uí Chennselaig, having their capital at Ferns, Co. Wexford, had been excluded from the rule of that province for the previous three centuries. In 1052 this man went one step further than either Brian or Máel Sechnaill when, having seized Dublin, he declared himself its king, and then bestowed it on his most favoured son, Murchad, ancestor of the famous line of the Meic Murchada (Mac Murroughs). From this newly-won position of power, Diarmait mac Maíl na mBó exerted his influence further afield so that when he died in battle in 1072, he was described as *rí hErend co ressabra*, 'king of Ireland with opposition'. This is an important title which emerges in this period to describe men who were claimants to the kingship of Ireland and had managed to get most of the other province-kings to acknowledge them as such, but to whom some provincial opposition always remained. The eleventh and twelfth centuries, therefore, witnessed great warfare in Ireland, but not meaningless violence: quite simply, the man who was high-king of Ireland *with* opposition was trying to become king *without* opposition, by forcing all the other province-kings to acknowledge his claim.

Diarmait mac Maíl na mBó was succeeded as the most dominant province-king by Tairdelbach Ó Briain of Munster, grandson of Brian Bóruma. Ó Briain was a man of some stature within Ireland and also had strong international contacts, who corresponded with the famous Pope Gregory VII, and with William the Conqueror's archbishop of Canterbury, Lanfranc. He also had as his capital the wealthy trading city of Limerick, and, in 1072, marched his armies on Dublin and was made king there, an indication of how important Dublin was becoming in the race for the high-kingship. Interestingly too, he also appointed his son Muirchertach as king of Dublin just as Diarmait mac Maíl na mBó had done a generation earlier. Muirchertach succeeded his father in 1086, though not without stiff

A Viking sword discovered in the grave find at Islandbridge, Dublin.

This tall, narrow cross at Tully in south Co. Dublin, though badly weathered, seems to portray a bishop, and the church nearby, dedicated to St Brigid, which dates from perhaps the 12th century, was known as Tulach na nEaspag ('Tully of the Bishops'), since it was the property of the priory of Holy Trinity at Christ Church Cathedral, Dublin.

Opposite: *The map shows some of the main features of the reform movement in the Irish Church in the late 11th and 12th centuries: the consecration at Canterbury of bishops for the dioceses established by the Ostmen of Dublin, Waterford and Limerick; the extraordinary career-path of St Malachy of Armagh; his fostering of the Cistercian order and the foundation of many of their abbeys in Ireland; the increased contact between Ireland and Rome as manifested by the appointment of papal legates to preside over synods; culminating in the four ecclesiastical provinces established under the terms of the Synod of Kells-Mellifont in 1152.*

opposition from within his own family. Because there was no fixed law of royal succession in Ireland, the path to kingship was potentially wide open. Provided a person had ability, charisma and access to the levers to power, he could stake his claim. To be a king's favourite son was a help, of course, because he could build up a power-base during his father's life-time. But arms and armies were not the exclusive possession of any one man, and for that reason power-struggles were common, and the enmity within dynasties was often as great as that between them.

Muirchertach Ó Briain changed the face of Irish politics when, in 1089, he took temporary control of the province of Leinster, and seems to have been intent on assuming the place of its own kings. In 1093 he went to Connacht and banished the reigning dynasty north to Tír Eógain, giving their lands to a minor local chieftain. In the following year, when he marched to Mide (Meath), he drove the ruling dynasty into Bréifne, partitioned the province in two and appointed minor local lords to rule both parts under his authority. But he never managed to assert real control further north, in particular, he failed to get the northern king, Domnall Mac Lochlainn of Cenél nEógain, to submit to him as over-king. The latter was every bit as innovative as Ó Briain. In 1112, for instance, Mac Lochlainn appointed his own son as king of the hostile neighbouring kingdom of Cenél Conaill. In the following year, he marched into the east Ulster kingdom of Ulaid, defeated and expelled their king, partitioned the kingdom, and took a large slice of it for himself.

What was happening here was the annexation of land and the attempt to exercise authority over traditionally alien territories, developments not far removed from those taking place in feudal society abroad where much of Europe was undergoing rapid change. Advanced methods of production led to an economic boom; improvements in armaments and military tactics gave kings, popes and potentates new power to conquer old enemies, and a population-surplus gave them the manpower to make those conquests permanent by a process of colonisation. As the Spaniards pushed back the forces of Islam, and Germans entered the lands of the Slavs beyond the River Elbe, and Frankish knights established crusading kingdoms in the Holy Land, so the Norman conquerors of England threatened the native rulers of Scotland and Wales, and, by the late twelfth century, Ireland.

Internationalising the Church

The Irish Church already had a long tradition of contact with the Church in Anglo-Saxon England, with places like Worcester, Winchester, Glastonbury and Canterbury. As the pace of reform in the English Church increased after the Norman conquest in 1066, these religious centres became vehicles for reform, and Irishmen, who were in the custom of training for priestly orders there, thus brought these ideas back to Ireland with them. The first evidence of this wind of change comes only eight years after the conquest, in 1074, when the Ostmen of Dublin chose as their bishop a man called Gilla Pátraic, whom they sent to Archbishop Lanfranc, who consecrated him as bishop, Gilla Pátraic having sworn canonical obedience to him. The archbishop of Canterbury was, therefore, the provincial superior of the bishop of Dublin. This procedure was repeated for each of Gilla Pátraic's successors at Dublin over the next half-century, and in the case of a bishop appointed to Waterford in 1096, and for one of the bishops of Limerick.

What is interesting is that the inhabitants of the Ostman towns had the full support of the Irish kings in looking to Canterbury for leadership. Evidently, they recognised that since Church law demand- ed that bishops be consecrated by canonically qualified superiors, which were not available in Ireland because it lacked a properly-structured diocesan system, Canterbury had to be involved, until, that is, the Irish Church under- went considerable reorganisation. In this movement towards reform Muirchertach Ó Briain of Munster took the lead. The first major reforming synod took place under his direc- tion at Cashel in 1101 and concerned itself with the sort of issues synods throughout Europe were dealing with at that time. It dealt with the laws on marriage, and with establishing the freedom of the Church from lay interference and taxation. It also made an effort to improve the quality of churchmen by insist- ing on them taking holy orders, and on being celibate, and it tried to eradicate abuses like simony, the purchase of ecclesiastical office. These reforms were, therefore, quite sweeping: the Irish Church was lagging behind that elsewhere in Europe, and these provisions were designed to bring it into line, with one major exception – the absence as yet of a proper diocesan structure. This was provided for at the synod of Ráith

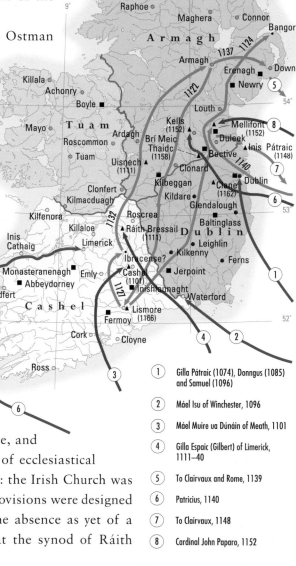

Reform of the Church

Tuam Ecclesiastical province, 1152

Synod of Kells–Mellifont, 1152

- Sees in the Province of Armagh
- Sees in the Province of Tuam
- Sees in the Province of Dublin
- Sees in the Province of Cashel
- Cistercian Abbeys founded by 1170
- Synods

→ Bishops of Ostman towns consecrated at Canterbury

→ Visits by Papal Legates

→ St Malachy's itinerary

1. Gilla Pátraic (1074), Donngus (1085) and Samuel (1096)
2. Máel Ísu of Winchester, 1096
3. Máel Muire ua Dúnáin of Meath, 1101
4. Gilla Espaic (Gilbert) of Limerick, 1111–40
5. To Clairvaux and Rome, 1139
6. Patricius, 1140
7. To Clairvaux, 1148
8. Cardinal John Paparo, 1152

Bressail in 1111, again under the auspices of Muirchertach Ó Briain.

The structure arrived at was one which respected the traditional division of the country into two halves. Two ecclesiastical provinces were established, the headship of the northern half going to Armagh, and that of the southern half to Cashel, each province being divided into twelve dioceses, Armagh having the primacy. This system was later modified, partly to reflect the growing power of Connacht (and its ecclesiastical capital at Tuam) and partly to recognise the importance of Dublin, so that at the synod of Kells-Mellifont in 1152 the country was divided into four ecclesiastical provinces, when the papal legate, Cardinal John Paparo, conferred pallia, the symbols of archiepiscopal jurisdiction, on the new archbishops of Armagh, Cashel, Dublin and Tuam (the archbishop of Armagh retaining primacy over all Ireland), a structure which has lasted to this day.

The Eclipse of Munster

The increasing power of Connacht to which the synod of Kells-Mellifont gave expression was first felt when Muirchertach Ó Briain fell from power in 1114. Thereafter, the balance of power shifted northwards and his place as the most powerful province-king was taken by Tairdelbach Ó Conchobair, king of Connacht. In his push for power Ó Conchobair marched on Dublin in 1118 and made himself king since, without Dublin, his claim to the high-kingship of Ireland would ring hollow, while in 1126 he became the fourth successive claimant to the kingship of Ireland to appoint his intended heir as its king. Tairdelbach was a remarkable military commander, notable for the use he made of naval forces and for the construction of castles and bridges. Like Ó Briain before him, he deposed other province-kings and partitioned their kingdoms, undermining, for instance, the status of the Ó Briain kings of Thomond by helping the revival of the Eóganacht, a branch of whom, bearing the surname Mac Carthaig (Mac Carthy), gained power in the kingdom of Desmond, a division from which Munster never recovered. He intervened to similar effect in Meath so that it became a cockpit of warfare between competing kings, ready like Munster to fall into the hands of any invading force strong enough to take it.

By the middle years of the century Ó Conchobair's place as king of Ireland was coming under threat from Muirchertach Mac Lochlainn, king of Cenél nEógain. He invaded Connacht and Bréifne in 1154, and came to Dublin, where the Ostmen proclaimed him as king, and two years later he campaigned as far south as Osraige (Ossory) in alliance with Diarmait Mac Murchada of Leinster, while in 1157 he partitioned Munster and laid siege to Limerick. The great Tairdelbach Ó Conchobair had died in 1156, and although his son Ruaidrí now sought to challenge Mac Lochlainn, by 1161 the latter had gained the formal submission of Ó Conchobair and Diarmait

Mac Murchada, who was now a firm ally, and was given in the annals the title 'king of Ireland without opposition'. This seemed to herald a promising new era of strong Irish kingship, but when Muirchertach treacherously blinded the king of Ulaid in 1166, Tír Eógain was invaded by the forces of Airgialla and Bréifne, and he was slain. His death gravely weakened the Mac Lochlainn family and paved the way for the restoration of the O'Neills to power in the north. More importantly, Muirchertach's ally Diarmait Mac Murchada was now left exposed and shortly afterwards took flight overseas, so that, indirectly, the death of Muirchertach Mac Lochlainn can be said to have caused the English invasion of Ireland.

The English Invasion

The English invasion, while something of an accident, was far from unforeseen. Following the death of Muirchertach Mac Lochlainn, Ruaidrí Ó Conchobair of Connacht succeeded to the high kingship. His leading ally was Tigernán Ó Ruairc of Bréifne, an inveterate enemy of Mac Murchada, king of Leinster. Ó Ruairc joined forces with others of Diarmait's enemies and forced him to flee. Without an ally in Ireland, on 1 August 1166, Mac Murchada, his wife and daughter, and a small group of followers, set sail for Bristol, where the exiled king was received by the city's reeve, Robert fitz Harding, a confidant of King Henry II of England, with whom he almost certainly had a prior acquaintance. From that moment on his fortunes never looked back, and within a year he was back in Ireland, back in power, and Ireland was facing invasion.

From Bristol, Mac Murchada went to Aquitaine in France where he eventually caught up with the king of England, and offered to become his vassal, and to hold his kingdom as a fief of the crown of England. In so doing, there can be little doubt that he foresaw the inevitable consequences of his action. King Henry accepted Diarmait's oath of fealty and issued him with letters authorising his vassals throughout his many lands to come to Mac Murchada's aid. So Diarmait went to South Wales, a very natural choice in view of its long-standing connections with the southern half of Ireland. Here he recruited help from a group of men of Flemish origin who had established a small colony in the Pembrokeshire area some decades earlier, and came back to Ireland with them in August 1167. They were led by Richard fitz Godebert, ancestor of the Roche family in Ireland, and with their help Mac Murchada won back the core of his kingdom, his ancestral lands of Uí Chennselaig.

Ruaidrí Ó Conchobair and Ó Ruairc marched to oppose Diarmait and fought two battles, one unsuccessful, the other victorious. After his defeat in the latter, Diarmait came to Ó Conchobair, and handed over hostages in return for his kingdom of Uí Chennselaig, but the kingdom of all Leinster

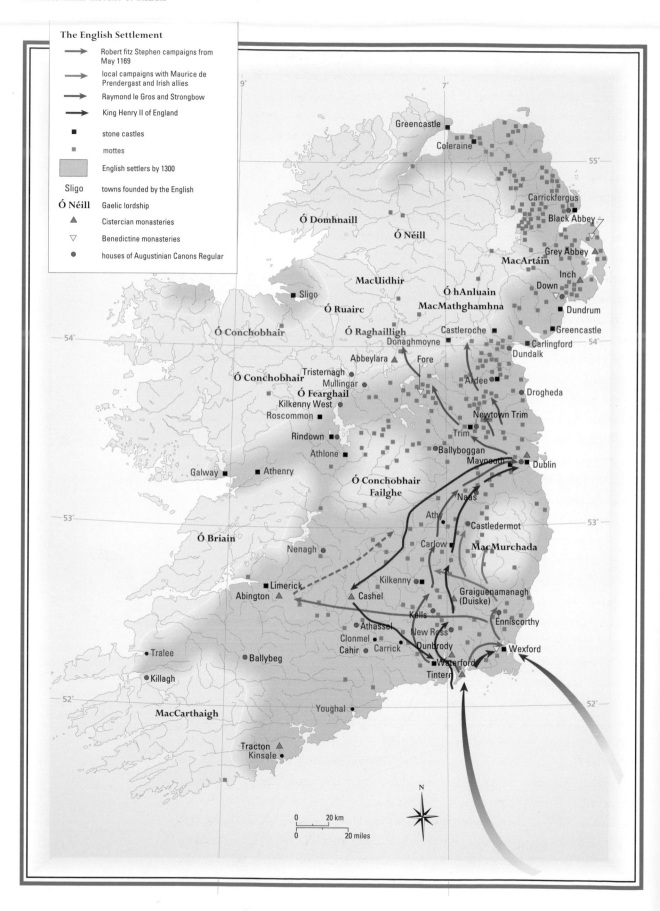

The English Settlement

→ Robert fitz Stephen campaigns from May 1169

→ local campaigns with Maurice de Prendergast and Irish allies

→ Raymond le Gros and Strongbow

→ King Henry II of England

■ stone castles

■ mottes

English settlers by 1300

Sligo   towns founded by the English

Ó Néill   Gaelic lordship

▲ Cistercian monasteries

▽ Benedictine monasteries

● houses of Augustinian Canons Regular

was still denied him, and this is what he sought to recover when, about 1 May 1169, the main body of his foreign allies arrived. There were 30 knights, 60 men-at-arms, and 300 foot-archers, and they landed in three ships at Bannow Bay in Co. Wexford, led by Robert fitz Stephen, uncle of the famous historian of the invasion, Giraldus Cambrensis, or Gerald de Barri, whose brother Robert was the first of the Barry family in Ireland. The next day they were joined by Maurice de Prendergast, a Pembrokeshire Fleming who brought with him two ship-loads of men-at-arms and archers. Having secured their landing, they proceeded to attack the Ostmen of Wexford, conquered the town, and Mac Murchada granted it to fitz Stephen and his half-brother Maurice fitz Gerald (the founder of the Irish Geraldines). Now Mac Murchada had sufficient resources to set about the recovery of Leinster.

Ruaidrí Ó Conchobair responded to this new challenge by leading an army to the province, where he accepted Mac Murchada's submission and allowed him to remain as king of Leinster, in return for the receipt of Diarmait's son as a hostage, and an undertaking to send back his foreign allies as soon as all Leinster had again been subdued. But it is doubtful whether Mac Murchada had any such intention and, indeed, according to Giraldus, he was now beginning to set his sights on the high-kingship. Contingents of reinforcements were still periodically arriving. At Baginbun, Co. Wexford, early in May 1170, another of the Geraldines, Raymond le Gros, arrived with fresh troops. But the invasion's real driving-force had yet to appear on the scene. While in Wales, Mac Murchada had met the lord of Pembroke and Strigoil, Richard de Clare, better known as Strongbow, and promised him his daughter Aoífe in marriage, together with the succession to his kingdom after Diarmait's own death. Strongbow did not land in Ireland until 23 August 1170, along with as many as two hundred knights and a thousand troops. They took Waterford, and there Strongbow married Aoífe as planned.

In September 1170, Strongbow, Mac Murchada and all the might of the Anglo-Norman military machine advanced on Dublin. Ruaidrí Ó Conchobair assembled the armies of his allies and marched to meet them, but while both sides were engaged in negotiations some of the English forces made an assault on the walls and overran the city, with considerable slaughter of the inhabitants. Although some the Ostmen escaped by boarding ship and heading for the Isles, many no doubt never returning, their king, Ascall Mac Turcaill, did launch an attempt to recover the city within weeks of the death of Diarmait Mac Murchada about May Day 1171, but he was captured and beheaded in the town. Ruaidrí Ó Conchobair then laid Dublin under siege, for a period of about two months, with the English forces being confined within the walls, without access to provisions by either land or sea, until eventually the besieged garrison decided to make a sortie, caught Ruaidrí's forces unawares (he himself was bathing, apparently in the Liffey), and thereby brought the siege to a humiliating end.

This proved to be a turning-point in Dublin's history, and a landmark in the English conquest of Ireland. It was also a major development in English politics. Strongbow was an important tenant of the English crown, in the south Welsh marches, in England and in Normandy, and was now the heir to a provincial kingdom in Ireland and controller of Dublin and Waterford, perhaps the country's two most important trading ports. There were, therefore, serious implications for King Henry II's authority involved in Strongbow's rapid rise to power in Ireland. Hence Henry now made plans to come to Ireland himself to take control. Strongbow sailed to meet the king and as a sign of good faith he handed over Dublin and the adjacent lands, as well as the other towns he had taken and all castles. But Henry persisted with his planned expedition.

He had, of course, always had an interest in acquiring Ireland and adding it to the already long list of his dominions, alongside England, Normandy, Aquitaine and Anjou, which had made him the dominant power from the Scottish border in the north to the Pyrenees in the south. In 1155, shortly after his accession to the throne, Henry had discussed plans for an invasion of Ireland. If the papal document *Laudabiliter* is genuine, it was obtained at this point from the English Pope Adrian IV, to provide justification for such an invasion (with the connivance of the archbishop of Canterbury, anxious to re-assert influence over the Irish Church). But the plans were shelved at this point and it was only when Diarmait Mac Murchada came to his court that the plan was resurrected. The fact that he accepted Mac Murchada's oath of fealty meant that he as Diarmait's overlord undertook a duty to protect him from his enemies, and thus, there can be little reason to doubt that he knew the implications, and that Diarmait's arrival provided an opportunity which Henry was happy to grasp.

The typical Anglo-Norman castle constructed in the early decades after the initial invasion was of the motte-and-bailey type familiar to them from their homeland. It could be constructed rapidly in a hostile environment, it offered protection from attack and while day-to-day life could take place in the outlying bailey in normal circumstances, the inhabitants of the manor could retreat into the safety of the timber-framed castle on top of the motte when danger struck.

Occupation and Settlement

Within a few short years of the events of 1169 the face of Ireland was transformed and the course of Irish history irreversibly changed. This process of settlement was part of a much wider movement of colonisation that affected many of the peripheral regions of Europe in this age. It brought enormous changes in the way land in Ireland was held and exploited, an agricultural and economic transformation, and the introduction of a radically new social system – though change was, of course, confined to those parts of the country successfully exposed to English colonisation, which never affected the entire island in the medieval period. When Strongbow succeeded to Leinster he inherited the kingdom built up by Diarmait Mac Murchada and his predecessors, but gaining such a massive territorial lordship was only a first step, worthless if he could not secure possession of it. He needed to defend it from those who might challenge his authority, and the method to which he had recourse was that which lay at the basis of 'feudal' society elsewhere: the division of his new lordship into manageable estates, and the allotting of this land to family, friends and followers, who might in turn sub-divide their grants, in a process known as sub-infeudation. He was a tenant-in-chief of the crown, but had his own tenants and, in turn, sub-tenants, and just as he owed military service to the king for Leinster, so those who held part of Leinster under him owed him military service or annual rents.

The same process was repeated elsewhere in the country. Hugh de Lacy, one of the largest land-holders in Herefordshire, was granted by Henry II the province of Meath (the modern counties of Meath and Westmeath, and parts of Longford and Offaly). Hugh made a reality of his new estate by dividing up his lordship among followers of his own, though, of course, like Strongbow, he kept some of the best land and most desirable locations as his own demesne lands. Hugh's tenants had the responsibility of defending Meath from Irish attack and he and they did so by a process of encastellation. The earliest efforts at castle-construction both in Meath and elsewhere involved the erection of earthen mottes or mounds, sometimes with a bailey or earthwork enclosure attached. The greatest density of mottes lies, understandably, in the eastern half of the island, and their construction was confined to the early decades of the conquest, the late twelfth and early thirteenth centuries.

When a motte or other earthwork castle had been constructed – or a stone castle in the case of the great lords – military control was quickly established. With domination of the surrounding countryside secure, the next step involved the conversion of the military outpost into an agricultural manor, since without tenants land was incapable of yielding a profit, and conquests would quickly evaporate without an effective occupation of the newly-won territory. One way of encouraging settlement involved the establishment of boroughs, which were given an urban constitution, although some were no more than agricultural villages. Divided up into burgage plots held by burgesses on favourable terms, and with their own court, borough status and the solid tenure it provided must have encouraged many to cross the Irish Sea and make a new home for themselves in Ireland. So, there followed for much of the next century the immigration into Ireland of large numbers of settlers from the neighbouring island, substantial enough to change for centuries to come the make-up of those areas which were heavily colonised, and to introduce into Ireland a category of inhabitant whose loyalties lay elsewhere and whose culture remained throughout the Middle Ages that of their transmarine homeland.

Ireland and the English Crown

Henry II's brief expedition to Ireland in the winter of 1171–72 was a highly successful one from his point of view. His biggest concern was that Strongbow might grow too powerful in Ireland and become a threat, and while he had no intention of removing him from power, he needed to demonstrate his superiority. Therefore, as well as taking Dublin, Wexford and Waterford into his own hands, Henry also granted Meath, as we have seen, to Hugh de Lacy to counter-balance Strongbow's growing power in the lordship. Meath was a crucial border-zone between the new colony in Dublin and Leinster, on the one hand, and Ruaidrí Ó Conchobair's kingdom of Connacht on the other, and it is not surprising that the 1170s saw widespread warfare there as de Lacy set about parcelling it out among those who had taken the gamble in following him to Ireland.

Ó Conchobair was not happy about this English presence on his doorstep, and he soon took the offensive in Meath, targeting the castles de Lacy and his men had built, such as the massive fortress at Trim, the origins of which can be traced to these years. The vulnerability of the lordship, and the need to reach a *modus vivendi* with Ruaidrí Ó Conchobair, prompted Henry II to agree to the so-called Treaty of Windsor in 1175. Under its terms Ruaidrí acknowledged Henry as his overlord, and would hand over an annual tribute of one hide out of every ten animals slaughtered, but excluded from the area of Ó Conchobair's control were Meath, Dublin, Wexford and all Leinster, and Munster from Waterford to Dungarvan. In return, Henry acknowledged Ruaidrí's position as king of Connacht and accepted that if any of the province-kings rebelled against either king, Ó Conchobair would have a legal entitlement to remove them from power, and he was given a promise of military aid to do so.

The treaty of Windsor was, therefore, a solid achievement by Ruaidrí Ó Conchobair, but the colonists had no interest in making it work since it implicitly drew a line on the map of Ireland, and dictated that the conquest stop there. It was clearly in their interests to provoke Ruaidrí into repudiating his fealty so that the treaty could be rendered void, and this seems to have been what happened. The colonists began extending the area under their control outwards from the area allowed under the treaty, trying, for instance, to annex Ó Briain's kingdom of Thomond, which included Limerick, and MacCarthaig's kingdom of Desmond, which included Cork, and there was little or nothing Ruaidrí could do about this. Likewise, in the early weeks of 1177 John de Courcy set off from Dublin and arrived at Downpatrick, the capital of the kingdom of the Ulaid, which he quickly overran, thereby winning for himself a kingdom. The Treaty of Windsor lay in tatters.

In May 1177, Henry held a council at Oxford at which he dropped all pretence of abiding by the treaty. He took Cork and Limerick into his own hands, and granted them to Englishmen. More importantly, Henry announced his intention of making his fourth son, John, king of Ireland – though he can have had no idea that John's older brothers would predecease him, and the lord of Ireland would become king of England, thereby attaching Ireland firmly to the English crown. Ruaidrí Ó Conchobair was no doubt opposed to Henry's plan to make his nine-year-old son king of Ireland, a position he himself claimed. Ruaidrí was, however, in a difficult position in that, not only was he trying to forestall English aggression, but he faced opposition even within his own family, and eventually in 1183 he abdicated and retired to the Augustinian abbey of Cong.

English Government in Ireland

Lord John did not come to Ireland until 1185. He brought a large army with him and, more importantly, some of Henry II's most experienced administrators and officials. The most successful work of the expedition was done by these men, who established the machinery of both local and central government in the lordship, and the normal civil law procedures that functioned in England were transferred to Ireland. The English king was now represented there by a deputy usually known as the justiciar (though by the late fourteenth century he generally bore the title of lieutenant). He was the lordship's supreme judge, head of the civil administration, and chief military commander. He had power to make war on the king's enemies by summoning the tenants-in-chief of the crown to a campaign, and had an armed retinue at his disposal. His office was an itinerant one, and he asserted his authority by travelling around the lordship, administering justice as he went, being

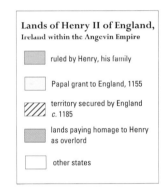

Lands of Henry II of England,
Ireland within the Angevin Empire

- ruled by Henry, his family
- Papal grant to England, 1155
- territory secured by England c. 1185
- lands paying homage to Henry as overlord
- other states

advised on matters of policy and on day-to-day government business by a council made up of some of the great resident magnates of the lordship.

The council was at first an informal affair but it gradually gained a fixed structure as the thirteenth century wore on, at which point too the practice emerged of holding parliaments, beginning in effect as specially enlarged meetings of the council, though by the end of the century they were judicial and legislative assemblies at which not only individuals but communities were represented, who were needed if consent for new taxation measures was to be obtained. Such taxes and other revenues were accounted for at the exchequer in Dublin, perhaps the oldest of its various departments of state. The chief clerk of the exchequer was the treasurer, second only in importance to the justiciar, though over the course of time he was gradually superseded in status by the chancellor whose office, the chancery, was the letter-writing office of government and the place where copies of official correspondence were maintained. The chancellor had custody of the great seal by which the government authenticated its documentation.

The business of government could not operate without an effective system of local government to extend the authority of the central administration into the localities. This was done by the adoption of the system of local government that already pertained in England, based on the shire and the office of sheriff, who was the principal local agent of the crown. In England shires were divided into hundreds, while the shire's Irish equivalent, the county, was divided into cantreds (later, and to this day, called baronies). The development of a scheme of counties in Ireland was protracted, and never extended to the entire island in the Middle Ages, for several reasons, but principally because large areas of the island remained in Irish hands and because much of the country was exempt from day-to-day governmental interference, being held by its lords as what were called liberties, with seneschals exercising the functions that sheriffs exercised in the royal counties.

In addition, the system of law that functioned in England was applied to Ireland from the late 1160s onwards, so that the common law of England became the law of the lordship of Ireland. English statutes applied in the courts of Ireland, though, increasingly, in the thirteenth century, legislation peculiar to Ireland was promulgated in Irish parliaments and councils. The net effect was that Ireland gained a system of government which radically altered the future course of its history. This period saw the birth of a parliamentary tradition which lasted uninterrupted until the Act of Union in 1800; it saw the establishment of a system of local government based on the county which has likewise endured; and it gained a common-law inheritance which has lain at the basis of the Irish legal system to this day.

John and Ireland

To the extent that the origins of this superstructure can be traced back to the lordship of John, credit must be given to him. In terms of colonial expansion too, there were successes which flowed from his 1185 expedition. To provide security for the borders of Leinster, he granted vast estates in the area to his trusted vassals, among them William de Burgh, ancestor of the famous Burke family, and Theobald Walter, ancestor of the Butlers. He also granted much of what is now Co. Louth to two of his chief officials and advisors, Bertram de Verdon and Gilbert Pipard. This may have been hard on the native rulers of the area, who lost their lands and were reduced to the status of tenants or were driven out to the badlands in the mountains and bogs, but from the point of view of the English crown and the settlers, it made sound political and economic sense. It was an arrangement for protecting what gains the English had already made in Ireland, while providing the bridgehead for a gradual forward expansion, which was clearly intended ultimately to encompass the whole island. Gone were the days of half-hearted conquest, gone were any thoughts (such as had been behind the Treaty of Windsor) of freezing the colony and arriving at a *modus vivendi* with the native rulers. Henceforth, there seems little reason to doubt that it would be royal policy gradually to erode the position of the native kings, and to expand the boundaries of the lordship correspondingly.

Dundrum is perhaps the most impressive of the Anglo-Norman strongholds built in Co. Down. It was probably begun by the self-styled 'Prince of Ulster', John de Courcy, not long after his conquest of the province in 1177. It is first mentioned in historical documents in 1205 when he attempted to recover it from the de Lacys (who had overthrown him), with the help of a fleet provided by his brother-in-law, the king of the Isle of Man. The picture shows the tall round keep or donjon which stands within the castle's upper ward. From here and the curtain walls there is a commanding view of Dundrum Bay below and across the Irish Sea.

However, some of the pioneers who had been in Ireland from the earliest days of the conquest resented John's attempt to impose these newcomers and this new restrictive authority on them. Those who had paved the way resented their easy acquisition of estates, and wondered why they were not being rewarded for their pioneering work. What we are seeing here is the emergence of a classic feature of the Anglo-Irish colony in generations to come: a resentment felt by those already settled in the lordship against newcomers from England. This development was somewhat ironic, in that at no stage during the Middle Ages did the Anglo-Irish colonists come to regard themselves as Irish; they were constantly at pains to point out that, no matter how long they had been settled in Ireland, they were 'the English of the land of Ireland', and yet when new men arrived from England, or English

Giraldus Cambrensis (Gerald of Wales), the great historian of the English invasion of Ireland, warned of the Irish that 'From an old and evil custom they always carry an axe in their hand as if it were a staff ... Wherever they go they drag this along with them. When they see the opportunity, and the occasion presents itself, this weapon has not to be unsheathed as a sword, or bent as a bow, or poised as a spear. Without further preparation, beyond being raised a little, it inflicts a mortal blow. At hand, or rather in the hand, and ever ready, is that which is enough to cause death.'

officials were sent to take charge of the Dublin administration, they would have none of it. In the course of time, therefore, differences emerged between the English born in Ireland and the English born in England, and we can see from the reaction of the established frontiersmen in the lordship to those who came over in John's wake that this was a feature of life in Ireland from the lordship's earliest days.

John also alienated the native Irish. Several of the Irish province-kings had willingly submitted to Henry II when he came to Ireland in 1171. They did so partly because they believed he would act as their protector against the aggression of the English barons. In the interval between 1171 and 1185 the Irish had become all the more aware of the need to find themselves a protector, because the expansion of the colony was proceeding apace and their status was being rapidly undermined. For many of them, perhaps, John appeared their last chance, but the policy he adopted pushed into rebellion even those who had earlier been willing to compromise. And the same was true of John's second expedition to Ireland, in the summer of 1210. This was of very great importance for the new English lordship in Ireland. During his brief stay he took steps to reorganise the government, strengthened English laws, regulated the coinage and such matters, and overthrew several of his more rebellious barons, seizing their lands and castles. But as regards John's dealings with the native Irish kings, it is clear that he left Ireland on bad terms with two of the most powerful, the northern king Áed Ó Néill, and the Connacht king Cathal Crobderg Ó Conchobair, brother of the late Ruaidrí. Thus, this 1210 campaign also failed to produce a settlement, and John left Ireland to the warfare that had consumed the country before his arrival. It was nearly two hundred years before another royal expedition took place.

The Church After the Invasion

There is little evidence that either Henry II or John displayed anti-Irish prejudice when it came to the Church. Of course, with a see as important as Dublin or Armagh, they would have liked to see someone in office who was

favourable to their own position: no king anywhere in Christendom acted otherwise. It helped, therefore, if the important positions in the Irish Church were filled by Englishmen, but they did not have to be. Both kings worked quite happily with Irish bishops, and neither insisted on the absolute exclusion of Irishmen from the episcopate. But after John's death the real power behind the throne during the minority of his young son Henry III was William Marshal, Strongbow's successor as lord of Leinster. Marshal was keen on expanding the boundaries of the lordship of Ireland, and, in January 1217, he ordered the justiciar in the

king's name to forbid any native Irishman to be appointed to a bishopric or other high church office. Obviously, the view was that they could not be trusted and that the expansion of the lordship would be facilitated if Englishmen occupied all the important positions in the Irish Church, and so it was an instrument of colonial expansion, nothing more.

In 1220, the Pope, Honorius III, objected to the policy but this and other papal pronouncements to the same effect were never entirely successful. As time went on, and as the lordship expanded, the cathedral chapters in many dioceses tended to have a majority of English extraction, and managed to secure the election of one from among their own ranks, although in those areas which were not so heavily settled, provided the king did not feel that a particular Irishman represented a political risk, he was usually prepared to allow such an appointment to proceed. Some dioceses, though, were split down the middle. Most of the archdiocese of Armagh remained in Irish hands throughout the Middle Ages, but it included Co. Louth, one of the most heavily anglicised areas. This caused a major problem, because the

The Cistercian Abbey at Knockmoy, Co. Galway, was founded about 1190 by Cathal Crobderg Ó Conchobair, brother of Ruaidrí, the last high-king of Ireland. It has a remarkable medieval wall painting, one of the scenes of which depicts the morality tale of the Three Live Kings and the Three Dead Kings, the latter warning them, 'We have been as you are, you shall be as we are.' The living kings are wearing crowns and seem to be engaged in the distinctly un-Irish sport of falconry.

English of Louth were frequently at war with the Irish of Armagh and Tyrone. The last native Irishman to occupy the primatial see in the medieval period died in 1306. For his successors, the cathedral city of Armagh was in hostile territory so that, in practice, the diocese became split in two. There was an *ecclesia inter Anglicos*, a church among the English, and an *ecclesia inter Hibernicos*, a church among the Irish. Anglo-Irish archbishops lived in the *ecclesia inter Anglicos* in Co. Louth, while that part of the diocese that remained *inter Hibernicos* was governed by an Irish churchman living at Armagh. Nothing typified more the divided loyalties that afflicted Ireland in the later Middle Ages.

The Expansion of the Colony

In certain respects, throughout the thirteenth century, but especially during the period of over half a century in which Henry III was to reign (1216–72), the English lordship of Ireland continued to expand and prosper. The process of territorial conquest and colonisation showed few signs of faltering. Land was being taken from the Irish, planted with peasant settlers from England and Wales, and being divided up into manors; and the methods of agricultural cultivation practised in England were being widely introduced. In each manor, typically, part of the land was held by the lord in demesne, and part divided into open fields held by the tenants. These great fields in turn would have been sub-divided into strips in such a way that each tenant would have a holding scattered among them, having a share of both good and bad land; much was under cultivation, with a three-course rotation of crops, part going towards the cultivation of winter corn, part spring corn and part lying fallow to give the land time to recover its fertility. As a result, the appearance of the very countryside was different, filled now with new manors and farms, new towns, castles, mills, churches and religious houses, and also peopled with a fairly high density of immigrant communities, speaking a different language from the native population, and paying their taxes to a different master.

It was not until about the year 1300 that the area under English control began to contract. From 1169 to approximately 1220, those men from Britain who conquered land for themselves in Ireland brought with them everything that was needed to establish a little England beyond the sea. It proved very successful, so that the east coast of Ireland from Carrickfergus to Cork was heavily anglicised, thickly settled, and substantially changed, and this region became the focal point of the lordship, and remained so throughout the later Middle Ages. However, the expansion that took place in Ireland after 1220 or thereabouts was mostly undertaken by people who were not new to Ireland, but rather the sons and grandsons of those first pioneers. The latter were usually substantial landholders in England or

Wales, and they did not have too much difficulty enticing their tenants to take the gamble on settling in Ireland. But when their sons and grandsons started to push west in the second phase of the conquest – from Cork into Kerry, from Limerick into Clare, from Meath into Galway, Roscommon and up into Sligo, from Louth into Armagh and from Antrim into Derry – they did not have access to the same numbers of English peasants. Therefore, even though the Anglo-Irish colony continued to expand throughout Henry III's reign, the expansion was often only superficial. On the ground, there was not the same programme of colonisation, and without that it was bound to fail.

Irish Resistance

One of the reasons the conquest faltered was due to Irish resistance. Opposition to colonial aggrandisement can be seen from the earliest stages of the conquest, but as the thirteenth century progressed it gradually intensified. Of the year 1247 an annalist says that 'the foreigners of Connacht had not experienced for many a long year the like of the war waged against them in this year'. By the summer of 1249 the war had been brought into Desmond by Finín Mac Carthaig, while further east 'the justiciar of Ireland led a great host into Leinster to attack the kings' sons who were spoiling and ruining the foreigners'. Connacht was in turmoil in this year also with, for the first time, the lead being taken by Áed, son of the reigning king, Feidlim Ó Conchobair. It was his leadership which made these uprisings a real cause of disquiet to the lordship's governors, especially when he made common cause with Brian Ó Néill of Tír Eógain, whose aim was nothing less than the overthrow of the earldom of Ulster. In 1258 they met at Cáel Uisce on the Erne, where they were joined by the son of the king of Thomond, Tadc Ó Briain. There, Ó Conchobair and Ó Briain abandoned their own dynasties' ancestral claims and acknowledged Brian Ó Néill's right to 'the kingship of the Irish of Ireland', while even the Dublin government admitted that he bore the title 'king of the kings of Ireland'. This was an extraordinary meeting which amounted to an attempt to revive the high-kingship after seventy-five years in abeyance.

In the following year Áed Ó Conchobair travelled to Derry and obtained as a bride the daughter of the Hebridean lord Dubgall Mac Ruaidrí, and a dowry of 160 galloglasses: Ó Conchobair was strengthening his army in preparation for a major campaign. Their plan appears to have had as a first move a strike at the capital of the earldom of Ulster, Downpatrick, and after the destruction of colonial power in Ulster would come an assault on the Connacht colony, on Ó Conchobair's behalf. However, the plan backfired. Tadc Ó Briain died prematurely in 1259, causing an annalist to remark that this was 'good news for the foreigners'. In the following year the attack on

THE ILLUSTRATED HISTORY OF IRELAND

Downpatrick was a disaster, with Brian Ó Néill losing his life in the contest, but the fact that his head was sent off to Henry III in London shows the significance that was attached to the victory.

English Misgovernment

In their efforts to overcome colonial domination Irish kings were facilitated by the misgovernment of the lordship at this time. In 1254 Henry III granted his eldest son Edward a vast estate that included Ireland, Gascony, and the Channel Islands, but the grant was made 'provided that the land of Ireland shall never be separated from the crown of England, and no one but Edward and his heirs, kings of England, shall ever claim or have any right in that land'. This was an important development because it meant that henceforth England and Ireland would remain tied in such a way that the king of one was *ipso facto* lord of the other. The advantage of this was that the future constitutional position of Ireland was secure; but the disadvantage was that Ireland's lord would inevitably be an absentee. As king of England, Ireland was only a small part of his estate, and far from the top of his list of priorities.

This was the case from the start of young Edward's take-over of power when he showed little sustained interest in Ireland. While it would be an exaggeration to say that the only real interest he had in Ireland was in exploiting its resources, there is an element of truth in it. When he ran up debts he used the revenues collected on his behalf in Ireland to pay them off. When he led an army on expedition in Wales or Scotland or Gascony or Flanders, he expected Ireland to supply food for his troops. The outcome was that revenues raised in Ireland were leaving the country and there was less money left in Ireland for running the government, and for combatting crime, disorder and warfare. As the latter increased, the profitability of the colony shrank: contemporary reports frequently refer to the destruction of crops, the fact that the cultivators of the crops were either dead or had fled, that fields therefore went untilled, and revenues uncollected. Ultimately, therefore, less money came into the exchequer, so that there were fewer resources available for Edward to siphon off.

All of this was ultimately very damaging for the Anglo-Irish lordship. To judge from the surviving court records from this period and the often pessimistic contemporary accounts, Ireland at the end of the thirteenth century was a country where lawlessness and disorder were rife and where the government was sometimes unable to cope. Contemporary accounts speak of the localities not being properly defended, of castles not being maintained, of the king's highways being overgrown, bridges collapsed, and so on. Most important of all, the parlous state of the government's finances and the diversion overseas of so much of its energy and resources meant that the revival in the power of the Irish kings proceeded apace and the domination over them which the colonists had earlier wielded began to be lost.

Carrickfergus, which means 'the Rock of Fergus', was a fortress since early historic times, the rock in question providing strategic access to Belfast Lough. Little wonder, then, that Ulster's larger-than-life conqueror, John de Courcy, should select it for the site of a castle of his own soon after 1177, and that it emerged as the principal town of Anglo-Norman Ulster. The castle drawn in black was completed by 1200, later additions in red by 1225 and in blue by 1250 (after McNeill).

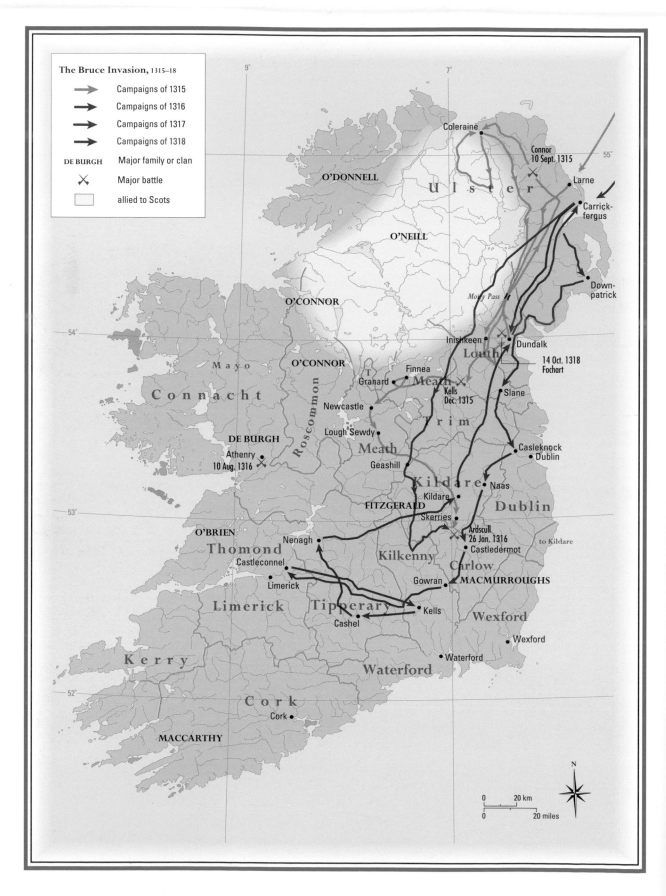

The Bruce Invasion, 1315–18

Campaigns of 1315
Campaigns of 1316
Campaigns of 1317
Campaigns of 1318
DE BURGH   Major family or clan
✕   Major battle
        allied to Scots

O'DONNELL

U l s t e r

O'NEILL

Coleraine

Connor
10 Sept. 1315

Larne

Carrick-
fergus

Down-
patrick

O'CONNOR

Moiry Pass

Inishkeen

Dundalk

14 Oct. 1318
Fochart

M a y o

Connacht

O'CONNOR

Finnea

Granard

Meath

Louth

Slane

Roscommon

Newcastle

Lough Sewdy

Trim

DE BURGH

Athenry
10 Aug. 1316

Meath

Geashill

Casleknock
Dublin

K i l d a r e

FITZGERALD

Kildare

Naas

Dublin

Skerries

O'BRIEN

Ardscull
26 Jan. 1316

Castledermot

to Kildare

Nenagh

Thomond

Castleconnel

Limerick

Kilkenny

Carlow

Gowran

MACMURROUGHS

Tipperary

Kells

Cashel

Wexford

L i m e r i c k

Wexford

Waterford

K e r r y

Waterford

C o r k

Cork

MACCARTHY

0   20 km
0   20 miles

N

CHAPTER IV

THE END OF THE GAELIC WORLD

By the early fourteenth century the English colony in Ireland was showing signs of neglect, its government not far from bankrupt because of the drain on its resources by the absentee lords of Ireland. The alarm-bells had begun to sound by 1297 when the Irish parliament assembled in that year 'in order to establish peace more firmly'. Those who gathered there complained about local communities not being properly armed to resist Irish raids, about absentees living in England but draining the profits of their Irish estates, without leaving sufficient for the bailiffs to defend the land from attack, and about the problem of degeneracy. *Gens* is the Latin for a people, a nation; to become 'degenerate' is to lose a sense of belonging to that nation. The survival of the colonists in Ireland depended, the government thought, on them retaining a sense of their separateness from the indigenous inhabitants of Ireland. They were 'the English of the land of Ireland'; they were not the Irish who were now, by their very birth, the enemy. To prevent them from being overwhelmed by the latter and to preserve their Englishness, the 1297 parliament banned those of English extraction from adopting the obvious traits of Irishness, including Irish-type clothing or hairstyle. Clearly, this was a colony under threat, and the most spectacular manifestation of the latter was the Bruce invasion.

The Bruce Invasion of Ireland

In the early summer of 1315 a fleet-load of Scottish veterans from the recent great victory over the English at Bannockburn put ashore on the coast of County Antrim. They were led by the only surviving brother of Robert the Bruce, Edward, recently ratified as heir-presumptive to the Scottish throne. It was a major expedition, planned well in advance, and although Scotland was then in the middle of a deadly struggle with England, for the next three and a half years a very significant proportion of her hard-pressed resources was devoted to it. Edward Bruce adopted the title 'King of Ireland', and was supported by some important Irish kings, principally Domnall O'Neill of Tír Eogain (Tyrone). He set up his own administration in Ireland to replace that of the English colony based in Dublin, and until his death in 1318

Robert the Bruce has had almost as potent a force in the Irish historical memory as that of the Scots, largely because of his success in combating English aggression, and the perception of him as an ally of the Irish, whose brother Edward can arguably be regarded as last high-king of Ireland. The illustration shows Robert's great seal as king of Scots; Edward too had a seal made to authenticate his pronouncements which bore the inscription 'by the Grace of God, King of Ireland'.

Edward Bruce sought to make his new kingdom a reality and to bring English rule in Ireland to an end.

One of the great question-marks which has hung over the Bruce invasion ever since is: did Robert really hope to turn Edward's invasion into a permanent conquest, or was he just trying to exploit Irish dissidence in order to force the then weak king of England, Edward II, to concede Robert's claim to be king of Scots? Many suggestions have been put forward through the ages. Some say that Bruce's aim was simply to rid himself of a troublesome younger brother, others that Edward was sent to try to cripple Ireland as a source of supply to the English, others still that Bruce wanted to create a diversion for Edward II by opening up a second front and splitting the English forces. But perhaps the most sensible view is that the Bruces were keeping their options open. Contemporaries believed that the Irish sought the help of Edward and Robert Bruce to free them from English rule, and maybe the Bruce brothers felt it was worth the investment. At the very least, an Irish revolt would indeed distract the English war-effort, and might even encourage the recently conquered Welsh to join in. And if the gamble paid off, the Bruces would end up ruling not one kingdom but two.

But why Ireland? Right from the moment when he seized the Scottish throne, Robert Bruce showed an interest in enlisting Irish support. He probably spent the winter of 1306–07 on Rathlin Island off the Antrim coast, and sent a letter to the Irish stating that they and the Scots 'stem from one seed of birth', have 'a common language and common custom', and proposed 'permanently strengthening and maintaining inviolate the special friendship between us and you, so that with God's will our nation may be able to recover her ancient liberty'. Here he speaks of the Scots and Irish as a single nation and this lies at the core of their plan for Ireland. The events of 1315–18 were a Scottish attempt to win support for their struggle with England by exploiting similar sentiment elsewhere. That sentiment lay in Ireland, and also in Wales. A contemporary source says of Bruce's invasion of Ireland that 'there was a rumour that if he achieved his wish there, he would at once cross to Wales, and raise the Welsh likewise against our king. For these two races are easily roused to rebellion; they bear hardly the yoke of slavery, and curse the lordship of the English'.

However, apart from the odd raid on Anglesey, there was no large-scale Welsh invasion. The reason for this is that the attempted conquest of Ireland got bogged down. The Bruces did have Irish support, and their arrival caused uprisings to break out all over the country, but they found it impossible to make that final push needed to overturn English rule, even after Edward was joined in Ireland by King Robert in the winter of 1316–17. They failed for a number of reasons. The Bruce occupation of Ireland coincided with one of the worst famines to inflict Europe in the Middle Ages.

For many, no doubt, political considerations came second to survival. It is also true that the Scots did not get sufficient support. Some of the Anglo-Irish colonists swapped sides during the invasion and joined the Scots, but most stayed loyal. And what Bruce needed was not just to defeat them – which he did in several battles – but to get them to join him. Without that, with just the support of the native Irish rebels, the long-term prospects were poor. However, even among the native Irish, support for Bruce was not universal. The political divisions in Gaelic Ireland were such that Bruce's support was limited to those who acknowledged Domnall O'Neill's supremacy. So, in practice O'Neill's allies were Bruce's allies and O'Neill's enemies were Bruce's enemies. And that is why, when Anglo-Irish colonists killed Edward himself in the Battle of Fochart, just north of Dundalk, on 14 October 1318, the new Scottish kingdom of Ireland died with him.

Aftermath of the Bruce Invasion

The invasion did, however, have long-term consequences. It wreaked a great deal of destruction throughout Ireland. There were parts of Ireland which provided taxes and rents for the government before the invasion but from which it never again drew revenue in the medieval period. Parts of Ireland which were formerly in what the government called the 'land of peace' were now in the 'land of war', or were march-lands between the two. As a direct result of the Bruce invasion, therefore, the area of Ireland under the effective control of the Dublin government shrank. The invasion also profoundly shifted the balance of power in Ireland. Previously, the most powerful man in the country had been Richard de Burgh, earl of Ulster and lord of Connacht, but the invasion gravely weakened his authority. After his death in 1326 he was succeeded by his young grandson who was eventually murdered by some of his own Anglo-Irish tenants in Ulster, an event which indicates the extent to which law and order and respect for authority had broken down among the Anglo-Irish. As for Domnall O'Neill, his plan of enlisting Scottish support may have backfired, but ultimately his dynasty won out, and soon the O'Neills re-emerged as the dominant force in Ulster and indeed throughout Gaelic Ireland.

The Problem of Absenteeism

As far back as the mid-thirteenth century several of the most important territorial blocs in Ireland had to be sub-divided between heiresses because they died out in the direct male line. The result of these partitions was that many English families came to inherit a relatively small landholding in Ireland, too small to retain their interest, and too insignificant to bother defending or investing in. However, this process of sub-division was taken a step further in the fourteenth century. For instance, the lordship of Leinster

This carving, from St Mary's Church at Gowran, Co. Kilkenny, is believed to be of the first Countess of Ormond , whose husband James Butler (d. 1338) was head of one of the premier families of Anglo-Norman descent in Ireland. They derived their surname from the fact that the first of their Anglo-Irish ancestors, Theobald Walter, was butler in the household of Prince John when he came to Ireland in 1185 and was granted extensive estates in north Munster and later in Leinster. The earldom of Ormond was not created until 1329 and takes its name from the area centred on Nenagh, Co. Tipperary, which was the principal seat of the family at that time.

was divided into five shares in the mid-thirteenth century, one of them being Kilkenny, but this in turn was divided in three a few generations later. Precisely the same happened to Wexford, while Carlow, part of another fifth share of Leinster, was subsequently split between two heiresses. And this same sort of thing happened elsewhere.

One by one, these small estates became vulnerable to the attacks of the Irish. In some cases the original Irish occupiers of these lands were still there, lurking in the badlands, awaiting an opportunity to recover their inheritance. The Mac Murchada family had been kings of Leinster before the province passed to Strongbow, then to the Marshals, then to the heiresses of the Marshals and their husbands, and then to their heiresses in turn. It is no coincidence that in 1328, for the first time since the English invasion, we hear of the inauguration of a Mac Murchada as king of Leinster. According to an Anglo-Irish chronicler based in Dublin, the Irish of Leinster gathered together and elected Domnall son of Art Mac Murchada as their king. He then ordered that his banner should be placed within two miles of Dublin (over which, of course, his ancestors had been king) and he then wanted to lead a conquest of all Ireland. It was an important development, which shows the resurgence that was taking place in native Ireland, but it was a resurgence that was made possible because Leinster was now weak, divided and vulnerable, much of it in the hands of absentees who showed scant attention to their Irish acquisitions.

The New Ascendancy

Since the great English aristocratic families had largely severed their links with Ireland, others emerged from within the colony as its natural leaders. During the early fourteenth century, therefore, the face of Ireland as it was to remain for the rest of the Middle Ages began to take shape. Power came into the hands of a small number of Anglo-Irish barons who generally had little or no land in England but whose families had been in Ireland since the early days of the conquest. John fitz Thomas, the Baron of Offaly, was made Earl of Kildare in 1316, James Butler was made Earl of Ormond in 1328, and Maurice fitz Thomas, the head of the Munster Geraldines, was made Earl of Desmond in 1329. The significant thing about the grant of these earldoms is that they were made in tail male, and could not be inherited by heiresses; if an earl died without sons his estate would pass to his closest surviving male relative. This meant that the splintering of the great conglomerations of lordships was brought to a halt, and the Geraldine earls of Kildare and Desmond, and the Butler earls of Ormond, were assured a continuous possession of their estates — provided they resisted the urge to commit treason — so that for the next two centuries the history of the Anglo-Irish lordship is essentially their history.

These men grew in importance partly because the government depended on them to keep the peace and maintain order in their localities. The revenues available to central government were shrinking all the time, from £5,000 or £6,000 during the reign of Edward I (1272–1307) to about £2,000 during the reign of his grandson, Edward III (1327–77). In theory, the parliament, council, and some of the courts were intended to circulate around the country, the justiciar at its head dispensing justice and maintaining order as he went. In practice, apart from the occasional assembly in Drogheda or Trim or Naas or Kilkenny, the location of government was becoming more and more restricted to Dublin; the effective area of operations of that government was becoming limited to parts of Leinster, Meath and Louth, and real authority in the localities was being delegated to the resident magnates.

The Rise of the Anglo-Irish

In the 1340s there first emerges a serious rift between the English born in Ireland and the English born in England. The people of England had little sympathy or understanding for the Anglo-Irish, while the latter resented the

A castle existed at Lea, Co. Laois, at least as far back as 1203, but it is unlikely to be that whose majestic remains still survive. These allow us to visualise something of its earlier grandeur. It was square in plan and had round towers at the corners, was three storeys high, with the entrance at first-floor level, and had a basement. It is a Geraldine castle, probably built when they were beginning to emerge as a powerful force in Leinster in the mid- to late-13th century, especially under the leadership of John fitz Thomas who became the 1st Earl of Kildare just before his death in 1316. (Photo: F. Gunn)

English, as demonstrated in 1341 when King Edward tried to revoke all grants of Irish lands made since 1307 (to be regranted to those whom he favoured), and to insist that only those who held land in England could hold office in Ireland (in order to ensure him greater leverage over them). This caused such a storm of protest that a Dublin chronicler says that 'the land of Ireland was on the point of separation from the land of England'. He adds that 'before that time there never was such a notable and manifest division between the English born in England and the English born in Ireland'. A parliament was held at Kilkenny, and a list of petitions drawn up in which the Anglo-Irish complained to the king about 'those who are sent from England to govern them, who have little knowledge of the land of Ireland, and who come here with little or nothing by which they can live and maintain their position, and so they use their offices to support themselves by extortion'. Edward, who was then at war with France, could not risk further disruption, and abandoned his scheme of reform.

Edward III's great preoccupation was with the Hundred Years War, and it was only in 1360 when hostilities with France came to a temporary halt that he was free to deal with other less pressing problems, including Ireland. Here, intervention was sorely needed. The early years of the century had witnessed one of the most severe famines in living memory, followed by a series of bad harvests, and, to cap it all, the outbreak of the Black Death in 1348–49, with periodic recurrences of plague thereafter. The effect of these natural disasters was to produce a prolonged agricultural depression and a massive shrinkage in population levels. This, combined with the raids of Irish and rebel English, meant that manors, villages and rural boroughs were deserted, and, instead of the inward migration of colonists, the colony began to experience a gradual haemorrhage of manpower.

The Statutes of Kilkenny

The most important absentee lord at this point was none other than Edward's son Lionel, who had inherited by marriage the de Burgh claim to Connacht and Ulster, and not long afterwards Edward decided to send him to Ireland as his lieutenant with a substantial English army. This was the first time that a member of the English royal family had led a military expedition to Ireland in over one hundred and fifty years, and was therefore an important development. Edward's aim was to take advantage of the lull in the fighting with France to turn the Irish government and economy around, so that it could once more become profitable. When, therefore, war with France broke out again, Ireland would be able to make a useful contribution. Therefore, in King Edward's view, spending a lot of money on Ireland in the short term would not be a waste; it would be an investment for the long term.

Though technically Earl of Ulster, Lionel had never been to Ireland and probably had little knowledge of the country; neither had he much previous experience, either militarily or administratively. Yet, it fell to him to reform the administration of Ireland and to begin the process of reconquest. Between May 1361 and February 1367 the total amount paid on his expedition was £52,000, of which £43,000 (or 83 per cent) came from the English exchequer. This, therefore, was a massive investment by Edward in Ireland. In spite of it, Lionel's expedition achieved little of lasting effect. He was successful in securing submissions from a number of Irish lords, but these did not last, and after his departure conditions were as bad as they were before.

The only thing for which Lionel's campaign tends to be remembered today is the parliament over which he presided at Kilkenny in 1366, at which the famous Statutes of Kilkenny were passed. The Statutes, though not unprecedented, represented an attempt to codify a whole series of enactments passed at various stages throughout the preceding two-thirds of a century. They dealt with economic matters, with the reform of the administration, with the preservation of public order, and, most notoriously, with the thorny question of the separate identity of the Anglo-Irish, and the method by which it might best be protected. Undoubtedly these amounted to a policy of racial exclusiveness on the part of the English in Ireland. For instance, they forbade Irishmen being appointed to certain church offices or from being received as members of religious houses in the 'land of peace'. They forbade Englishmen using the Irish language, mode of riding without saddles, and dress, or from patronising the Irish learned classes of poets and musicians. They forbade marriage, concubinage and fosterage between the Irish and the English, and other forms of contact. Clearly the intention was to maintain a sharp distinction between the two societies in Ireland, but as with Lionel's expedition in general the Statutes of Kilkenny failed in their purpose.

Irish Dynasties and English Settlement
c. 1300

allegiance of Irish chiefdoms to:

the King of England
the Earl of Ulster
the Lord of Connacht
the Lord of Trim
the Lord of Thomond
counties and liberties
Irish chiefdoms

The Failure of Richard II

Lionel is of significance as marking a turning-point in Anglo-Irish affairs, with the commencement of a period of large-scale military intervention in Ireland, largely financed by the English exchequer, under William of

13

Hec est copia carte dni Cristofori de Preston militis fact dnis [...] Ric Secundi [...]

Gormaneston

Indentura de couenantz sup adquisicione manii de Gormaneston p[...] de Preston [...] de seint Amand, e de antiquo tempe [...] [...]

Cest endente tesmoigne q come mons Anmayi de seint Amant le piere e mons Robt de preston [...] finalment accordz, du bargain du manoir de Gormaneston oue les apptenances [...] [...] le dit mons anmayi eit p ces chartres grantez, au dit mons Robt deux centes chartres [...] de soixante, linjes e [...] de [...] linjes a pendre de son dit manoir [...] sont [...] aussi eit pair [...] dit mons Robt [...] del vne rente [...] del autre come p ces lres endentez, [...] appent e auxint eit fait chartes de feffement du dit manoir au dit mons Robt e a ces heirs e as entres [...] luy nomez, e [...] eit fait [...] et auxint eit fait quatre lres auxi [...] e a dius [...] nomez, p le dit Robt p la cosine de ceo e de ses vint e quatre [...] de [...] vne [...] de [...] dit [...] de [...] mez dibat au dit mons Robt e ses compaignons deliuerez et [...] en la [...] le dit mons Robt et ses ditz compaignons luy eit fait tros relees de tout son droit du dit manoir quele chartres faite, [...] susdites le dit mons Anmay as fait enseller en sa presence demesne de son [...] seal e les as deliure au dit mons Robt et le dit mons Anmay as plenerement recen du dit mons Robt toute la some entre eux accordz, qnele il dist auoir p le dit bargain et [...] ceo le dit mons Anmay loialment empient de trauailler a la court le Roy et en haste come il [...] [...] e [...] [...] les deux chartres de cent chartre p la chartre de feffement e les relees susditz, e les [...] estre ensculles, as costages du dit Robt come en [...] [...] [...] ses relees Et auxi il empient loialment q toutz les eumenes chartres muniments, [...] e remembrances touchantes le dit manoir q sont devs luy ou [...] vsoient il [...] seyches oue tout la haste qil [...] e les [...] deliuer au dit mons Robt sanz delay Et auxint il empient loialment [...] de fois q le dit mons Robt vendra coueitez nouelles [...] ou manoir auantdit tieles come le dit mons anmay luy as fait auie q le dit mons anmay les [...] a luy faire sanz delay as costages du dit Robt, En tesmoignance de quen chose a cestes lres endentez, les auantditz mons anmay e Robt a cestes endentez ont mys lors seals. Don le mescredy lendemein de lassumpcion de nre dame lan du regne nre seign le Roy Edward tierz, puis la conquest [...]

Indentura Anmay fit R ad implendu conuentes pais sui [...] e R p domini [...]

Ceste endente faire entre mons Anmay de seint Amant le fiz e mons Robert preston de preston tesmoigne q come mons Anmay de seint [...] mant le piere eit finalment

Windsor from 1369 to 1372 and from 1374 to 1376, and under King Richard II in person in 1394–95 and 1399. Both Lionel and Windsor failed because the English government could not afford to maintain a large enough army in Ireland for long enough to provide a lasting solution. Still, before the end of the century one further attempt to solve 'the Irish problem' was made by King Richard II.

In 1394 he became the first king of England since 1210, and the last until 1689, to visit his lordship. He did so believing that his presence, combined with that of a large army, could turn back the tide: the army was the stick which would force the Irish, and those Anglo-Irish who were now just as rebellious, to submit to his royal authority, but unlike his predecessors he came too with a carrot, dangling the promise of more security of tenure for them if they stayed loyal in the future. It is certainly the case that he had some initial success, principally in getting the powerful king of Leinster, Art Mac Murchada Cáemanach (McMurrough Kavanagh), to promise allegiance, but again the arrangement proved a temporary one and collapsed soon after his departure in the following year. Not undaunted, King Richard returned to Ireland in 1399, but the circumstances were not as favourable as before on all fronts: the Irish proved elusive, while his Lancastrian cousins and enemies at home seized the opportunity of his absence to instigate a coup, leading to his deposition and death.

In the end, therefore, Richard II failed in Ireland as in England. To be fair to him, he showed some foresight in seeking to bring the Irish in from the cold, and in recognising the legitimacy of some of their complaints. But, when their goals conflicted with the objectives of his English subjects in Ireland, he failed to find a means of squaring the circle. A resurgence was taking place within native Ireland over which neither he nor his ministers had any control. This was a political resurgence, but was more successful at a cultural level, the colonists conforming to the norms of Gaelic society, becoming patrons of the Gaelic learned classes, and in time being accorded a place of honour in poets' and hereditary historians' scheme of things.

The Emergence of the Pale

If the interventions of Richard II and his predecessors had shown anything it was that, even to maintain the English position in Ireland, demanded a huge injection of resources in money and manpower. The Irish government was incapable, because of incompetence, corruption and shortage of funds, of financing itself without subsidies, which were something the new cash-starved Lancastrian kings found it hard to come by. In these circumstances, the government had to reconsider the scale of its military commitments and the very nature of its operations. Efforts continued to try to get those who held lands in Ireland to return to protect them, but if anything the drain was

Opposite: *Gormanston Register, 1398, the ancient register book of the Preston family of Gormanston, Co. Meath.*

worsening, with parliament complaining to the king in 1421 that 'tenants, tradesmen, and labourers … daily depart in great numbers from your said land [of Ireland] to the kingdom of England and remain there'. The major military offensives of previous years tended to be replaced by small-scale defensive measures, the aim of which was less that of reconquest and more to do with securing the colony's frontiers.

In this new era of realism the boundaries of the area over which the government claimed effective control increasingly became confined to the coastal littoral from Dundalk to Dalkey, including portions of Cos. Louth, Meath, Dublin and Kildare, an area which by the mid-fifteenth century was known as the English 'Pale', and which in part at least came by the late fifteenth century to be enclosed by an earthen bank and ditch. The emergence of the Pale is of great significance, since what the government was doing was recognising that it could no longer continue to exercise its normal functions beyond this attenuated area. It was not washing its hands of the rest of the country, merely handing over the reins of authority in these areas to the great lords who dominated the localities, and that included both Irish and English.

This produced a new equilibrium in Ireland. The Dublin government did its best to maintain the rule of law within the Pale, and to keep the inhabitants of this cordoned enclave (and their stock) free from the raids and exactions of those beyond, and from demanding 'black-rent' (protection-money), but the rest of Ireland was largely given over to a few men who exercised command there by any means at their disposal and by a form of lordship that was sometimes little short of tyrannical. These methods allowed the activities of the Irish lords elsewhere to go largely unchecked. Increasingly we find them seeking alliance by marriage with the Anglo-Irish magnates. The White Earl of Ormond (d. 1452), for example, was related to both Mac Murchada of Leinster and O'Néill of Ulster. By means of such alliances, he could ensure peace for his lordship, and build upon his position of power. As a result, the White Earl, who already held the liberty of Tipperary, came to exert near total control over the royal county of Kilkenny, and in a famous set of ordinances actually regulated the imposition of 'coyne and livery' and other such illegal exactions; these onerous demands – which involved his armies living off the countryside which they were otherwise protecting – are sometimes thought to be confined to the native Irish but in fact men like the White Earl depended on them to retain their supremacy.

In the fourteenth century men like the earls of Ormond and Desmond had on occasion refused to take on the task of being chief governor, because they would have to foot the bill themselves. But in the fifteenth century, the Lancastrian governments badly needed to recruit their governors from among those who were powerful landowners in Ireland, since they could not depend upon the availability of subventions from England. In order to coax the magnates into accepting the post, the degree of financial scrutiny was relaxed and lieutenants were given the prerogative of appointing and dismissing whom they pleased to some important offices of state. This gave them control over the king's council in Ireland, and, through it, parliament. As a result, the chief governor was less and less answerable to outside control, had wide-ranging rights of patronage at his disposal, and real power. As a result, the post of lieutenant became a considerably more attractive one for the three great resident magnates, the earls of Ormond, Desmond and Kildare.

Aristocratic Home Rule?

This new development had advantages since the participation of the great nobles in government meant strong and stable rule. The disadvantage was that aristocratic government led to aristocratic domination, and, instead of government being impartial and open to all, it became a cause of faction and power-struggles. As the great lordships became more autonomous, what some historians would see as a separatist tendency began to emerge among the Anglo-Irish. This had been smouldering for generations, as resentment with interference from England and from English-born officials grew, but it took an organised form in the mid-fifteenth century in the public assertion that Ireland was not bound by statutes out of England. At a parliament held in Drogheda in 1460, it was declared that 'the land of Ireland is, and at all times has been, corporate of itself by the ancient laws and customs used in the same, freed from the burden of any special law of the realm of England save only such laws as by the lords spiritual and temporal and commons of the said land [of Ireland] had been in great council or parliament there held, admitted, accepted, affirmed and proclaimed'.

It can be argued that what this statute amounted to was a statement of the legislative independence of Ireland. It is true that there were exceptional circumstances surrounding its promulgation. Richard, duke of York, who had earlier enjoyed a relatively successful career as lieutenant in Ireland, had been attainted by the English parliament in 1459 for treason against the Lancastrian king, Henry VI, and was now a fugitive in Ireland, where Yorkist supporters dominated the government. His Irish supporters passed the famous 1460 statute partly to prevent English writs ordering York's arrest from having force in Ireland. But just as Richard used his following within the Irish parliament to shield himself from prosecution, so the Anglo-Irish, it would seem, used his vulnerability to make a declaration which was in accord with their own pre-conceived notions of autonomy.

The Kildare Ascendancy

Soon after the passing of the 1460 Declaration, the Yorkist cause prevailed in England and the Butlers of Ormond, who had supported the other régime, saw themselves out of favour. A temporary eclipse in the fortunes of the earls of Desmond then turned the spotlight on their Geraldine cousins, the earls of Kildare. Prior to this point Kildare had not been the most powerful of the Anglo-Irish lordships, though it was composed of a vast amount of land, and its geographic location was of great significance: since political influence in the colony was increasingly centred on the Pale, the advancement of the interests of the Palesmen was crucial for the success of government. That is why when Edward IV sought effective but economically efficient government he turned in 1471 to the greatest nobleman in the Pale, Thomas fitz Maurice, the seventh earl of Kildare, and from this point onwards, with few interruptions, an earl of Kildare was to govern Ireland until their power was smashed by Henry VIII in 1534.

Ladies from the region of the Pale are shown here with 'Kerns', warriors armed in the traditional fashion. This illustration was intended to contrast the civilisation of the Pale with the perceived barbarism of the west.

Once they gained the deputyship the seventh, eighth and ninth earls in turn used their control of government to increase their lands further, by passing laws allowing them to occupy the lands of absentees, to use the rents and profits of absentee estates for their own ends, and to possess what lands they could recover from rebels. Kildare's enemies became the government's enemies, and government revenues were used to prosecute them. By a vast array of strategic marriage-alliances, and by securing the right to billet their standing army on the countryside, and by gaining control of government revenues without an absolute duty to account for expenditure, the earls came to dominate Irish life, and did so within a very short space of time. One of the keys to their power lay in control of the council. In theory, the earls did not have the right to appoint and dismiss ministers of the council, but in practice they exercised just such a right.

Attempts to remove or undermine the position of the eighth earl, known in Irish sources as Gearóid Mór, were made during the reign of Edward IV and the brief reign of his brother Richard III, as part of a policy aimed at reasserting royal control over the Irish administration, but in neither case was it carried out. It is, though, probably anachronistic to view this as a struggle by Kildare to achieve separatist or 'Home Rule' policies at the expense of the English crown. Under the earls of Kildare significant successes were obtained in pushing back the frontier with Gaelic Ireland; old castles were re-taken from the Irish, new ones were erected to defend the territory gained, and the king's writ ran over a more extensive area. This was, of course, Kildare expansion, but in doing so they were strengthening the

English lordship of Ireland. That is why the earls of Kildare were retained as deputy: they provided a cost-effective method of safeguarding vital English interests in Ireland. A delicate balance existed between the aspirations of the earls and the interests of the king. The earls were not indispensable. As masters of the Pale the earls of Kildare helped to keep secure the administrative headquarters of the colony, but equally Kildare needed to occupy the position of deputy in order to enhance his own status within the colony. There were, therefore, mutual benefits for both king and earl in the Kildare supremacy.

Early Tudor Ireland

After the Battle of Bosworth in August 1485, and the accession of Henry Tudor as King Henry VII, the prospects of the Butler family in Ireland underwent a sea-change and it may have been this, or sincere Yorkist fervour, which encouraged the Great Earl to support the cause of the pretender Lambert Simnel and to secure his coronation in Christ Church cathedral in Dublin in May 1487. Although the plot came to nothing in the end, it was a startling reminder of the dangers inherent in neglecting Ireland, and an illustration of the way in which Ireland had come to play a role that was critical to the conspiracies that dominated the age. Crucially too, instead of the customary title 'king of England and France, and lord of Ireland', Simnel was crowned 'king of England, France and Ireland', a measure of the extent to which the constitutional position of Ireland within the English realm was beginning to become an issue. Kildare had clearly acted treasonably, but

Castle and round tower of Kildare from an engraving made in 1833.

again he survived, Henry Tudor being unwilling as yet to do without him. What forced Henry's hand was the appearance in Ireland in November 1491 of yet another Yorkist pretender, Perkin Warbeck, to whose cause Kildare was at best neutral. The earl was dismissed from office almost immediately, and although he was eventually restored to the king's favour and to high office, in the interval Henry VII decided upon a major intervention in Ireland, and a determined effort to strengthen royal control.

In August 1494 he nominated several new men to office in the lordship and on 12 September 1494 appointed Edward Poynings as his deputy. It was part of Poynings' mission to ensure that Perkin Warbeck did not receive sufficient support in Ireland by which to launch a Yorkist invasion of England. In this he succeeded, although Warbeck eluded capture for a few more years.

Another of Poynings' tasks was to reform the financial administration of Ireland, so that the collection of revenue would become more productive and the auditing of accounts more efficient. In this, as might be expected, he and his officials were rather less than successful. But Poynings had one more task yet to fulfil. Henry Tudor had decided to reinstate Kildare, and intended both to clip his wings and to ensure that no governor of Ireland in the future could evade royal control in the manner in which the earls of Kildare had come to do. Therefore, Poynings was issued with explicit instructions as to legislation which Henry intended to have passed by the Irish parliament, comfortable in the knowledge that the new English officials dominating the Irish council would secure its passage.

Poynings' Parliament

The parliament met at Drogheda on 1 December 1494, and continued in session until the following March. The legislation passed confirmed the king's intention of asserting real control over the governance of his lordship. Ireland's chief ministers were henceforth to hold their offices at the king's pleasure, and not for life as Kildare had sought to secure for his cronies. Furthermore, this parliament decreed that the government of Ireland was subordinate to that of England and that all royal commandments were to be duly obeyed. It annulled what it called the 'pretensed prescription' of the 1460 parliament, which had decreed that those resident in Ireland could not be summoned from the country by orders issuing from England, and that English seals were inoperative in Ireland; instead, the great seal of England, the privy seal, and signet, were henceforth to be obeyed in Ireland.

Piers Butler, 8th Earl of Ormond, from his tomb in St Canice's Cathedral, Kilkenny

But it is for the ninth act, what has become known as Poynings' Law, that this parliament is best remembered, an act which thereafter changed the procedures for the passage of legislation by Irish parliaments. From now on, no parliament could be held in Ireland without the king's explicit licence, and no legislation could be enacted until the proposed legislation had been inspected and approved by the king and his council in England. The aim here was clearly to ensure that the Irish parliament never again (as had happened when Kildare secured the recognition of Lambert Simnel as king) passed measures which were contrary to the interests of the king of England. A constitutional check on the administration of the king's lordship of Ireland was thereby introduced. But inherent in the legislation was the assumption that the government of Ireland would again be entrusted to somebody of Kildare's ilk, since such stringent safeguards would have been unnecessary if government through loyal English officials such as Poynings was to become the norm. And therefore the Great Earl was soon reappointed but had to swear to abide by the provisions of Poynings' Law, so that if writs were issued out of England ordering the delivery to the king of those whom he considered rebels or traitors, those writs had to be obeyed.

Malahide Castle, Co. Dublin, is arguably the most distinguished of all Irish private castles, no other house in Ireland being in continuous occupation by the same family for longer, until the death of the 7th Baron in 1973. The Talbots of Malahide were established there almost exactly 800 years earlier, but only gradually rose through the ranks of the Pale gentry as the Middle Ages wore on. The great hall of the castle is a unique survival in Ireland in its original form and dates, approximately, from the 15th century when the family's fortunes were in their prime.

Poynings' Law was passed to meet a certain set of circumstances (in particular, no doubt, to ensure that the supporters in Ireland of the pretender Perkin Warbeck did not use parliament, as had happened in the case of Simnel, to effect a coup d'état) and it is probably the case that its framers would have been surprised to know that it was still operative three centuries later. Nevertheless, Poynings' parliament was the most important to meet in Ireland from that which passed the Statutes of Kilkenny in 1366 to the Reformation Parliament of 1536. Although some of the enactments of the parliament were later repealed, and others were simply ignored, most did take effect, and as a result royal control in the lordship of Ireland was significantly increased. The legislation was not intended to be a direct challenge to Gearóid Mór or a deliberate assault on the powers of the chief governor. The intention was simply to ensure that the king had knowledge of the decisions made in his name and the prime role in the decision-making process. That achieved, Kildare could be safely restored to office, as was to happen in August 1496. With proper safeguards built into the system, as Poynings had ensured, Kildare would be an asset to the king: a local magnate, able to provide strong and cost-effective government, yet constrained by law, and a water-tight promise of good behaviour, from overstepping the mark.

Tudor Strategic Concerns

The two separate conspiracies to overthrow the Tudor régime in the late fifteenth century were significant in that, in both cases, the pretender landed in Ireland, finding support among some of the Anglo-Irish and many of the native Irish. This was not an entirely new phenomenon – Scots and Welsh opponents of the English had tried this in the past – but the difference now was that these pretenders had the backing of England's major European enemies, and hence, as the sixteenth century began, so too there emerged arguably *the* major theme in English strategic considerations regarding Ireland until recent times: the possibility that England's enemies might use Ireland as a base from which to launch an invasion of Britain. It was for this reason that Henry VII sought not just to strengthen English influence in Ireland, but to increase direct royal control, as manifested in Poynings' Law.

Then under Henry VIII a tendency began to fill appointments, especially the top positions in the administration, the judiciary and the episcopacy, with English-born officials (whom historians call the New English), rather than people of English extraction born in Ireland, the Old English. This was not good for government, for many reasons. Of course it alienated the Old English, who saw newcomers assuming influential positions over which they had formerly had a monopoly. Also, many of these New English were Henry VIII's courtiers, being rewarded with positions in Ireland in return for services elsewhere, and were no better than absentee landlords. These individuals, being new to the Irish scene, frequently came to rash judgements as to how the government of Ireland could be improved, reports which were listened to at court and which produced unhelpful and sometimes pointless interventions into Irish affairs. One such was Henry VIII's decision in 1520 to remove the ninth earl of Kildare, Gearóid Óg, from the Lord Deputyship, and send an ill-considered military expedition to Ireland under the generalship of the earl of Surrey.

This expedition was an unmitigated failure, partly because Surrey lacked the military resources to engage in anything other than temporary peace-keeping operations, and partly because Kildare's supporters in Ireland made life as difficult as possible for him. But it provides us with a very important insight into sixteenth-century English thinking on the subject of Ireland and how to deal with it. To Surrey and to people like him, the only solution to the perennial problem of warfare in Ireland was to institute a full-scale military conquest – to complete the job started 350 years earlier – so that the native Irish could be overrun, so that English renegades in Ireland could be made amenable to the law, and English law and government made applicable throughout the entire island. It would need a large standing army, the construction of new castles and towns, and the introduction of new English settlers, and it would be very expensive, but the problem would be solved once and for all.

But while Surrey was in Ireland, Henry VIII began to formulate another solution to the Irish problem, though circumstances intervened to ensure that he did not attempt it until much later. Henry's solution involved a complete reassessment of the constitutional position of the native Irish. Why were they, of their nature, 'the enemy'? Why not treat them precisely the same as any other subject of the crown? Perhaps their constant rebelliousness was a consequence of genuine grievances, the principal one being that they were denied access to the law and therefore to legal title to their lands. If they were granted the right to hold lawfully and to pass on to their heirs lands to which they had a traditional claim, maybe they could finally be brought in from the cold: if they were given the benefit of the law, then perhaps they would learn to abide by the law.

A Clash of Civilisations

This conflict between conquest or accommodation lay at the heart of English policy towards Ireland for the rest of the Tudor period, and indeed, in a modified form, the same conflict between coercion and conciliation underlay British policy towards Ireland until the twentieth century. It accounts for the many inconsistencies in approach to Irish affairs that characterised each of the Tudor monarchs throughout the sixteenth century until the so-called Elizabethan conquest of 1603. In a very real sense, it was the choice between a military solution and a political solution. And not all advocates of military methods did so out of sheer bloody-mindedness.

Many contemporaries were aware that Tudor Ireland was the scene of a clash of civilisations, in this respect: Irish society, and in particular Irish law, differed to such an extent from its English equivalent, especially in matters relating to inheritance and succession to title, that the Irish could not simply be 'brought in from the cold' by the passage of an act of parliament. The job of making English landlords out of Irish warlords might eventually prove possible, but not without a lot of effort pushing square pegs into round holes. The principle of primogeniture that underpinned English common law – the system by which the eldest legitimate child succeeds to all property and titles – ran directly counter to Irish practice, where bastard sons had as much right as legitimate offspring, lordship could not pass through the female line, and, most importantly, there was no automatic right to succession by an eldest son: if he succeeded his father it was because he had proved himself to be the obvious choice, frequently only after a lengthy and bloody succession dispute with, perhaps, a brother or cousin. For this reason, the advocates of coercion won out in the end, and the English government committed itself to whatever it took – a short sharp shock or a war of attrition – to bring about a conquest. But the conciliatory approach was tried first.

Dublin Castle, the administrative centre of English power in Ireland until 1922, gained its present form largely after 1700, but a not inconsiderable portion of its medieval fabric remains intact, including the Record Tower (above). This witnessed the only siege of importance that the castle ever suffered, that by Silken Thomas, son of Gearóid Óg, in 1534, though he was unsuccessful in taking it.

The Kildare Rebellion

The position of ascendancy held by the earls of Kildare was smashed by their unsuccessful rebellion in 1534. Its causes are complex, but it was probably a reaction, admittedly miscalculated, against the increasing centralisation of Tudor policy. During the final period spent by Gearóid Óg, the ninth earl, as Deputy, successive appointments to office in Ireland were made contrary to his wishes by Thomas Cromwell, Henry VIII's most senior advisor, and considerable resentment built up as a result. By August 1533 Kildare was secretly removing military supplies from Dublin Castle and, when summoned to England early in the following year, only reluctantly obliged, appointing his son Lord Offaly, better known as 'Silken Thomas', as his deputy. On 11 June, Thomas denounced royal policy before a meeting of the Irish privy council, as a result of which his father was sent to the Tower of London, where he died some months later. Meanwhile, Thomas had instigated a full-scale rebellion, proclaiming a Catholic Crusade, and laying siege to Dublin Castle. But when an

The fine tower house at Portaferry, Co. Down, was built to guard the entrance to Strangford Lough. It may be as late as the 16th century and was probably built by the Savage family. They were Anglo-Normans who settled in Ulster in the aftermath of de Courcy's conquest of 1177 and subsequently became dominant in the Ards Peninsula which the main branch of the family ruled from their magnificently strategic motte castle at Ardkeen. In time, especially after the last resident Earl of Ulster was murdered in 1333, the Savage family became the leading 'English' family in Ulster, through they were heavily 'Gaelicised'. In 1482, Sir Janico Savage, Lord of Lecale, held the post of seneschal of the earldom and was described as 'the most famous of the English of the province for his exploits against the Irish', but he had revolted against the Crown by 1515 and was described as 'one of the English great rebels'.

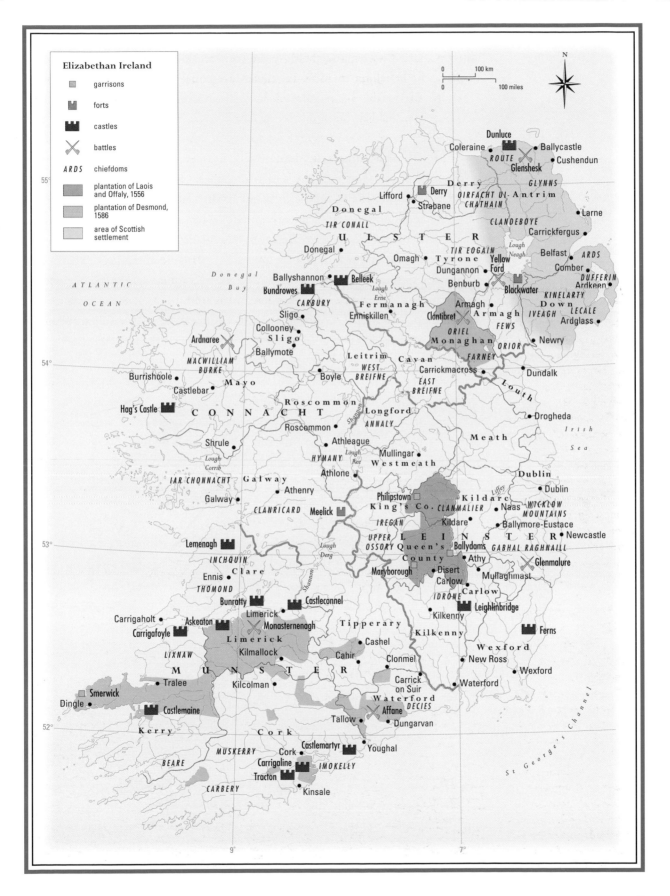

Elizabethan Ireland

- garrisons
- forts
- castles
- battles
- ARDS chiefdoms
- plantation of Laois and Offaly, 1556
- plantation of Desmond, 1586
- area of Scottish settlement

THE ILLUSTRATED HISTORY OF IRELAND

Hugh O'Neill, Earl of Tyrone, was brought up among English settlers in the Irish midlands and fought on the side of the English in Munster and Ulster. Aspiring to a leadership role in central Ulster, he realised that the spread of English administration into the province represented a challenge to his position. Eventually he opted to head the confederacy of Ulster chieftains who had begun a major campaign against English garrisons and officials in Ulster in 1594. Aided by a disciplined army, he achieved many successes in the war to 1599. Thereafter the English under Mountjoy asserted their supremacy despite the landing of Spanish troops in Kinsale in 1601. The ensuing treaty of Mellifont guaranteed O'Neill's headship of his clan and his title to the earldom but pressure from officials in Dublin caused him to flee Ireland in 1607.

army arrived from England he was soon on the defensive and by August 1535 he was forced to surrender. Soon afterwards he was sent to London, and although he had been promised that his life would be spared, he and five of his uncles were executed, and the massive Kildare estate was confiscated.

'Surrender and Regrant'

The failure of the Kildare rebellion marked the effective end of England's medieval lordship of Ireland, and the beginning of a period of what we nowadays would call 'direct rule'. In reaction to rule by a military garrison and Henry VIII's enforced introduction to Ireland of the Anglican Reformation, many of the leading native Irish lords joined forces in an unprecedented nation-wide confederacy known (misleadingly) as the Geraldine League. Though it was soon overcome, the League convinced Henry to attempt a compromise solution to the Irish problem by commencing a process known to historians as 'Surrender and Regrant'. This involved the Irish lords acknowledging Henry as their liege lord, and agreeing to adopt English law, language and customs, in return for a charter granting them their lands, which they would hold of the crown in perpetuity (provided they remained faithful); they would henceforth be peers of the realm, and be given a new title. To symbolise this new start Henry's own title was changed in 1541 from 'lord of Ireland' to 'king of Ireland': the intention was that the new restored 'kingdom' of Ireland would embrace the inhabitants of the whole island, Gaelic and English, who would all be subject to English law and institutions and have the same constitutional rights.

This was a constitutional revolution which might have produced a settlement of the Irish question, but the experiment lapsed with the death of Henry VIII in 1547. Meanwhile, young and ambitious English nobles and gentry, looking around them for a theatre of warfare where they could make their reputations, were presented with few opportunities other than Ireland, however small-scale the campaigning. Using their influence at court these people secured a change in policy towards Ireland which manifested itself first in increased numbers of troops, then the imposition of garrisons in key border areas, and, most ambitious yet, the attempt to win the territories of Laois and Offaly from Irish hands, and establish a plantation of English settlers there which began in 1557.

Reformation and Reaction

The Old English had little say in these developments, though they were expected partly to finance them, and of course the native Irish were at the receiving end. If one bears in mind the fact that hand in hand with this change in policy went an intensified campaign to promote Protestantism in Ireland, then one can see why the Reformation made slow progress there: the Old English now felt alienated from government and less inclined to follow its edicts, while the Irish saw the Protestant Reformation as just an instrument of military conquest and forced Anglicisation. Therefore, by the time Elizabeth I came to the throne the political climate in Ireland had deteriorated very considerably since the days of her father, Henry, and the native Irish were very reluctant to believe that she aimed at anything other than their outright expropriation. They were not entirely unjustified in this view. The sixteenth century, of course, saw the beginnings of European colonisation in the New World, and with it the development of justification-theories, by which the wholesale annihilation of indigenous societies was explained away as the inevitable and necessary progress of civilisation at the expense of peoples who were no better than primitive savages. Those advocating a soldier's solution to the Irish problem found no difficulty in applying the same theory there.

The leading dynasty in Gaelic Ireland were, as we have seen, the O'Neills of Ulster, and Ulster, then the least Anglicised province in Ireland, presented the most severe challenge to those anxious to subdue the country by force. There, Shane O'Neill, the first Irish lord to train and arm the peasantry of his lordship of Tyrone, was able to claim that he represented the defender of the Roman faith in Ireland in the face of English heresy, and by 1566 was encouraging a French invasion and offering the kingdom of Ireland to Charles IX, as well as colluding with Mary, Queen of Scots. Ten years and vast resources in money and troops were spent unsuccessfully trying to overcome him, but only death by assassination finally removed him. By the 1570s, it was fears of a Spanish landing in the south of Ireland (which eventually materialised) that led to the idea of a new English plantation of Munster, but the atrocities that were associated with its initiation, while temporarily dampening unrest, hardened attitudes further in Gaelic Ireland.

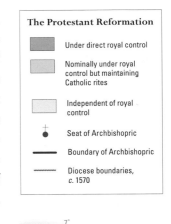

The Protestant Reformation

- Under direct royal control
- Nominally under royal control but maintaining Catholic rites
- Independent of royal control
- ✝ Seat of Archbishopric
- ▬ Boundary of Archbishopric
- ┄ Diocese boundaries, c. 1570

Dissolution of religious houses
- ■ by Henry VIII
- ▨ by Edward VI
- ▦ by Elizabeth I
- ▪ by James I
- □ 1 house
- ▢ several houses

The Nine Years' War

In Ulster, young lords like O'Donnell and Maguire reacted to the government's tightening grip by forming a confederacy which aimed at winning the support of Philip II of Spain for an independent Catholic Ireland under the latter's suzerainty. The only question was whether Shane O'Neill's nephew, Hugh, who had the 'Surrender and Regrant' title of Earl of Tyrone, would take command of the confederacy or remain loyal to his English courtly background.

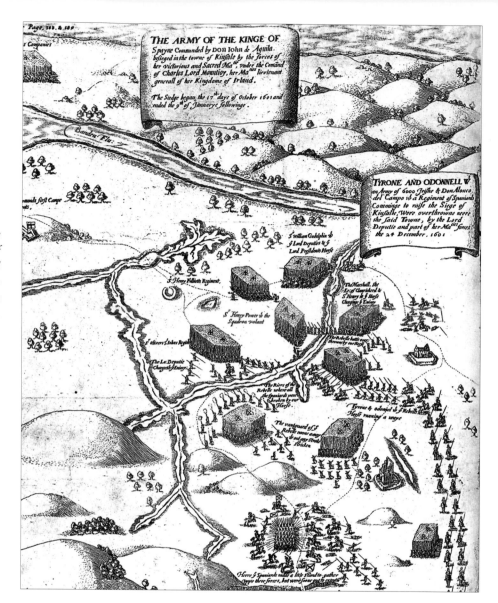

The Royal Army meet the combined armies of Tyrone and O'Donnell together with their Spanish allies at Kinsale on Christmas eve in 1601.

When he chose to go into rebellion in 1595, having created his own professional standing army on the English model, he utterly transformed the military balance in Ireland, and successfully confronted English armies in the field. When the young Philip III of Spain became convinced that the rebellion was a religious war to defend Catholicism, he sent a new Spanish armada, but the Nine Years' War that followed was essentially an Irish nationalist uprising against English rule. The Spanish fleet sailed from the port of Lisbon on 3 September 1601 and landed at Kinsale, Co. Cork, on the 21st. O'Neill and his allies marched south from Ulster to meet them but the confederate army and their Spanish allies were roundly defeated in battle there on Christmas Eve.

The Battle of Kinsale effectively ended the revolt, O'Donnell setting sail for Spain three days later, where he died soon afterwards. By 1607, the suspicions that continued to surround O'Neill and the new O'Donnell lord made them feel vulnerable still, while the aggressive and intrusive efforts to settle, colonise, and Anglicise Ulster no doubt convinced them that they had outlived their time, with the result that they too sailed off into permanent exile in what is known to history as the 'Flight of the Earls'. A Gaelic poet wrote that 'If Providence has ordained that Ireland, a new England in everything but name, should henceforth be in the hands of enemies, it is fitting to bid farewell to that island'. A single military defeat had led to the collapse of a political order, and the collapse of that order had undermined a civilisation.

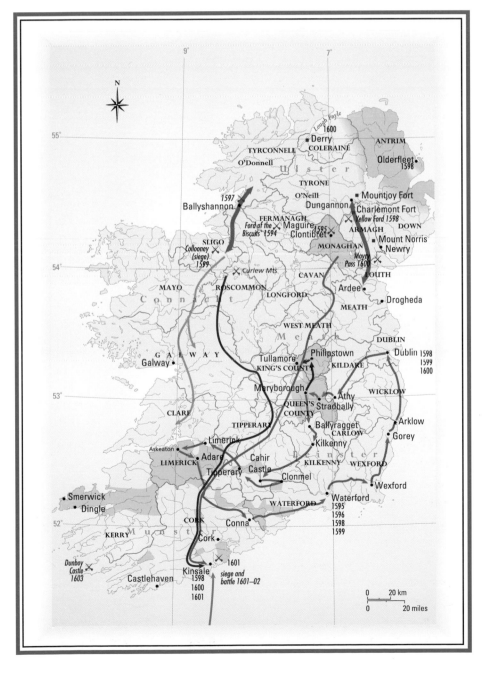

O'Neill's Rising, 1595–1601

1600	Landings
X	Battles
—— 1598 ── 1599	The marches of the Earl of Essex
⟷	Main passages into and out of Tyrone and Tyrconnell
→	Raids by O'Donnell
→	O'Donnell's march
→	O'Neill's march
→	Spanish arrival
■	Forts constructed by Mountjoy and Dowcra
▨	'Planted' before 1595

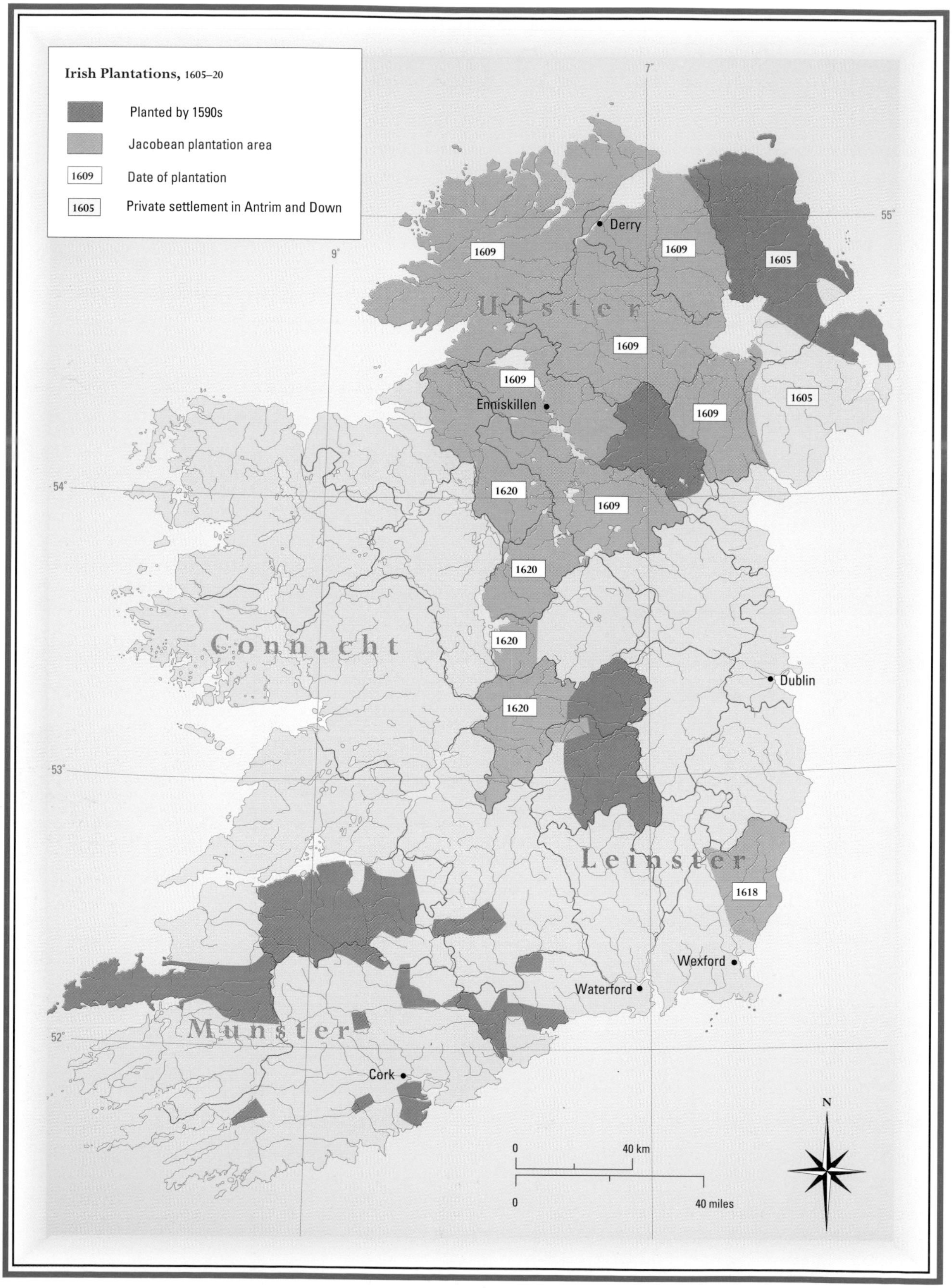
Irish Plantations, 1605–20
Planted by 1590s
Jacobean plantation area
1609 Date of plantation
1605 Private settlement in Antrim and Down
Ulster
Connacht
Leinster
Munster
Derry
Enniskillen
Dublin
Wexford
Waterford
Cork
1609
1605
1620
1618
55°
54°
53°
52°
9°
7°
0
40 km
40 miles
N

CHAPTER V

CONFISCATION, PLANTATION AND ASCENDANCY

'Nothing is more dangerous than middle counsels, which England of old too much practiced in Ireland': so wrote Fynes Moryson, based on his experience as an Elizabethan official in Ireland at the time of the Battle of Kinsale. And in its aftermath 'middle counsels' were well and truly dispensed with. The commander of the English forces, Lord Deputy Mountjoy, followed the defeated Hugh O'Neill into Ulster, where he established strategic garrisons, and brought the province to its knees by a combination of warfare and famine. In a gesture filled with symbolism, he demolished the stone at Tullahogue on which the O'Neills had for centuries been inaugurated and a demoralised Hugh O'Neill soon afterwards submitted under the terms of the Treaty of Mellifont. It was this treaty which completed the Tudor conquest of Ireland, yet it was agreed on 30 March 1603, a week after the death – concealed from O'Neill until later – of the last of the Tudors, Elizabeth I.

Life in the Early Seventeenth Century

After the devastation wreaked by the Nine Years' War, it took some time for the country to recover economically, but recover it did: over-population was not as yet a problem (there may have been as few as a half-million inhabitants before the huge influx of English and Scottish settlers later in the century rapidly doubled that number), and the economy was basic, and resilient. Since the bulk of the population depended on the land, the return of peace brought a measure of stability, and, since the economy was based on subsistence rather than the market, the poor condition of the country's communications and the debased state of its currency

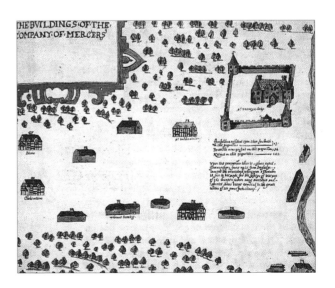

A contemporary plan of Mercers' settlement in Derry made during the plantation of Ulster.

can have effected only a minority, while the pirates who roamed off its coasts were not unduly attracted by its exports to England, France and Spain of fish and cattle, and products derived from the latter and from sheep. The one thriving engine of the Irish economy in this period was the destruction of its vast woodlands, which began as a military tactic under the Tudors, but accelerated at a rate that was alarming even to contemporaries in the seventeenth century, as a ready market was found overseas for Irish timber and wood-products, notably staves for the manufacture of wine-casks.

With few exceptions, of which Kilkenny, home of the Butlers of Ormond, is most notable, Irish towns were coastal ports of some antiquity established under external aegis. Dublin, being the centre of government, was by far the biggest and it and Waterford the most Anglicised, though the latter did trade also with France and Spain. The silting up of the Liffey over many centuries weakened Dublin's status as a port, and perhaps the two most significant trade-routes were Waterford to Bristol and, increasingly in the seventeenth century, Drogheda to Chester. Spain is where the western town of Galway looked for its associations, and its apogee had been reached by perhaps the turn of the seventeenth century, as the beauty of the contemporary town houses of its merchant classes still affirms. Though it later declined markedly, at this point it stood head and shoulders above its Munster rivals, Cork and Limerick, the former more important as a political centre than a trading port and the latter only notable for the majesty of its castle and strength of its town walls. In spite of its dominant position within Connacht, Galway too was proud of its English heritage, the most famous statement of which is its civic ordinance of 1581 to the effect that 'Neither O nor Mac shall strut nor swagger through the streets of Galway'. By that stage the only remnants of a town in Ulster were the proud surroundings of Carrickfergus Castle, though the bridgeheads established under the Tudors at Derry and Newry soon saw rapid expansion.

Anglicisation and Reformation

With the overthrow of the Gaelic order came major social change. Irish and Old English lords had maintained large private armies of 'kerne' or 'swordsmen' who were landless individuals dependent entirely on their martial skills and their lord's patronage. The displacement of the latter meant that they put their arms to other use and emerged as brigands who posed a threat to the peace that lasted well into the eighteenth century, and always had the potential of being applied to a political, rebellious purpose. Anglicisation was another feature of the Irish social landscape after Kinsale, though it would be a mistake to think that some sections of the native Irish were not already beginning to adopt English ways, including English language and fashion styles, in the sixteenth century. This was to some extent the product of intermingling with the Old English, but partly too the result of a growing wish among the Irish lords, who were increasingly involved in intrigue with their Catholic counterparts elsewhere in Europe in the Counter-Reformation period, to fit in: although the Irish had not yet developed an 'inferiority complex', their language was unique to them and their kindred in Gaelic Scotland and their dress-styles were viewed as uncivilised, while the many peculiarities of Irish custom undoubtedly began to appear to hold the Gaelic nobility back from assuming their place in the European mainstream, and a gradual voluntary abandonment began.

Remarkably though, the Irish nobility showed a great reluctance to Anglicise where it involved the adoption of Protestantism, and since this 'Recusancy' was something they shared with many people of English extraction within Ireland, namely the 'Old English', there emerged in Counter-Reformation Ireland a new communion of interest between both groups, where ethnic origin for the first time since the English invasion of the twelfth century took second place to religious affiliation. Queen Elizabeth had been reasonably tolerant of Recusancy in Ireland, partly for fear of alienating the Old English, and the number of Protestants in Ireland remained small throughout her reign, confined mostly among government officials and new settlers. By contrast, the numbers of Roman Catholics remained high and they were zealously ministered to by a plentiful supply of Continentally-trained priests, among whom the Jesuits were predominant: the latter were so successful in performing their task that by the end of Elizabeth's reign they had won the hearts-and-minds battle among the populace, as regards the choice between Catholicism and Protestantism. By the time a university, Trinity College, was established in Dublin in 1592, in part to provide for the better education of potential ministers in the new religion, and by the time too that the first Irish translation of the New Testament was published, in 1603, in an effort to spread the reformed faith among native-speakers, it was too late and the Protestant Reformation had failed in Ireland. Nevertheless, the scene was set for a monstrous struggle over religion which was to dominate Irish life for generations to come.

The Stuart Accession

Following the ascent to the English throne in 1603 of the son of Mary, Queen of Scots, James Stuart (James VI of Scotland, James I of England and Ireland), Catholic hopes were raised: among the native Irish the element of shared ancestry in the Stuart genealogy may have caused the more romantic to ponder notions of a restored Irish-Scottish ascendancy; among the Old English it was his late mother's devotion to Catholicism that brought hope, leading townsmen to seize the churches and restore Roman Catholic services. Mountjoy, however, quickly stamped this out, famously telling the citizens of Waterford that he would cut the charter of liberties granted them by King John with the sword which he wielded in the name of King James. Mountjoy's replacement, Sir Arthur Chichester, took an even stronger stance, ably assisted by the attorney-general, Sir John Davies. Catholic clergy were banished from the kingdom and, believing that if the leaders of society conformed to the Protestant Church the general populace would soon follow, fines were imposed for non-attendance at reformed church services.

No parliament had been held in Ireland between 1586 and 1613, a delay to some extent caused by the need to 'fix' the composition of the House of Commons in order to secure a Protestant majority. Under Chichester and Davies this was done by doubling the number of boroughs entitled to be represented in parliament, and making sure that the town corporations which elected the new members of parliament were Protestant-controlled. Yet the penal legislation against the Recusants that some advocated did not as yet secure its passage through parliament and, on the whole, government policy towards the Roman Catholics was a cautious one: for so long as their loyalty was not in doubt they were tolerated. Instead, government hopes rested on a policy of plantation which would in theory see the Catholic population outnumbered by the settlement in Ireland of large numbers of English and Scottish Protestants.

James I in 1621 from a portrait by David Mytens.

The Problem of Ulster

Having submitted to Mountjoy in 1603, O'Neill was confirmed as Earl of Tyrone and Rory O'Donnell was made Earl of Tyrconnell, converting them overnight into very substantial landholding aristocrats on the English model, but the independence of Gaelic Ulster was gone. The province was divided up into counties, royal courts established, and the traditional authority of O'Neill, O'Donnell and the other lords cut from under them by creating a class of native freeholder who was no longer subject to his hereditary lord, but only to the English king. Perhaps it was the knowledge that this erosion of their status would continue inexorably, or perhaps the fear that an excuse would eventually be found to convict them for their previous rebellion or some rumoured later treason; whatever the reason, in a well-planned move O'Neill and O'Donnell and about 100 followers sailed off from Ireland in August 1607, as we have seen, in what has become known as 'the Flight of the Earls'. They seem to have been bound for Spain but, via the Spanish Netherlands, eventually found refuge at the papal court in Rome, where, however, their hopes for obtaining military aid to secure a restoration (if such was their intention) fell on deaf ears.

While the departure of O'Neill and O'Donnell set English minds at work on a planned re-settlement of the province, the short-lived rebellion soon afterwards by O'Doherty of Inishowen created an environment at court receptive to a very much more radical solution. Six new counties within Ulster – Armagh,

Cavan, Fermanagh, Tyrone, Derry and Donegal – were declared crown property, and a scheme for their plantation drawn up, which would see only small numbers of 'deserving' native landholders retain their status, and even then on condition that they provided proper legal leases for their tenants, and adopted English styles of dwelling and methods of farming. The rest of the land, apart

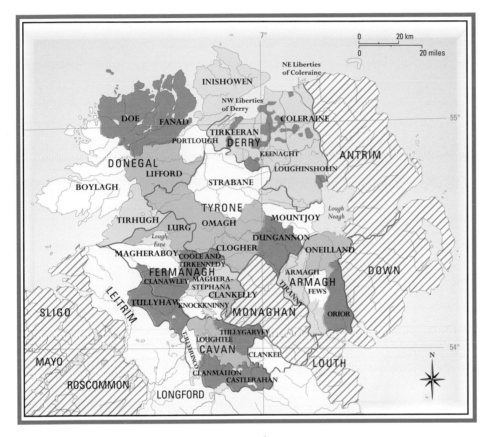

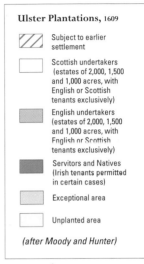

Ulster Plantations, 1609

- ⫽ Subject to earlier settlement
- ☐ Scottish undertakers (estates of 2,000, 1,500 and 1,000 acres, with English or Scottish tenants exclusively)
- ▦ English undertakers (estates of 2,000, 1,500 and 1,000 acres, with English or Scottish tenants exclusively)
- ▨ Servitors and Natives (Irish tenants permitted in certain cases)
- ☐ Exceptional area
- ☐ Unplanted area

(after Moody and Hunter)

from church property, was set aside for colonisation by 'servitors' (men who had served the crown in Ireland) and by 'undertakers' who agreed to bring over new English and Scottish immigrants and establish new village communities, and to provide for their defence in terms of fortifications and arms. But since the implementation of this ambitious scheme was a massive exercise there were inevitable shortfalls. A very substantial influx of Anglo-Scottish colonists did indeed follow but instead of creating strong, water-tight communities, insulated from a native population dispersed elsewhere, many of the new undertakers and servitors, finding it difficult or too much trouble to recruit sufficient numbers of willing 'planters', accepted native tenants on their holdings. This, from the point of view of government policy and future security, had disastrous implications – as time would tell – since it meant that scattered throughout the province there remained a substantial native population, disaffected and resentful and reduced to tenant status, and living in such proximity to the settlers that they would continue to pose a threat.

One of the more unusual aspects of the Ulster Plantation was the role played by the City of London in the affair, when, in 1610, it agreed to undertake the re-settlement of what was then the county of Coleraine, and the rebuilding of the towns of Coleraine and Derry, soon to be renamed Londonderry. They formed themselves into a joint-stock body made up of various London companies and began to plant the county and build towns named after them, hence Draperstown and Salterstown. Another unusual aspect is the exclusion from the scheme of what might nowadays be regarded as the two most radically transformed counties, Antrim and Down. These, however, had already begun to feel the effects of Scottish immigration and this was accelerated in the early seventeenth century under the leadership of James Hamilton, who was granted the title of Viscount Clandeboye in acknowledgement of his success in wresting it from its traditional lords, the Clandeboye O'Neills, and Hugh Montgomery from Ayrshire, who likewise became a Viscount, Montgomery of the Ards, having successfully colonised that peninsula in Co. Down. The towns which these men founded, or re-founded, and the settlers from the Scottish lowlands whom they introduced into this part of Ulster, transformed its appearance and re-shaped its identity, giving the area the strong Ulster-Scots flavour it retains to this day.

The Graces

James I was succeeded by his son Charles in 1625 at a time of open war between England and Spain, and considerable fear abounded that the Catholics of Ireland might welcome an invasion by the latter or rise up in support. The pro-Spanish feeling in the country was first dealt with by repressive means, but the government was in such financial straits that Charles I decided to embark on a policy of conciliation, in an attempt to win the support of the Irish Recusants, particularly the Old English gentry of the Pale, and their agreement to make a financial contribution to the public coffers. The arrangement which he made with them in May 1628 amounted to a list of 51 concessions which, because they were entitled 'matters of grace and bounty' have become known as the Graces. In return for three annual subsidies of £40,000 each, the Recusants had merely to swear an oath of allegiance instead of the Oath of Supremacy, to which Catholics objected on religious grounds, and the refusal to take which had severely hampered their entitlement, for instance, to enter into their inheritances or practice law.

Although there were benefits from the Graces for the, as yet, tiny Protestant community in Ireland – they provided, among other things, more secure land-titles for the 'undertakers' of Ulster – Protestants were, needless to say, unhappy with the advantages they afforded to Roman Catholics. And since more than a quarter of the land of Ireland was now in Protestant hands, they would have to contribute heavily from the profits of this land towards the annual subsidies. In the aftermath of their award, therefore, the Dublin government led by Richard

Boyle (the archetypal self-made man who had arrived in Ireland penniless and ended up as the extremely wealthy Earl of Cork) did its best to discriminate against the practice of Catholicism: no functioning Catholic hierarchy was tolerated, the mass itself was banned, 'mass-houses' and monasteries pulled down or confiscated, and their occupants forced to flee. Finally, when the three annual subsidies agreed under the terms of the Graces had been collected and spent, the fine for non-attendance at reformed Sunday services, abolished under the Graces, was reintroduced.

Wentworth in Ireland, 1633–40

With the lapse of the annual subsidies coming from Ireland, Charles I found himself faced with a problem familiar to every English monarch since Edward II: how to make Ireland again a source of profit to the crown, and how to do so without posing a threat to security. His method was to send to the country a man, Thomas Wentworth (later created Earl of Strafford), with a proven record as a tough and efficient administrator in the north of England, who spelled out his policy for Ireland thus: 'The truth is, we must there bow and govern the native by the planter, and the planter by the native'. Playing one side off against the other in this way did pay dividends, in that Wentworth was able to manipulate parliament into voting more money for his administration, but it meant that neither Catholics nor Protestants trusted him and ran the risk of them burying their differences in order to secure revenge, as later transpired. The only people, in fact, upon whom Wentworth could rely were English officials who came to Ireland with him, causing precisely the same sort of resentment in Dublin to outside intruders that had been manifest since the reign of Edward III precisely three centuries earlier.

While in Ireland, Wentworth did nothing to ease the sense of alienation felt by the native Irish. Furthermore, he revised plans for a plantation of Connacht which would have serious consequences for the Old English of the province. He also victimised important members of the 'New English' establishment like the earl of Cork, and he treated harshly the Ulster undertakers, including the London companies, increasing their rents and making their terms of tenure more onerous. In the field of religion, he sought to bring the Church of Ireland into line with the Church of England by purging its puritan spirit, opposing the anti-episcopal views of Scottish ministers in Ulster in particular, and fostering a more orthodox Anglicanism (while turning a blind eye, some felt, to the activities of Roman Catholic clergy). And, to top it all, he imposed high export duties and expensive export licenses. Not surprisingly, no matter how much money he thereby raised for government purposes, and no matter how much more efficiently he made the administration run, his régime quickly began to be perceived as tyrannical by every powerful interest group in the country, all of whom he managed to alienate.

Meanwhile, the growing conflict in Britain between the king and his subjects was beginning to have an impact on Ireland. Wentworth was called home to take charge of affairs when the Scots Presbyterians united against Charles I's imposition of orthodox Anglicanism and his increasingly authoritarian rule. It was only a matter of time before the Ulster Scots, who shared their grievances, made common cause with their compatriots. However, it was thought safe for Wentworth to leave Ireland, and indeed for the king to draw troops from the country to intensify his war against the Scots, because Ireland seemed out-wardly calm. But a common hostility to Wentworth, now Earl of Strafford, united Catholics and Protestants in the Irish parliament, who during 1640 and 1641 drew up lists of complaints against the administrative practices he had instituted and pressed to have the Graces confirmed. That alliance lasted as long as Strafford held a position of authority, but when their mutual hate-fig-ure was executed at the insistence of the English Parliamentarians in May 1641, their deep-set divisions would inevitably resurface — it was only a matter of when and how.

The 1641 Rebellion

The Catholic component within the Irish parliament was almost entirely Old English, and the native Irish gained little from their activities. The latter saw the danger inherent in the upper hand which the Parliamentary faction was obtain-ing in England, since its puritan ethos was likely to be a lot less tolerant of Catholicism than King Charles and even Strafford had been. Besides, the threat of civil war in England presented the best opportunity in a generation for an attempt to overthrow English rule and it was an opportunity which the Irish, led to begin with by Rory O'More of Laois, realised they should grasp. They were encouraged to do so by Eoghan Ruadh O'Neill, a nephew of the great Hugh and an officer of thirty years standing in the Spanish service, who assured the rebels' emissaries of foreign military aid. Their insurrection got off to a bad start when the plan to seize Dublin Castle on 23 October 1641 was foiled, but the ground-swell of support for it, especially in the north, meant that a widespread revolt erupted nonetheless in Ulster under the leadership of Sir Phelim O'Neill. The rebels first seized Dungannon at the heart of the province and Mountjoy Fort, on the shores of Lough Neagh, and then Charlemont Castle somewhat further to the south, before spreading to Co. Down, and taking Newry.

In these early days of the rising many English settlers were slaughtered and thousands more driven from their homes, and such was the fear among the Protestant population throughout Ireland, and indeed Britain, that credence was given to even the most far-fetched rumours of atrocities, the belief being that it was the rebels' intention to massacre the entire Protestant population. Such atrocities as did take place, and they were many, were not so much the deliber-ate policy of the rebel leaders as manifestations of undisciplined hatred and thirst for revenge on the part of the native Catholic insurgents. In fact, the aims of the rebel leaders were quite conservative, to the extent that they did not view themselves as rebels at all. They protested their loyalty to the crown and claimed to wish to safeguard royal prerogatives in the face of the growing puritan faction. They stated their goal as no more than the defence of their religious liberties, although there can be little doubt that the recovery of lost lands was part of their agenda. The latter is surely the only explanation for the return to Ireland in July 1642 of Eoghan Ruadh O'Neill to take command of the rebel forces: he was viewed by the Irish of Ulster as their natural leader, and many must have seen in his arrival the prospect of overturning the conquest.

By now, the temporary alliance of Old English and New English in the Dublin parliament had been sundered, because the latter could view the rebels with a degree of clarity denied the former: they were papists and they were Irish and that made them the natural enemy of both English and Protestant interests in Ireland. By the end of 1641 the Ulster rebels had overrun much of Co. Louth, and the Old English of the Pale, with whom they shared little other than their Catholicism, joined forces with them, however reluctantly. Thereafter the rebellion became a national movement as others of the Catholic gentry throughout Leinster, Munster and Connacht joined the cause, and by the early months of 1642 only a few pockets of loyalism remained, principally defended towns and forts, many of them under siege. But the rebel forces were poorly armed and poorly led, their commanders seemingly lacking any concerted plan. It was only when Church leaders took the initiative that the insurgents managed to bring some order to their activities: in May 1642 they set up a provisional government, which organised elections for an assembly that finally met at Kilkenny in October.

The Confederation of Kilkenny

Calling themselves 'the Confederate Catholics of Ireland', those gathered at Kilkenny set out their aims as the restoration of the rights of the Catholic Church, the maintenance of the king's prerogatives, and the defence of Ireland's liberties. In theory, it was an assembly of all Ireland, and was the only such sustained experiment in Irish self-government at a national level before 1919. But Protestants were, of course, excluded, and there were divisions apparent from the start, the most serious of which was the age-old distrust between the native Irish and the Old English. The latter, needless to say, had a great deal more to lose should this gamble in self-government fail, since the Irish had already lost by confiscation most of their estates for earlier such acts of rebellion. Having said that, there were those among the Confederate allies who did try to steer a middle course between the two ethnic groups, and these moderates were quite successful in marginalising the extremes: they were not revolutionaries and they were not even separatists, in that they promoted above all loyalty to the Stuart

*Giovanni Battista
Rinuccini (d. 1665),
Archbishop of Fermo and
Papal Nuncio to Ireland,
was given the impossible
task of securing from
Charles I the public
restoration of Catholicism.
He proved a divisive force
among the confederated
Catholic leadership, the
Gaelic Irish largely
supporting his militant
Counter-Reformation
stance, but the Old
English, whom he regarded
as Catholics in name only,
resented his unwillingness
to reach a realistic
compromise with the king.*

monarchy, but they were certainly reforming nationalists, whose philosophy was not unlike that later pursued by Grattan or Parnell, since they advocated the construction of an Irish kingdom which would be tolerant of diversity, whether ethnic or religious.

Since the English civil war had broken out in August 1642, Charles I sought to make peace with the Confederates in order to free up the forces of the Dublin government for service against his Parliamentary opponents in England, and a year's cessation was concluded in September 1643. The cessation was never complete, since it was ignored by the Ulster Scots and also in Munster by, of all people, Murrough O'Brien of Inchiquin, a staunch Protestant, and thus a desultory half-peace continued in being for the next two years, disunity and personal jealousies affecting the conduct of affairs on both sides. What ended the stalemate was the arrival in October 1645 of the papal nuncio, Archbishop Giovanni Battista Rinuccini, who had strong clerical and popular support in opposing a compromise treaty with the king and the Dublin government, and a powerful ally in Eoghan Ruadh. When the latter scored a surprise victory at Benburb, on 5 June 1646, over the Ulster Scots led by General Robert Munro, it seemed that the Confederates were in sight of victory, but instead of consolidating his success in Ulster O'Neill marched south, joined Rinuccini, and together they entered Kilkenny and seized command of the Confederate supreme council. Their plan was to march on Dublin but the usual quarrels among their generals lost them the initiative, and the capital's commander, the royalist Earl of Ormond, faced with a choice between losing the city to an Irish Catholic army or the Protestant forces of the English Parliamentary faction, reluctantly chose the latter option.

Their arrival in Dublin transformed the balance of power. Disunity among the Confederate forces had now brought them close to civil war. Rinuccini had lost the support of the Confederates and eventually left Ireland in February 1649, while Eoghan Ruadh and his army, back in Ulster, showed few signs of a decisive breakthrough. Meanwhile, the Parliamentary victory that resulted in the execution of King Charles in January caused a total realignment of forces. Royalists, both Catholic and Protestant, joined together against his executioners. The Confederacy was dissolved and the Earl of Ormond took command of the royalist army of Ireland. Drogheda and Dundalk were quickly recovered but when Ormond advanced on Dublin he made it only as far as Rathmines, where his forces were shattered on 2 August by the Parliamentary general, Michael Jones. Two weeks later, Oliver Cromwell and 3,000 Ironsides landed in Ireland.

Cromwellian Ireland

Cromwell came to Ireland with more than enough resources of manpower and military skill to enforce a settlement, and, in his own words, to accomplish his 'great work against the barbarous and bloodthirsty Irish'. He began with his infamous siege and sacking of Drogheda on 11 September 1649. Much of the, ironically English, royalist garrison and Catholic clergy were put to death as were some of the townspeople, though not all, as later tradition had it. Eoghan Ruadh O'Neill, already a sick man, died shortly afterwards, and the Parliamentary forces were soon in command of the north. Cromwell himself headed south and stormed Wexford, where his troops ran amok and by his own

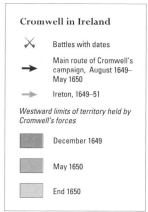

Cromwell in Ireland

✗ Battles with dates

➜ Main route of Cromwell's campaign, August 1649– May 1650

→ Ireton, 1649–51

Westward limits of territory held by Cromwell's forces

December 1649

May 1650

End 1650

This woodcut features a pillaging soldier and was printed on the cover of a tract published in 1642, entitled The English-Irish Soldier. *It was intended to depict the manner in which those who sought military careers in Ireland needed to sustain themselves on the countryside.*

estimate killed 2,000, and he later took New Ross, and forced the surrender of Cork, Youghal and Kinsale. Waterford held out against his forces until the following August, but he managed to take Kilkenny, and by the time he left Ireland in May 1650, even the staunch defenders of Clonmel had been brought to heel.

Cromwell left his son-in-law, Henry Ireton, to mop up any outstanding resistance, having achieved what he had set out to do, that is, as he himself put it, 'by the assistance of God, to hold forth and maintain the lustre and glory of English liberty in a nation where we have an undoubted right to do it'. Although Limerick withstood a lengthy siege until October 1651, and Galway only surrendered in the following May, opposition elsewhere gradually crumbled. Irish officers in the field surrendered on terms which allowed them and their recruits to take service abroad, while those reduced to beggary were soon being transported in their thousands to the West Indies. The last outposts of defiance in Ulster and Connacht finally succumbed in the summer of 1652, to bring Cromwell's blood-soaked conquest to an end.

The next stage of Cromwell's settlement involved the appointment of parliamentary commissioners, who were sent to Ireland to suppress Catholicism, to make provision for a puritan ministry and for the education of reliable and 'godly ministers of the gospel'. They were suspicious of the Ulster Scots who had organised themselves on the Scottish Presbyterian model and had links with the Scottish General Assembly. But 'popery' was considered a far greater evil which they were intent upon eradicating. Roman Catholic clergy had a price put on their heads, were hunted down, and killed, imprisoned or banished overseas. Yet, these measures seemed only to increase their numbers, and while narrowing the divisions between native Irish and Old English, they served only to widen the gulf of hatred between Protestants and Catholics, convincing the latter that they would never be safe under a Protestant government. The commissioners also knew the danger of having large numbers of disbanded Irish troops in the country and so actively encouraged them to seek employment in friendly countries overseas. Many thousands left, though those who remained often turned as before to brigandage, becoming known as 'tories' and later 'rapparees', some of whom like Redmond O'Hanlon were Robin Hood-type characters in the popular imagination, at least among the native population who saw them as playing something of a patriotic role since they preyed largely upon the settlers.

'To Hell or to Connacht!'

The other major plank of the commissioners' policy was further large-scale plantation, a scheme which was very opportune in view of the large numbers of rebel proprietors whose lands were now deemed forfeit. An Act of Settlement was passed in 1652 which detailed those who would lose their lands, or part of their lands, depending on the seriousness of their alleged crimes. However, even those who were deemed entitled to hold onto part of their estate would be transported west of the Shannon, including Clare (hence the origin of the phrase, ascribed to Cromwell, 'To hell or to Connacht!') and would be allocated their entitlement of land out of confiscated estates in that province. Their former lands would be granted by Cromwell's government to whomsoever it pleased. Needless to say, this radical plan was extraordinarily difficult to put into effect, and was never fully completed. But many thousands of people were forced to abandon their homes and farms and to transport themselves, their families, their stock and their possessions, and move west over the Shannon. The transportation scheme, of course, only involved forfeited proprietors; it did not include landless labourers, since they would be required to serve the needs of the new settlers, though many small tenants did choose to follow in the footsteps of their old landlords.

To speed up the process of land confiscation and re-allocation, a survey of forfeited lands was begun by the remarkable William Petty (his suggestion that the lands be noted down on maps gave it the name 'the Down Survey') and it was completed in little more than a year. The net effect, despite the incomplete nature of the confiscation, transportation and plantation scheme, was a sweeping change in the ownership of land in the country, the importance of which can hardly be overestimated. It greatly increased not just the number of Protestants in Ireland, but, more importantly, the amount of land in their possession, and also their power: they now enjoyed an almost complete ascendancy throughout the countryside and, because Catholic Confederates in the cities and towns also had their property confiscated, Protestant control over urban life, both politically and in terms of trade, was not far short of absolute.

The Stuart Restoration

Oliver Cromwell died on 3 September 1658, to be succeeded as Protector by his son Richard, while his younger son Henry was Lord Deputy of Ireland. However, in less than two years the English parliament had come to terms with its

Cromwellian land confiscations, 1652–57

- Government reservations
- Land given to veterans of the Parliamentary Army and adventurers (including one mile coastal strip in Connacht)
- Additional land provided for the army
- Land reserved for transplanted Irish

king, Charles II, and he was restored. The change from Commonwealth to monarchy was seized by all those who had lost estates in Ireland as an opportunity to recover them, and in 1662 another Act of Settlement was passed, the purpose of which was to sort out the sorry mess that existed between the many conflicting claims to the same parcels of land. Indeed, the recently elevated 'duke' of Ormond wrote, at about this time, that 'There must be new discoveries made of a new Ireland, for the old will not serve to satisfy these engagements'. There was no easy solution to the problem and Charles opted for a middle course which modified some of the harsher elements of the Cromwellian settlement, but certainly did little to redress the imbalance between Catholic and Protestant land-ownership, despite his own sympathies for the Catholic position. Although it is difficult to be precise, about three-fifths of the land of Ireland was in Catholic hands at the outbreak of the 1641 rebellion, and under Charles II's land settlement they held not much more than one-fifth. They had also, in the interval, been excluded from all positions of political and commercial influence. Little wonder that they dreamed of a return to happier times, and that their Protestant masters could never lose their sense of insecurity and suspicion.

It was an age filled with fears of 'fanatical' religious conspiracies, and the rumours of a 'popish plot' that surfaced in England in 1678 were widely believed and found a ready audience in Ireland. The viceroy, Ormond, though not convinced by some of the more outlandish rumours, took precautions by putting the army on a state of alert and reviving the militia, and he yielded to pressure from England by banishing Catholic bishops and clergy from the kingdom, and ordered lay Catholics to surrender their arms. When accusations were made against the archbishop of Armagh, Oliver Plunkett, who was arrested for treason in November 1679 on the patently false evidence of discredited witnesses, Ormond knew enough about the character of the man to be certain of his innocence, but could not prevent him being brought for trial to London. Charles II too, no doubt, knew of Archbishop Plunkett's innocence but failed to intervene, with the result that he was convicted of high treason and suffered a traitor's fate in July 1681, the last notable victim of the 'popish plot'.

James II and Ireland

Four years later Charles II was dead and was succeeded by his brother James, who immediately set about what was called the 'Catholic design'. He granted Richard Talbot, one of the leaders of the Irish Catholics, the title Earl of Tyrconnell and gave him charge of Irish affairs, causing one contemporary to remark that this was done 'to the astonishment of all sober men, and to the evident ruin of the Protestants of that kingdom'. Tyrconnell began with the army, which he rapidly built up and filled almost entirely with Catholic officers, and then turned to the administration which he similarly restructured. Catholics became a majority on the judiciary and were appointed to the corporations of

Opposite: Richard Talbot (1630–91) was a member of a Meath branch of the Old English gentry family of that name, who fought with the Catholic and Royalist forces during the period of the Confederacy, served the future James II in the French and Spanish armies, and became the leading Irish Catholic spokesman at court following the Restoration of the monarchy. It was no surprise that when James succeeded to the throne he should sponsor Talbot, making him the 1st Earl of Tyrconnell, and agreeing to his radical plans for Catholicising the army and administration and revising the Restoration land settlement.

cities and towns, and it was clearly Tyrconnell's plan, having dealt with the matter of religious representation, to turn to the even more sensitive issue of land. This was one of the main subjects dealt with at the so-called 'Patriot Parliament' held in Dublin in 1689, which was almost exclusively Catholic in composition, and sought to turn the clock back in terms of land-ownership to the situation that pertained prior to the Cromwellian and Restoration settlements. But meanwhile Protestants had understandably panicked, and throngs fled to England, while many dismissed army officers made for the court in Holland of King James's son-in-law, Prince William of Orange. However, it was when James himself brought Irish troops to assist him in England that the tide turned against him there, because in the public mind this was blatant evidence of an attempt to destroy the Protestant constitution by means of papist force.

William of Orange landed in England in November 1688 and he and his wife Mary, King James's daughter, were received as king and queen. Early in December, the Protestants of Derry shut the city gates to block access by a new garrison, and Enniskillen followed suit, both soon becoming crowded with refugees. Protestant troops were raised by newly-formed county associations throughout the province, and messages of allegiance sent to William and Mary.

On 12 March 1689 James II landed in Ireland and later advanced on Derry. Its commander, Robert Lundy, whose name forever afterwards has been synonymous with treachery in the Ulster Protestant imagination, thought to surrender but the 30,000 occupants of the city refused and the most famous siege in Irish and British history began. It

Tyrconel arming ye Papists in Ireland.

lasted fifteen weeks, and many thousands within Derry's walls starved, until a relief ship broke through the besiegers' boom across the Foyle, bringing ample supplies of food to the famished refugees. The next day the Jacobite army retreated south and King James's cause was beginning to wilt. Within a fortnight 10,000 Williamite troops had landed near Belfast under the command of Marshal Schomberg and gradually took over each remaining Jacobite stronghold in Ulster. James, lacking the resources to maintain resistance, issued his notorious 'brass money' to help pay his way, but was also beginning to lack the spirit to fight on, even when joined by 7,000 French reinforcements in March 1690 (half of whom, ironically, were Protestant Walloons and Germans).

The Boyne and Beyond
On 16 June 1690 James advanced from Dublin as far as Dundalk, but retreated

back over the Boyne when news arrived that King William had landed at Carrickfergus two days earlier: having an inferior army, the river would provide a useful defensive barrier. William's forces arrived at its northern bank on 30 June and next day, Tuesday 1 July (July 12th in the old calendar, on which day it is still commemorated) the most famous – if not necessarily decisive – battle in Irish history began. There were Ulster Protestants in William's army, but the great bulk of his forces came from much further afield; along with the English,

Williamite artillery in action at the Battle of the Boyne.

Scots and, of course, Dutch, there were as many as 7,000 Danes, and contingents of Swiss, Brandenburgers and French Huguenots. They forced a passage across the Boyne and James's infantry broke and fled, while his cavalry's brave charges only delayed a Williamite victory that was now inevitable. James fled south and sailed off with the French into exile on 4 July.

The Battle of the Boyne was important in a number of respects. It was a con-

CONFISCATION, PLANTATION AND ASCENDANCY

test between two kings to determine which of them would rule England, and it decided the issue in favour of William. In a European context, it was a victory for Protestantism and yet was hailed, ironically, by the Catholics of Spain and Austria, since it weakened the position of the French under Louis XIV. But above all else it represented the climax of a century of bloody conflict in Ireland over land and religion. That war was not yet over but the end was in sight. Irish casualties at the Boyne had not exceeded 1,000 and their forces still held Athlone and – thanks to the exploits of Patrick Sarsfield, the most popular of their generals – Limerick. Thus, when William left Ireland on 5 September the Jacobite forces were still relatively intact. In May 1691 Irish hopes were raised by the arrival of French reinforcements at Limerick under the Marquis de St Ruth, but William's army, led by the Dutch General Ginkel, soon took Athlone and crossed the Shannon. It was his victory over St Ruth on 12 July, at Aughrim in Co. Galway, that sealed the Jacobite fate. Nearly 7,000 Irish were killed, making it as momentous a day in the Catholic folk memory as Boyne was for Protestants, if for entirely contrary reasons. A month later the siege of Limerick began, on 3 October the Treaty of Limerick was signed, and, on 22 December, 12,000 Jacobite troops led by Patrick Sarsfield set sail for France. What became known as the 'Flight of the Wild Geese' had begun and the Williamite war was over. Power henceforth would rest with the Protestant minority and the hopes of the Catholic nobles and gentry of recovering their lands and status were finally extinguished. The Protestant Ascendancy was secured.

The Penal Laws

The first article of the Treaty of Limerick had guaranteed Roman Catholics such rights to practise their religion as they had enjoyed under Charles II, but this was completely ignored. About a million acres of land were confiscated from 'rebels', leaving only about one-seventh of the country in Catholic hands. Almost immediately a series of penal laws against them began to be introduced and this reduced their land-holdings further throughout the course of the eighteenth century. Members of parliament, which rapidly became a greatly more powerful institution than previously, were required to take an anti-papal oath which thereby debarred Catholics from taking their seats. They were not allowed to bear arms, to own a horse worth more than £5, or to send their children abroad for education, and Catholic clergy were yet again expelled from the country. In order to prevent any increase in land held by Catholics, the Irish parliament in 1704 prohibited their acquisition of land from Protestants, either by marriage or inheritance, and limited leases to a maximum of 31 years. It also forbade them from making wills and decreed that land should be divided equally between the sons of the deceased, unless the eldest conformed to the Church of Ireland, whereby he inherited all. Later, Catholics were forbidden from maintaining schools, and finally, in 1728, they were denied the vote.

Of course, the strict letter of the 'popery laws' was by no means always enforced, and, in any case, under their terms Catholics could still practice their religion, but they must do so from a position of utter inferiority, political, social, and economic. It is important too to note that in addition to Catholics, Protestant dissenters were also kept in an inferior position. The 1704 Act had a clause enforcing a sacramental test repugnant to dissenters, the refusal to take which debarred them, like Catholics, from public office and from military employment. What worried the establishment in part was the close-knit organisation of Ulster Presbyterians, who had dominated the municipal corporation in Derry and in the rapidly-expanding Belfast until the 1704 sacramental test drove them out. Yet worries about the dissidents proved groundless when, during the Scottish Jacobite risings of 1715 and 1745, the Ulster dissenters forgot their grievances and stood four-square behind the Protestant cause, ready to defend Ireland should there be a sympathetic Catholic uprising or a Jacobite invasion.

The Emergence of Protestant Nationalism

As the Protestant ascendancy in Ireland took firmer root, so too did a growing sense of security. And as the Catholic threat appeared to recede, Protestant Ireland could afford to question its degree of dependence on the British government. At the core of this debate was the fundamental constitutional issue of whether or not the British parliament had the right to legislate for Ireland, an issue that went as far back as the passage of Poynings' Law in 1494–95, and beyond. The Irish parliament itself was, of course, a very flawed institution. It was exclusively composed of members of the established Church, the House of Lords being dominated by conservative and docile bishops, the Commons by representatives from the boroughs who were the pawns of wealthy patrons and from the counties who were landlords' men, more concerned with winning posts or pensions for themselves and their cronies than tackling constitutional issues. Yet, such issues did soon come to the fore. One concerned the question of whether a person who had lost a case in the Irish House of Lords could appeal to the Lords in Westminster. The latter sought to ensure that this was the case by the passage in 1720 of what was known as the 'Sixth of George I', an 'Act for the better securing the dependency of the Kingdom of Ireland on the Crown of Great Britain', which aroused considerable indignation in Ireland.

Soon afterwards, when an Englishman named William Wood was given the license to mint halfpence for Ireland, without any prior consultation with the Irish parliament, it caused an uproar. Ostensibly, this was a row over currency, but the 'Wood's halfpence' affair revealed deeper tensions: Irish objections to the right of the British government to grant such a patent without the approval of the Irish parliament. Two years earlier Jonathan Swift had published his '*Proposal for the universal use of Irish manufacture ... utterly rejecting and renouncing everything wearable that comes from England*', which was primarily concerned with the way in which the British parliament had done its best to stifle the Irish woollen trade, but the core point of which was that England was the cause of Ireland's poverty. The 'Wood's halfpence' affair now caused Swift to publish his series of Drapier's Letters which again had an ostensibly narrow focus but whose real theme was the constitutional relationship between Britain and Ireland, and in which he told 'the whole people of Ireland' that 'by the laws of God, of nature, of nations, and of your own country, you are and ought to be as free a people as your brethren in England'. Here, Swift was articulating something which was only just in its infancy: the identification of the Protestants of Ireland with what, for most of them, was their new home. Ireland, they recognised and now insisted, was a distinct nation. Protestant Irish nationalism had been born.

Powerscourt House, Co. Wicklow, symbolises for many the grandeur of the Protestant Ascendancy in Ireland and is probably the most famous of all Irish country houses. Designed by Richard Castle, building began in 1731 though the interior was left unfinished for many years. Its owner was a member of the Irish parliament named Richard Wingfield, who subsequently became the 1st Viscount Powerscourt.

The Rise of the 'Patriots'

Those who represented this new nationalist spirit among the Protestants in the Irish parliament had as their predominant concern the securing of Ireland's constitutional rights and the denunciation of English encroachment, and were, since as far back as the 1720s, known as the 'patriots'. One of the developments they most vigorously opposed was, not unlike their medieval antecedents, the appointment of English-born officials to important Irish offices. The latter was British government policy: Archbishop William King of Dublin was one of the leaders of the opposition to the English interest in Ireland, described in 1714 by the then Lord Lieutenant as 'to a ridiculous extravagance, national', and not long before his death, when he was visibly ill, one of the architects of British policy in Ireland declared that 'his majesty's service absolutely requires that, whenever he drops, the place be filled with an Englishman'. This kind of interference was matched by a jealousy in the British parliament at what appeared to be any sign of progress in the Irish economy, which manifested itself in the regular imposition of restrictions on Irish trade. This, needless to say, was another target of the 'patriots', and their criticism of British policy in this regard was augmented by the gradual emergence of a commercial middle class. Men made wealthy by their involvement in the export, for example, of linen or provisions, and well-informed by the proliferation of pamphlets and newspapers as the eighteenth century wore on, were eager to find a role in the political life of the country. Since the new middle class resented the restrictions placed on Irish merchants and manufacturers by the Westminster parliament, they backed the 'patriots' because both groups in essence had a common interest: the weakening of Ireland's dependence on England.

Among the new middle class were many Roman Catholics, since the legal obstacles put in the way of their land-owning meant that trade was one of the few avenues of enterprise open to them. And by the mid-eighteenth century, as Protestants began to fear them less, many of the penal laws, while not repealed, were not rigorously enforced. Catholics had, as a result, greater access to education, and the Catholic clergy were more free to perform their ministry. There was no question as yet of them being granted full rights of citizenship, but the growing sense of identification with Ireland among sections of the Protestant community did have important implications: if the welfare of Ireland was a matter of concern to both Catholics and Protestants, the latter could not but come to regard the Catholics as their fellow-countrymen, and if both were concerned to promote Irish rights, then the religious differences between them must inevitably matter less. The English-born Lord Chancellor of Ireland expressed it well in 1761 when he wrote: 'formerly Protestant or Papist were the key words; they are now court or country, referring still to constitutional grievances'.

The splendour of Georgian Dublin was best displayed in its newly laid-out squares and thoroughfares, the classic symbol of which were the majestic doorways with their elegant fanlights.

One other development had important implications for the Irish parliament in this period. It had been British government policy, in the words of one contemporary, 'to bring back the administration to the Castle', in other words, to have decision-making in the hands of Dublin Castle officials, appointed from London, rather than the members of the Irish parliament. One way of keeping parliament quiescent was to avoid general elections, and so throughout the eighteenth century general elections took place only on the death of the monarch, until, that is, 1768, when the lifetime of parliament was limited to eight years. This had the effect of increasing the power of public opinion, since members of parliament had to face their electorate far more frequently than before: the days were numbered, therefore, when government could turn a deaf ear to public demands or ignore trends in society outside its walls or even, for that matter, withstand for long the ripple-effect of events happening far from Ireland's shores.

The growing quarrel between Britain and her American colonies was a case in point, especially when that quarrel turned into open war in April 1775. Few could fail to see the parallels between the position of the colonies and of Ireland. Irish public opinion was, therefore, opposed to Britain's American policy and the war was unpopular in Ireland. Thus, when the American Congress asserted the freedom of the Thirteen Colonies from Great Britain, on 4 July 1776, their Declaration of Independence had an explosive impact on Ireland.

Nicholas Ward was an English government official who settled in an estate on the shores of Strangford Lough, Co. Down, in 1610 and whose family fortunes mirror the Ascendancy period. As their estates in the Lecale district grew, partly through the benefits that accrued from loyalty in time of crisis, partly by judicious marriages, Bernard Ward, afterwards 1st Viscount Bangor, was ready by the mid-18th century to build Castleward, a grand house for an all-powerful local landlord on a sumptuous site overlooking Strangford Lough. Begun in 1760, it took 13 years to complete, at a cost of £40,000.

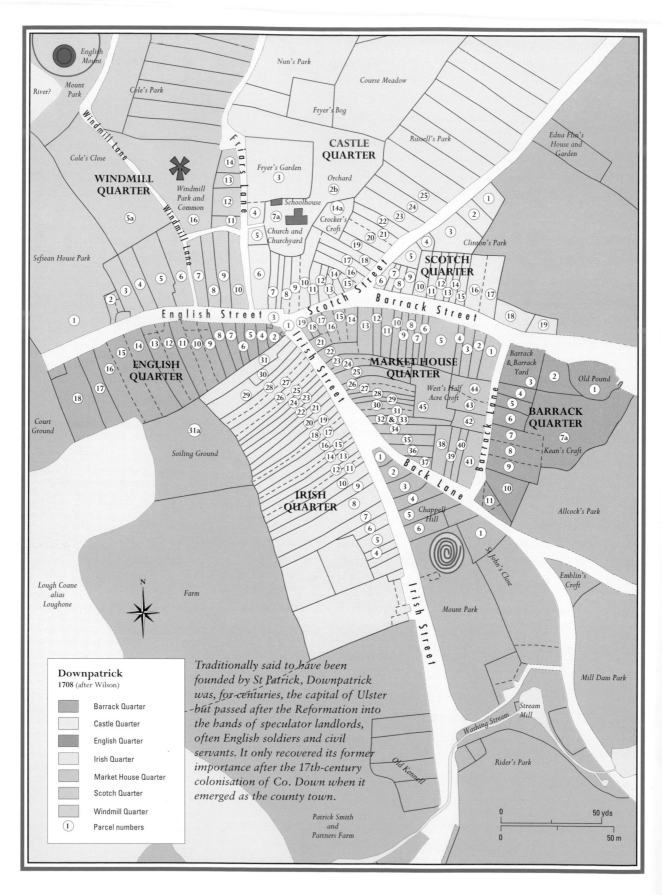

English Mount

Mount Park

River?

Cole's Park

Nun's Park

Course Meadow

Fryer's Bog

Russell's Park

Edna Flin's House and Garden

Cole's Close

Friars Lane

CASTLE QUARTER

WINDMILL QUARTER

Windmill Lane

Windmill Park and Common

Fryer's Garden

3

Orchard

2b

25

24

1

2

Schoolhouse

14a

Crocker's Croft

23

22

3

Clinton's Park

14

13

12

11

16

5a

4

7a

Church and Churchyard

5

20

21

19

18

17

SCOTCH QUARTER

4

Sefsean House Park

5

16

17

7

6

8

5

10

11

12

14

16

17

18

6

4

5

6

7

9

8

10

6

9

11

10

13

12

15

14

13

15

19

3

2

1

ENGLISH STREET

3

1

19

18

17

16

14

13

12

10

8

7

5

9

4

3

2

1

Scotch Street

18

19

15

14

13

12

11

10

9

8

7

6

5

4

3

2

1

Barrack Street

18

15

16

16

17

14

11

12

10

9

ENGLISH QUARTER

15

16

17

18

21

22

31

30

28

29

27

26

25

24

23

23

24

25

26

27

28

29

30

31

32 & 33

34

MARKET HOUSE QUARTER

West's Half Acre Croft

44

45

43

42

Barrack & Barrack Yard

3

2

4

5

6

7a

Old Pound

1

BARRACK QUARTER

Kean's Craft

Court Ground

31a

Soiling Ground

20

19

18

17

16

15

14

13

12

11

10

9

8

7

6

5

4

35

36

37

38

39

40

41

1

4

5

6

7

8

9

10

11

Allcock's Park

IRISH QUARTER

Back Lane

Barrack Lane

Chappell Hill

1

Emblin's Croft

St John's Close

Mill Dam Park

Lough Coane alias Loughone

N

Farm

Irish Street

Mount Park

Stream Mill

Washing Stream

Old Kennell

Rider's Park

Patrick Smith and Partners Farm

Traditionally said to have been founded by St Patrick, Downpatrick was, for centuries, the capital of Ulster but passed after the Reformation into the hands of speculator landlords, often English soldiers and civil servants. It only recovered its former importance after the 17th-century colonisation of Co. Down when it emerged as the county town.

Downpatrick

1708 (after Wilson)

- Barrack Quarter
- Castle Quarter
- English Quarter
- Irish Quarter
- Market House Quarter
- Scotch Quarter
- Windmill Quarter
- ① Parcel numbers

0   50 yds

0   50 m

DOWNPATRICK SETTLEMENT PLAN 1708

No.	Denominations	Principal tenant	Tenants in possession

SCOTCH QUARTER

Scotch Street (south and east side)

No.	Denominations	Principal tenant	Tenants in possession
1	Peery's tenement	James M'Knight	John Perry
2	McGawsy's tenement	James M'Knight	John McGawsy
3	Barn and haggard	James M'Knight	Do.
4	John Lane's tenement	Samuel Heron	Untenanted
5	Kiln tenement	John Brison	Do.

Barrack Street (north side)

No.	Denominations	Principal tenant	Tenants in possession
6 } 7	Aston's tenement	Hector McNeile / Sibilla Aston	John McKilnoe / Rev. Mr James Kelly
8	McDoell's tenement	John M'Doell	Do.
9	Duffy's tenement	John Duffy	Do.
10	Savage's tenement	William Savage	Pat Lanan and James Smith
11 } 12	Neagle's tenement	Patrick Savage / Hannah Hall, widow	Do. / Do.
13 } 14 } 15	Widow Pressick's tenement	Richard Strany / Hercules Welsh / Edmund O'Hanlan	Do. / Do. / Do.
16	Neil Smith's tenement	George Savage	Untenanted
17	William Bane's tenement	Charles Carr	Do.
18	Oliver's tenement	James Neelsons	Do.
19	Thomas Smith's tenement	Elizabeth Clendillon	Do.

MARKET HOUSE QUARTER

Barrack Street (south side)

No.	Denominations	Principal tenant	Tenants in possession
1	Cricket's tenement	Robert Cricket	Robert Cricket, William Brison and Savage
2	Wat Welshe's tenement	Nurse Smith	Richard Fitzsimon
3 } 4	Clinton's tenement	Rev. James Kelly and John Ekin / Sold to Charles Pelson	Charles O'Hara / Charles Pelson
5	Teer's tenement, barn, malthouse and kiln	Rowland Brown	Rowland Brown and John Sloan
6 } 7	Jasper Jelly's tenement	Patrick McCreery / Pat Savage	His wife / Dennys Borne, clothier
8 } 9 } 10	Arbison's tenement	Alexander Gillaspy / John Teer, baker / Abraham Crocket	Do. / Do. / Do.
11	Murrow's tenement	Daniel McAlister	John Sprat and Widow Murrow, unbuilt
12	Gilbert Brew's ¹/₂ tenement	Daniel McAlister	John Sprat and Widow Murrow, unbuilt
13	Shaw's tenement	Francis Shaw, goaler	Do. and John Mullen

Scotch Street (south side)

No.	Denominations	Principal tenant	Tenants in possession
14	Macavea's tenement	James McKnight	Jno. McCrery and Sara Hanne
15	Carson's tenement	James Carson	William Shannon and John Ellis
16	Audley's ¹/₂ tenement	William Irwyn from Peter Ore	Untenanted
17	Brison's tenement	Jane Brison	Do.
18	Wregg's ¹/₂ tenement	Richard Cadle	Robert Fyscild

No.	Denominations	Principal tenant	Tenants in possession
Irish Street (east side)			
19	Market House	The Lord of the Manor	Built by Lord Ardglass; the town and manor
20	Cadley's shop	Richard Cadley	Richard Cadley
21	Allcock's tenement	Samuel Heron	John Alcock
22	Old Correction House tenement	Seneca Hadzor	Untenanted
23 } 24 }	Glencrosse's tenement	William Carson, James Carson, Samuel Heron and Elizabeth Thompson	Widow Carson Daniel McAlister
25	Paterson's tenement	James Hamilton	Do.
26 } 27 }	McKnishe's tenement	James Smith, gauger John McKnish	Thomas Kibbon George Stewart
28 } 29 }	McKilboy's tenement	Nurse Smith Thomas Blackwood	Do. Do.
30 } 31 }	Widow Black's tenement	Christopher Conner John Glencross	Do. Peter Dun
32 } 33 }	Yarrow and Curry's tenement	Charles Parks	$^1/_2$ waste
34	Widow King's tenement	Set to Sadler and Callow since All Saints' 1708	
35	Finiston's tenement	—Thompson	William Callow
36	McCrery's tenement	Widow McDouell	Do.
37	Himlen's tenement	William Himlen	Do.
37a	Himlen's croft	William Himlen	Do.
38	Johnson's tenement	Mark Carson	William Irwyn
39 } 40 }	Arwaker's tenement	Nathaniel McCreery Anthony McKee	Unbuilt Unbuilt
41	Sloan's tenement	John Alcock	Do.
Barrack Lane (west side)			
42	McMullan's tenement	John Sankey	Hugh McMullan
43	Tumulty's tenement	(this holding is called	Daniel Tumulty
44	Fenan's tenement	West's half acre)	Andrew Fenan
45	Sankey's croft		

BARRACK QUARTER

No.	Denominations	Principal tenant	Tenants in possession
Barrack Lane (east side)			
1	The Old Pound	Charles Carr and Seneca Magarry	
2	Hannah's Garden	Robert Cricket	Do.
3	Horse Barrack and Barrack Yard	The Queen	
4	Galt's tenement	John Galt, smith	Do.
5	Cullen's tenement	Jane Waterson	Do.
6	Harrison's tenement		James Finiston (a barn)
7	Kean's tenement	Finiston	Unbuilt
7a	Kean's croft		Good arable
8	Patrick Boy's tenement	James Finiston	Unbuilt
9	Cavanagh's tenement		Unbuilt
10	Old Gallows Hill	Waste	
11	Widow Kirby's tenement	Dr Mercer	Barn and haggard
		Gilbert Brown	Do.

No.	Denominations	Principal tenant	Tenants in possession
CHAPEL HILL			
Irish Street (east side)			
1	Johnston's ½ tenement	Elizabeth Thompson, widow	John Ross and Thompson (the idiot)
2	Mercer's tenement	Waste	Unbuilt
3	Sloan's kiln tenement	Waste	Unbuilt
4	Beaghan's tenement	Alexander Dickey	Thomas Blackwood
5	Drake's tenement	William McComb	Do.
6	Stevenson's tenement	Daniel Colt	Do.
7	Finiston ½ tenement	John Brown	Robert Dixon
MOUNT PARK			
Back Lane (west side)			
1			Laughlin Cavanagh, etc.
2	St John's close	John Brown	Do.
3			Andrew McPrior
4	Gordon's tenement	John Brown	Samuel Gordon
Irish Street (east side)			
	Mount Park properly continued	Alexander Dickey	Do.
STREAM MILL HOLDING			
1	House stead, kiln and garden		
2	Mill dam	James Hamilton, Esq.	Alexander McKee
3	Mill common		
Washing Stream (south side)			
4	Peterson's garden	Unbuilt	Waste
5	Sanders Moor's do.	Unbuilt, Bryan Omoney	Waste
6	Murphey's tenement	Patrick Murphey	Do.
OLD KENNEL			
Washing Stream (west side)			
1	Gregorie's tenement	John Gregory	Do.
2	Venable's tenement	Rowland Brown	Do.
3	Boyd's tenement	William Con	Do.
4	Widow Russel's tenement	John Hays	Do.

Downpatrick, Co. Down, was one of those Ulster towns that experienced the effects of the Jacobite Plantation. The map shows the way in which the old town became divided in the aftermath of the Plantation into quarters housing the new English and Scottish settlers, the native population being confined, for the most part, to the Irish Quarter at the west side of Irish Street. The names of the tenants in possession of the town's various properties in 1708, however, reveal that a considerable native Irish, and probably Catholic, population remained intact throughout the town.

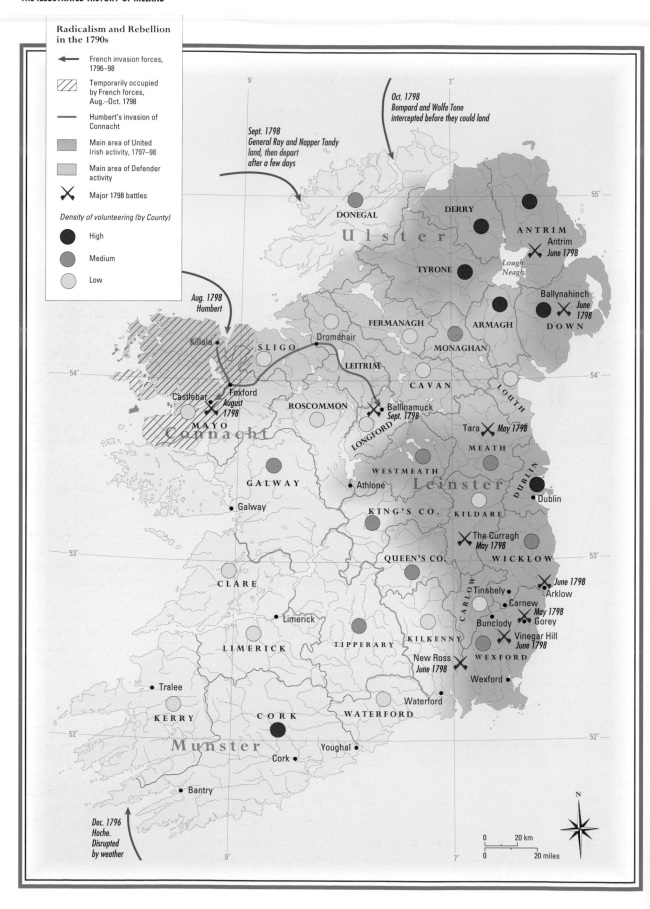

Radicalism and Rebellion in the 1790s

← French invasion forces, 1796–98

⧄ Temporarily occupied by French forces, Aug.–Oct. 1798

— Humbert's invasion of Connacht

▨ Main area of United Irish activity, 1797–98

▨ Main area of Defender activity

✕ Major 1798 battles

Density of volunteering (by County)

● High

● Medium

○ Low

Oct. 1798 Bompard and Wolfe Tone intercepted before they could land

Sept. 1798 General Ray and Napper Tandy land, then depart after a few days

Aug. 1798 Humbert

Dec. 1796 Hoche. Disrupted by weather

U l s t e r

DONEGAL

DERRY

ANTRIM

Antrim June 1798

TYRONE

Lough Neagh

Ballynahinch June 1798

FERMANAGH

ARMAGH

DOWN

MONAGHAN

LEITRIM

Dromahair

CAVAN

LOUTH

Killala

S L I G O

Castlebar

Foxford August 1798

MAYO

C o n n a c h t

ROSCOMMON

Ballinamuck Sept. 1798

LONGFORD

Tara May 1798

M E A T H

WESTMEATH

Athlone

L e i n s t e r

DUBLIN

Dublin

GALWAY

Galway

KING'S CO.

KILDARE

The Curragh May 1798

QUEEN'S CO.

WICKLOW

June 1798

Arklow

CLARE

CARLOW

Tinahely

Carnew May 1798

Gorey

Limerick

TIPPERARY

KILKENNY

Bunclody

Vinegar Hill June 1798

WEXFORD

LIMERICK

New Ross June 1798

Wexford

Waterford

Tralee

KERRY

CORK

WATERFORD

Youghal

M u n s t e r

Cork

Bantry

N

0   20 km

0   20 miles

CHAPTER VI

THE MOST DISTRESSFUL COUNTRY

In 1771, the great American statesman Benjamin Franklin visited Ireland and held meetings in Dublin with the leading parliamentary 'patriots', in which he proposed co-operation between them and the American colonists in their heightening struggle against the British, later noting: 'I found them disposed to be friends of America…[and] endeavoured to confirm them with the expectation that our growing weight might in time be thrown into their scale, and, by joining our interests with theirs, a more equitable treatment from this nation [Britain] might be obtained for themselves as well as for us'. Many Irish, particularly the Presbyterians of Ulster, were indeed friends of America since the ships that brought the flax seed which fed Ulster's thriving linen industry had, since the late 1710s, been returning with ever fuller complements of emigrants, seeking greater religious tolerance and, of course, cheap land, in New England, Pennsylvania, Delaware and south to the Carolinas. They were by no means all Ulster Scots, or even Protestants: perhaps as many as 100,000 Irish Catholics emigrated to North America in the eighteenth century, and, combined with the quarter of a million Protestant emigrants from Ulster who crossed the Atlantic in the same period, it would not be far off the mark to suggest that at the outbreak of the War of Independence about half the American colonial population was of Irish stock.

Little wonder, then, the favourable response that greeted their war in Ireland, summed up in the reminiscence of the famous Dublin radical, James Napper Tandy, one of the founders of the United Irishmen, that 'when America revolted against the tyranny of Great Britain my heart rejoiced within me, and I should at that time have joined her standard if not prevented'. As for the northern Presbyterians, the then Lord Lieutenant of Ireland bluntly declared that they 'are in their hearts Americans'. For the British government, the main concern was to ensure that Ireland did not become another America, in addition to which the closure of the American markets increased the importance of Ireland as a destination of British trade, and Irish troops and supplies were badly needed for the war. This crisis, therefore, helped soften the government's stance on issues of concern to the patriot party in Ireland who, to begin with, started pressurising them to repeal British laws limiting Ireland's freedom to trade.

James Napper Tandy (c. 1737–1803) was prominent among the 'patriot' party in Dublin and active in the city's guilds and Corporation. He became commander of the Dublin Volunteers and was active in seeking parliamentary reform and voting rights for Catholics. He later became the first secretary of the Dublin United Irishmen. He sailed with the French to Ireland in 1798, was returned to Ireland after being arrested in Hamburg, and although sentenced to death was deported to France in 1802.

They followed the American example – originally, of course, proposed by Dean Swift – of establishing 'non-importation' associations whose aim of boycotting English goods was taken up with an enthusiasm and a hitherto unheard-of organisational efficiency throughout the country. Within the Irish parliament, the lead was taken by a young barrister by the name of Henry Grattan, who had entered parliament in the very year of the American Revolution and who, in that great age of parliamentary eloquence, had no rival, and behind whom the patriots now rallied. It was he, in October 1779, who moved the amendment calling for the abolition of restrictions on Irish exports to which the government was eventually forced to concede, the first of his parliamentary triumphs, and part of the reason why, to this day, the late eighteenth-century Irish House of Commons has been universally known as 'Grattan's Parliament'.

The Dublin Volunteers saluting the statue of William III on College Green, 4 November 1779.

The Irish Volunteers

Public opinion, now a force to reckon with in Ireland, was four-square behind the patriots, expressing itself in a proliferation of pamphlets and such newspapers as *The Freeman's Journal*, founded in 1763 by the remarkable Dublin-based apothecary and MP, Charles Lucas. What public opinion needed, though, was an organisation through which to channel its energies. Because Ireland lacked a militia, when the standing army was heavily depleted by the withdrawal of troops to fight in America, groups of armed men volunteered to form associations to support the regular army – in the event, for instance, of a rumoured French invasion – and during 1778 the Volunteer movement began to attract recruits at a startling rate, so that within a year there was a full-scale Volunteer army in existence nation-wide, the local landlords providing the officers, its members almost exclusively Protestant since Catholics were still forbidden to bear arms. Though formed to augment the army, the sudden strength of the Volunteer movement and the wave of euphoria which accompanied its spread,

THE MOST DISTRESSFUL COUNTRY

meant that the will of its members carried quite some weight. The majority of them were as concerned with securing Irish free trade and opposing English governmental interference in Ireland as they were in repelling the French, so that it very quickly became a vehicle for demonstrating public support for the patriots in parliament.

The latter, led by Grattan, were by and large in favour of relaxing the Penal Laws against Catholics, partly because this was an age of greater religious tolerance, partly because old fears had eased, and partly out of political motives. The Dublin parliament was exclusively Protestant, and Irish Roman Catholics tended to look, however forlornly, to Westminster for an answer to their grievances; but there was always a temptation on the part of the British government to keep these divisions alive in order to weaken Irish opposition. Men like Henry Grattan realised this; hence his famous assertion that 'the Irish Protestant could never be free till the Irish Catholic had ceased to be a slave'. And so it was he who, in 1778, championed the Catholic Relief Act which repealed many of the provisions relating to the tenure and inheritance of land introduced under the Popery Act of 1704, causing perhaps the greatest of his Irish contemporaries, Edmund Burke, to remark, in a letter to the speaker of the Irish House of Commons: 'You are now beginning to have a country'.

It was in the following year that the demands for free trade reached their climax, the parliamentary debates being supplemented by great public demonstrations of the Volunteers, most memorably that held, significantly, on the birthday of William of Orange, 4 November 1779, before his statue in College Green. The tensions thus raised had the desired effect and a series of acts followed, under the provisions of which Ireland emerged with virtually the same rights to trade as those of Britain, the Irish parliament securing the freedom from that day on to regulate Irish trade. The British government had been compelled to yield to Irish demands, and the joy that greeted it throughout Ireland was deafening – and, of course, success breeds success. Grattan and the other patriots knew that what Britain had granted it could just as easily take away, unless, that is, the Irish parliament could legislate for its own affairs without the say-so of Westminster, something it had not been able to do for nearly three centuries, since the passage of Poynings' Law in 1494. This now became the patriots' next target.

Irish Parliamentary Independence

Fresh from the 'free trade' success of 1779, and with a united country behind him, Grattan moved his 'declaration of independence' in the Irish House of Commons on 19 April 1780, to the effect 'That the King's Most Excellent Majesty, and the Lords and Commons of Ireland, are the only power competent to enact laws to bind Ireland'. Grattan's demand for constitutional reform was not met, but this stirred the Volunteers into further activity. They held a convention at Dungannon, Co. Tyrone, in February 1782, at which the resolutions passed were drawn up by the leader of the patriots in the Irish House of Lords, the earl of Charlemont, along with Grattan and Henry Flood, former patriot leader in the Commons, his reputation now somewhat tarnished for having temporarily taken up government office.

Their resolutions spelled out the patriots' demand for legislative independence, concluding: 'We know our duty to our Sovereign, and are loyal. We know our duty to ourselves, and are resolved to be free. We seek for our rights and no more than our rights' – a very strong statement of national feeling. Of course, when the Volunteers spoke, they spoke for the Protestants of Ireland, but it is worth noting that the final resolution of the Dungannon Convention stated that 'as men and as Irishmen, as Christians and as Protestants, we rejoice in the relaxation of the Penal Laws against our Roman Catholic fellow-subjects'.

The Dungannon Convention stirred the country and Grattan soon afterwards again moved his declaration of independence in parliament, but it was once more defeated. Only a change of government in Westminster, with the Whigs in power and a new Lord Lieutenant in charge in Dublin Castle, brought the prospect of success, and on 16 April 1782 Grattan left his sick bed to move his declaration for a third time, declaring before the Commons : 'I am now to address a free people...I found Ireland on her knees. I watched over her with a paternal solicitude. I have traced her progress from injuries to arms, and from arms to liberty...Ireland is now a nation, and in that new character I hail her, and, bowing to her august presence, I say, Esto perpetua (Be it ever so)'. Grattan's resolution was passed unanimously and a statement of Ireland's constitutional claims sent to the King. In response, the British government agreed to repeal the infamous 'sixth of George I', the act, passed in 1720, 'for the better securing the dependency of the kingdom of Ireland on the crown of Great Britain'.

The effect was that the Irish parliament had the sole right to legislate for Ireland, and the Irish House of Lords was affirmed as the country's final court of appeal. Poynings' Law was modified so that Bills transmitted from Ireland could not be altered, though the right of the King to suppress them in certain cases was retained. This is what is sometimes known as 'the constitution of 1782'. Thus was the formal independence of the Irish parliament and judiciary established. The fact remained, though, that the country was still governed by a Viceroy sent from England and by officials based in Dublin Castle answerable to Westminster as much as to the Irish parliament. The 1782 'constitution' was a fragile object. Only time would tell whether its achievement was as real as it was apparent.

Grattan's Parliament

The trade concessions won in 1779–80 and the parliamentary changes of 1782, however important their effect on contemporary affairs, were by no means a per-

Grattan's Parliament is the name given by a later generation of Irish nationalists to the period between the achievement of 'legislative independence' and the Act of Union, when the previously hated parliament of the Establishment seemed to take on board more of the characteristics of a national parliament. It was looked back on as something of a Golden Age but it never became a truly representative body and the Catholic majority remained excluded from membership.

manent settlement of Ireland's constitutional position vis-à-vis Great Britain. Different factions sought different benefits from the new developments: the landlords regarded themselves as 'the Lords and Commons of Ireland' and looked to the new dispensation for a guarantee of their ascendancy, but middle-class Protestants hoped they would benefit by having greater control over elections, while Roman Catholics sought at least the right to vote, if not actually to sit in parliament. The latter were the first to be disappointed.

Grattan was in favour of extending their entitlements, declaring that 'as the mover of the Declaration of Rights, I should be ashamed of giving freedom to but 600,000 of my fellow-countrymen, when I could extend it to two million more', but his rival, Henry Flood, told parliament that while 'I admit the merit of the Roman Catholics', nevertheless maintained that 'I will not consent to their having any influence in choosing members for this House'. Lord Charlemont, commander-in-chief of the Volunteers, tended to Flood's view, and so the pressure which the Volunteer movement had earlier brought to bear in winning other crucial changes was absent in this instance and the measure was doomed.

Next it was the turn of the Protestant middle classes to be disappointed. Although Grattan and Flood were both strong advocates of reform of the parliamentary system, Grattan was worried about the extent of the extra-parliamentary pressure which the Volunteers could muster, while Flood was keen to exploit this to the full. When a Volunteer Convention met in the Rotunda in Dublin in November 1783 it drew up a plan of reform of which Flood was largely the architect, and on 29 November he marched from there to the House of Commons in College Green, in his Volunteer uniform, and proposed a Bill 'for the more equal representation of the people in parliament'. Opposition to the Bill was led by John Fitzgibbon, later the infamous Lord Clare, but even moderates were uneasy about the way in which the proposal originated among the armed Volunteer movement and it in turn was defeated.

The Volunteers had failed in this peaceful attempt to secure reform, and the unity which had existed among the Protestants of Ireland a year earlier was fractured. Fitzgibbon, committed to safeguarding the Protestant ascendancy, vehemently opposed to Catholic emancipation (a phrase now becoming current), and a firm believer in maintaining as close as possible a link with Westminster – by, if necessary, a parliamentary union – emerged strengthened from this contest and was probably the most powerful man in Ireland in the last decade or so of the eighteenth century. As for the Volunteers, they gradually broke free from the leadership of the landlord classes, and came to reflect more radical views as both leaders and men now originated lower down the social scale.

Impact of the French Revolution

When the French Revolution erupted in 1789 reaction to it in Ireland, as with the American War of Independence before it, was generally positive. Those who sought reform in Ireland looked to France and saw the establishment of religious equality, the new open electoral system, and even the abolition of tithes to the Church as achievements worthy of support if not emulation. The execution of Louis XVI and his queen, and the declaration of a republic, were especially popular among the Presbyterians of Ulster, where the Volunteers remained strongest, and their sympathy for the new religious tolerance in France led many of them to advocate similar equality for Catholics in Ireland.

In the summer of 1791, a young Protestant (though not a Presbyterian) named Theobald Wolfe Tone published an influential pamphlet entitled *An argument on behalf of the Catholics of Ireland,* calling for the abolition of all penal laws, and on 14 October of that year he helped found in Belfast the Society of United Irishmen, with the aim of bringing together Irishmen of all creeds, establishing complete religious equality, and radically reforming the government of Ireland. Their remarkable newspaper, *The Northern Star*, first appeared in February 1792 and proved critical in making Belfast a centre of conspiratorial activity, taking its ideals from the French Revolution but much of its inspiration from Ireland's ancient history and antiquities which they sought to foster and preserve.

Tone was active too in promoting the cause of the United Irishmen in Dublin, where their first meeting was held on 9 November 1791, and was soon afterwards appointed secretary to the Catholic Association. A Catholic Relief Act passed through the Irish parliament in 1792, which removed restrictions on Roman Catholic education and allowed them to practice law, but it made no provision for their right to vote. The response of the Catholic Association was to imitate the Volunteers and organise a Catholic 'Convention' which met in Dublin in December in the Tailors' Hall in Back Lane, thereby acquiring its nickname, the 'Back Lane Parliament'.

A list of petitions was drawn up for presentation before the king and as its delegates travelled through Belfast the streets were lined with cheering Protestant crowds wishing their Catholic fellow-countrymen well on their mission. The British cabinet, under William Pitt (the younger), looked favourably on their demands, partly because of fears arising out of the deterioration in relations with France, and soon afterwards, therefore, the Irish parliament passed another Relief Act granting Catholics the right to vote in local and parliamentary elections, to bear arms under certain conditions, and to hold all but the most senior of civil and military offices. Yet still they were excluded from membership of parliament.

To make matters worse, this carrot of reform was matched by a repressive stick. Fear of popular agitation, and the danger of French revolutionary spirit spilling over into Ireland, caused the government to introduce a Convention Act, forbidding the holding of public assemblies. This was accompanied by a prohibition on the unlicensed distribution of arms, and also by the establishment of a militia, intended both to strengthen the government's security and to draw support away from the Volunteers. The result was that the reforms pleased nobody. They were deemed half-hearted by Catholics and by Protestant radicals alike, and thus the alliance between them grew stronger as hopes of French intervention rose. As for reactionary Protestants fearful of reform, they were beginning to lose faith in the capacity of their own parliament to maintain their

Members of the Society of United Irishmen take an oath to rise against English rule.

Opposite: *In Ireland, the French Revolution inspired a wave of radical enthusiasm which the authorities suppressed with military repression, and which led ultimately to something akin to a civil war. From the period of the revolution can be traced the strong element of democratic republican ideals which became part of Irish popular political culture. For the French, Ireland was seen as a weak spot in England's defences and hence they responded favourably to Wolfe Tone's appeals for military assistance by sending an expeditionary force to Ireland in December 1796 under the leadership of General Lazare Hoche.*

ascendancy. For the former, it seemed, a more revolutionary programme of action was called for, while some of the latter began to think the unthinkable: that if their own Irish parliament could not guarantee their future status, then perhaps it was time to get rid of it.

The United Irishmen

When war finally broke out between Britain and France, the United Irishmen represented a considerable threat to British interests, since among their ranks from the start were men and women whose goals were no longer the reformation of the Irish government but rather its overthrow and the declaration of a republic along French lines. In May 1794, therefore, the government announced the suppression of the Dublin United Irishmen, but this had, as ever, the opposite effect to that intended: instead of an open organisation led by relative moderates, holding public meetings and calling for democratic reforms, the government was soon faced with an underground secret society in which those of radical views prevailed, whose aim was now the formation of an alliance with France and securing complete independence from Britain. Furthermore, while formerly having been largely Protestant and strong only in Ulster, Wolfe Tone realised the importance of attracting Catholics throughout the country to the movement, since the popular revolution he had in mind could hardly survive without their participation, and there remained the risk that the government might try to buy their loyalty with further small concessions.

To Tone and his comrades, the future lay in attracting to their cause not comfortably off, if idealistic, members of the middle classes but the repressed poor. Agrarian unrest was ongoing throughout the country and, although the impetus was largely resentment against oppressive landlords and tithe-collectors, there is evidence that the egalitarian principles of the French revolution were seeping through to the wider public consciousness even in rural Ireland. The only barrier which stood in the way of winning them over to the revolutionary cause was religion.

Sectarian Tensions and Orangeism

Apart from the fact that the upper ranks of Catholic society were far from enthused by the anti-clericalism of the French Jacobins, the agrarian demands of the Catholic peasantry very easily led to local sectarian tensions. In many parts of the country, but especially in south Ulster, Catholic and Protestant tenants were in competition with each other for land, all the more so since the rapid population-expansion – which culminated in the cataclysm of the Great Famine a half-century later – was already well underway. So the Protestants formed themselves into armed groups, the 'Peep O'Day Boys', and the Catholics set up their own 'Defenders', and clashes between them were ugly and frequently fatal. The nastiest was the so-called Battle of the Diamond fought in Co. Armagh in September 1795, when the Defenders were roundly defeated by their Protestant neighbours, who then set up the 'Orange' organisation to defend their ascendancy. In the months that followed the 'Orangemen' persecuted the Catholics of Armagh and of neighbouring counties and drove thousands of them out of the province entirely. No doubt many of the cruelties alleged against them were untrue or exaggerated, but fear and hatred of them swelled the ranks of the Defenders.

Catholics believed that the government at least condoned Orange atrocities, especially since the new movement was soon joined by members of the Protestant establishment and even government officials. The result was that in many places there was a very considerable overlap between membership of the Defenders and the United Irishmen, the one dedicated to protecting Catholics from a perceived imminent extermination, the other convinced that a constitutional means of securing reform was now hopeless and that Ireland's ills could only be resolved by the overthrow of the old régime, though still anxious to secure this by uniting men of all creeds together.

The government's response to the heightened threat of armed rebellion was further repression. An Insurrection Act passed in March 1796 introduced the death penalty for unlawful oath-taking, and curfews in districts considered disturbed where those found with unlicensed arms or considered guilty of disorderly offenses could be press-ganged into the navy. Finally, since the recently-established militia was considered suspect as containing large numbers of Catholics, an almost exclusively Protestant Yeomanry force was raised, in effect arming the Protestants against them. In mid-September the Belfast leaders of the United Irishmen were arrested but their conspiracy continued to spread even after the printing-presses at *The Northern Star* offices were smashed. A brutal policy of repression followed, spearheaded by the notorious General Gerard Lake, during which the yeomanry burned houses, flogged their occupants, and sent hundreds of suspects off to the fleet. They managed to seize much of the United Irishmen's weaponry and cowed the resistance of the majority of its supporters, leaving intact only a small number of committed republicans, mostly

Opposite: *No organisation has captured the political imagination of the Irish of succeeding generations more than the Society of United Irishmen founded in Belfast in October 1791 and in Dublin on 9 November. The Belfast society was predominantly Presbyterian and middle class, that in Dublin a good mixture of Protestant and Catholic, but again largely middle class with the occasional recruit from the aristocracy. Though its goals were many and diverse, what has preserved the affection in which it has continued to be held is its overriding commitment to a union of all Irish people irrespective of religious denomination.*

Vinegar Hill, near Enniscorthy, was the main camp of the 'boys of Wexford' in the 1798 rebellion, until it was stormed by General Lake and a force of 10,000 men on 21 June. Today, it is remembered largely in sorrow as the turning point in the fortunes of the rebels.

Presbyterians, still dedicated to achieving the United Irish ideals.

Further bad news for the conspirators came from the south when Wolfe Tone, having travelled first to America and then to France, was prevented by bad weather from making a landing in Bantry Bay in December 1796 with a French expeditionary force of 43 ships containing up to 15,000 men. The military repression inflicted on Ulster was now extended to Leinster and Munster, but the United Irish leadership persisted, nevertheless, with their plans for a rising. They worked closely with the Defenders and recruited on a massive scale throughout the country, while continuing to try to win over the French into making a large-scale commitment of men and arms to Ireland. Their problem was that the Dublin Castle authorities were kept abreast of their plans by a network of spies and informers and could afford to watch and wait and then finally swoop just before the call to arms was made by the leadership, all the while continuing with their brutal regime of martial law which was formally proclaimed in March 1798.

'Ninety-eight'

It was in mid-March 1798 that the Castle decided the time had come to arrest the leaders of the Dublin United Irishmen. Oliver Bond was captured at a meeting of the Leinster 'Directory' of the United men in his premises on Bridge

Street, and most of the others were taken in another raid on the same day. Of those who escaped arrest the most notable was the romantic and charismatic Lord Edward Fitzgerald, scion of the house of Kildare and brother of the duke of Leinster, though he was eventually cornered in a house in Thomas Street on 19 May, and mortally wounded after a gallant attempt at resisting arrest. According to papers found in Lord Edward's possession a total of 279,896 had already taken the United Irish oath – an extraordinary testimony to their popularity. But his capture was a crushing blow to the plans to fix a rising in Dublin to begin four days later on the night of 23 May. The city was saturated with troops, the populace were terrorised, and a house-to-house search produced in the region of 20,000 pikes, the weapon ever afterwards associated with the men of '98.

The collapse of the plan for Dublin meant that the rebellion got off to a disastrous start and all hope of seizing the country's centre of power had to be abandoned. Instead, isolated risings broke out in various Leinster counties, principally Wexford, and, to a lesser extent, Carlow, Kildare and Meath. The rebels were poorly armed and organised, and were outnumbered by the government forces – over 75,000 of them, including 40,000 yeomen – who were also better trained and armed. The action was concentrated on attempts to seize some of the smaller provincial towns, on ambushing enemy forces, and on attacking the houses of the hated local magistrates. Within days, though, the insurgents suffered heavy defeats at the Curragh of Kildare and the hill of Tara and it was only in Co. Wexford that success looked more likely.

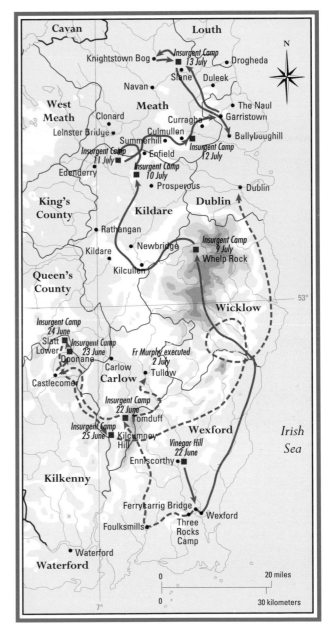

Here the rebels seem to have had the advantage of surprise and were led by some Catholic and a few Protestant gentry, merchants from the towns and some remarkable priests, of whom Fr John Murphy of Kilcormack is the best-remembered, thanks to the popularity of the later ballad celebrating his actions at Boolavogue. They seized the towns of Enniscorthy and Wexford, which they held for three weeks, but they failed to take New Ross and so push outwards beyond the county boundary, and when about 20,000 of them faced a 'redcoat'

army of perhaps half that size, under General Lake, at Vinegar Hill on 21 June, they were routed with heavy casualties.

Though the survivors took to the Wicklow Mountains, the cause of 'the Boys of Wexford' was now lost. They certainly did not lack for courage, but it was not matched by an equal display of discipline, and many of the Wexford rebels, far from championing the ideals of the United Irishmen, saw the enemy in their Protestant neighbours every bit as much as Dublin Castle, whom they indiscriminately plundered and even slaughtered. In Wexford as elsewhere the great majority of those taking part, on both sides, were Irish-born, and in some respects therefore the 1798 rebellion had much of the flavour of a civil war.

It was in east Ulster that the United Irish doctrine of revolutionary republicanism found its truest expression, but here too the rebellion proved a bitter disappointment. Risings broke out in early June, led by the remnants of the Antrim and Down United leadership, largely Presbyterian in composition. Among their idealistically-spirited number, perhaps the name of a young Belfastman, Henry Joy McCracken, shines most brilliantly still in the popular memory, but their Antrim successes were confined to a brief seizure of Antrim town by up to 4,000 men before the government forces re-took control. In Down, things looked a little more hopeful, especially after the insurrectionist capture of Saintfield, whereupon their general, Lisburnman Henry Munro, led up to 7,000 United men in a march on Ballynahinch. There, however, on 13 June, they were defeated with disastrous consequences, and Munro and McCracken were among the leaders hanged.

The 1798 rebellion in Ulster was over, the gallantry of its leaders passing into legend. They were Anglicans and Dissenters, fighting for an independent Irish Republic which the bulk of their Roman Catholic compatriots had yet to embrace, and even after their separatist republicanism had given way to loyalism and support for union with Great Britain it was still with an element of pride that they sang, in memory of McCracken:

> *Ah, lads, for Ireland's cause we fought, for home and sire we bled,*
> *Tho' pikes were fed, still our hearts beat true, and five to one lay dead.*
> *But many a lassie mourned her lad, and mother mourned her boy;*
> *For youth was strong in that gallant throng, who followed Henry Joy.*

The West's Awake

The final scenes of '98 were played out in that part of the country previously least affected by the revolutionary impulse: Connacht and west Ulster. When news of the Leinster uprisings reached Paris a small force of troops was dispatched to Ireland, part of which landed at Killala in late August under the command of General Joseph Amable Humbert. Their first serious engagement was at what became known as 'the races of Castlebar' where Humbert was spectacularly successful against a much superior force under General Lake himself, after which success they enjoyed brief control of Mayo. But the United Irishmen were not organised in the region and, although many of the local populace did rise to their support, the French were soon marooned in a sea of government forces and their proposed march eastwards across the country ended up a forced surrender at Ballinamuck, Co. Longford.

A larger French fleet attempted to land further north in Donegal in October, but six of its ships were captured before they could effect a landing, and their crews brought ashore: one of the uniformed 'French' officers turned out to be none other than Theobald Wolfe Tone. He was recognised and straightaway brought to Dublin, court-martialled, and condemned; it appears he took his own life when denied his request to be shot rather than hanged.

Wolfe Tone spent much of his life, and indeed died, seeking Catholic Emancipation, constitutional reform and, ultimately, the complete separation of Ireland from Great Britain. He was a revolutionary and a republican far ahead of his time and of the great mass of his fellow-countrymen, whom he thought he could unite in furtherance of his ideals regardless of their creed or social standing. It is true that the strength of the army which the British and Irish governments brought into the field against him contributed to his failure – during his lifetime – and the half-hearted assistance of his French allies must have been a source of disappointment, but the real failure lay not with Tone himself or his goals but in the hearts and minds of his compatriots who never succeeded in being as Wolfe Tone sought to make them – 'United Irishmen'.

The Legacy of '98

Somewhere between 30,000 and 50,000 Irish men and women rose up in rebellion in 1798, in significant numbers in seven counties and to a lesser extent in about eleven others. In that one summer as many as 20,000 people may have lost their lives, the vast majority among the rebels and their communities. Why did it fail, and why did it happen in the first place? It failed because of the government terror-campaign that preceded it and continued throughout '98; because of the latter's success in arresting the leadership, disarming the recruits, and gaining intelligence on their plans; because of the confusion in the United Irish ranks after the leadership structure collapsed, especially the breakdown of communications between the Ulster and Leinster 'directories'; and it failed because foreign aid was necessary to overthrow British rule and this was not available in sufficient force.

In retrospect, too, we can see that the 1798 rebellion was a failure because it was dependent on the strength of the bonds between Presbyterian radicals, rural Catholic Defenders and the urban Catholic middle class, and that alliance did not hold; and it did not hold because the rebels' objectives were not uniform. For some of the participants the impulse for rebellion was economic, even selfish, if concern for one's livelihood and the welfare of one's dependents can be deemed such. By the late 1790s the population of Ireland was five million or more, double what it had been a half-century earlier. Throughout the country people were disaffected because available land was becoming scarce, rent and tithe-payments were increasing while at the same time wages were falling, and the war with France had led to higher taxes and sharp fluctuations in the prices farmers received for their milk and grain: it is perhaps no coincidence that Wexford was famed for its barley and that its growers were facing financial crisis in the very year of the rebellion.

There was also, of course, a strong political impulse at work. The Catholic middle classes were becoming more assertive and were angry at the piecemeal approach to relaxing the penal legislation, particularly the fact that parliament's doors remained closed against them. It should be remembered that many Protestants had championed this cause and they too must have been angry at the government's foot-dragging: surely this is the explanation for the involvement of Protestant gentry figures in the Wexford rising, most notably perhaps their young commander-in-chief, Beauchamp Bagenal Harvey, hanged on Wexford Bridge for his efforts. His motives were as selfless as those of the thirty Presbyterian ministers who were among the ranks of the Ulster insurgents. But the Anglican elite, the Dissenter radical, the urban middle-class Catholic, and the rural masses who followed them with such enthusiasm into battle, all shared one thing in common: a deep sense of alienation from the state and an urgent desire to wring change in the way that Ireland was governed.

Turkeys Voting for Christmas?

Even before the events of 1798, the idea of abolishing the Irish parliament had been many times mooted. The constitutional changes wrested under Grattan had led to concern in some quarters that Great Britain and Ireland might drift further apart, while the outbreak of war with France had heightened invasion fears. The British Prime Minister, Pitt, saw the disturbed nature of Ireland in the 1790s as a danger to both countries and became convinced that government control of the situation would be firmer and stronger if a legislative union took place, all the more so during and after 1798. His main task was convincing the Protestants of Ireland to vote their own parliament out of existence, but his most effective weapon was fear: fear of a French invasion, fear of being overwhelmed by the Catholic majority, the fear which many of them now felt that the days of their continued ascendancy in Ireland were numbered, and that Union with Britain would bolster their position – this, rather than conviction, was what would bring them around to Pitt's view. Still, the parliamentary arithmetic was not in his favour and the business of obtaining a 'yes' majority would not be easy.

The first step was the appointment as Chief Secretary in Ireland of Robert

Stewart, Viscount Castlereagh, a man now fully won over to the cause of Union who took to the role with relish. Like Pitt, Castlereagh was of the view that Union should be accompanied by Catholic Emancipation, but for those Protestants – like Lord Clare (John Fitzgibbon) – who favoured Union as a way of protecting their ascendancy this made little sense, so the issue was quietly dropped. But it was made clear to the Roman Catholic leaders, including the bishops, that Catholic Emancipation would never come from the Irish parliament and that their only hope lay with Westminster. This had the desired effect: influential Catholic opinion was largely pro-Union.

The immediate occasion for the Irish Act of Union, negotiated by Cornwallis and Castlereagh under the active supervision of the British Prime Minister, William Pitt, was the 1798 rebellion. This convinced the British establishment that direct control needed to be taken of this neighbouring dependency because its instability was becoming a serious threat. The only problem was convincing the membership of the parliament itself that they should vote themselves out of existence, and this was done by the normal 18th-century recourse to bribery and patronage, and a very public campaign fought by both sides through pamphleteering, petitions and public meetings.

As for the mass of Catholic opinion, they had no great love for the Dublin parliament, and no reason to think that laws enacted in London would be any different. Catholic tenants would shed few tears over the extinction of an Irish parliament perceived as being the property of the ruling landlord class by whom they were oppressed. As for the Presbyterians of Ulster, their revolutionary zeal was already beginning to wane; they, like Catholics, owed few favours to an Irish parliament which had long discriminated against them too; and they had cause to hope that Union would bring closer commercial ties with Britain, which might aid economic development and the linen industry in particular.

For the Protestants of Dublin, and the easily-aroused Dublin 'mob', what was most worrying in the proposed loss of its parliament was the threat to its position as a capital city and all the advantages, commercial and otherwise, that went with it. Here was the voice of self-interest, by no means unique to Dublin, and self-interest was something the government could deal with a great deal more easily than principle. Government office, favour, and patronage were withheld from those opposed to Union, and were used as a way of gradually building up a parliamentary majority. Peerages, positions of influence, and pensions were handed out to those willing to swap sides in the chamber of the Irish House of Commons. Where promises failed, threats sometimes worked, and some anti-Union MPs were 'persuaded' to vacate their seats and make way for Unionist replacements.

The Act of Union

Parliament finally met to debate the issue on 15 January 1800, and an angry all-night session followed. Towards dawn, Henry Grattan, whose health had recently declined, entered the chamber dressed in his Volunteer uniform, deathly pale and barely able to walk. He spoke for two hours, apparently with all his customary fire and eloquent oratory, but to no avail. Oratory was no match for fear and favour, and Castlereagh had his way. The final terms for Union were accepted on 28 March, the Bill for Union was introduced on 21 May, it received royal assent on 1 August, and on 1 January 1801 the 'United Kingdom of Great Britain and Ireland' came into being. Thirty-two Irish peers would assume places in the Westminster House of Lords, while the House of Commons would have 100 Irish MPs, twice as many as Scotland: two members from each county and the cities of Dublin and Cork (a total of 68), one from a further 31 cities and boroughs, and one from Trinity College, Dublin.

To seal the Parliament's fate for ever, the magnificent Parliament Buildings in College Green were sold to a commercial bank (in whose possession they still remain), and the sale specified that the chamber of the House of Commons be totally reconstructed so that it displayed no reminder of its former use (though the House of Lords remains largely intact). Thus was an institution of over six centuries' duration brought to an end. It had never truly been an 'Irish' parliament, and was, rather, an importation from England and the voice of the people who called themselves 'the English of Ireland'. Yet, however deficient and unrepresentative, 'Grattan's Parliament' had shown its capacity to move with the times and perhaps in due course to become a parliament for all the people, while the very existence of a parliament in Ireland served as a reminder of the country's separate existence as a European nation. Hindsight would show that its abolition would have the most tragic consequences.

Robert Emmet (1778–1803), younger brother of the United Irish leader Thomas Addis Emmet, first emerged into the light of publicity when he was expelled from Trinity College, Dublin, in April 1798 along with all other students suspected of being involved in radical activity, and emerged as one of the new group leading the revolutionary movement after the 1798 defeat. After the failure of his own insurrection in 1803 he was executed.

Robert Emmet

The coming into effect of the Act of Union marked the beginning of a lengthy period of political stagnation in Irish life with one brief, tragic exception – the rebellion of Robert Emmet, younger brother of one of the leaders of the United Irishmen, Thomas Addis Emmet. As a teenager and student in 1798 Robert was secretary of one of the four branches of United Irishmen in Trinity College, Dublin, and had already acquired a reputation for fiery oratory in the College's Historical Society. After a spell in exile in France where he discussed Irish independence with Napoleon, he returned to Ireland in 1802 and began preparations for a new rebellion. Former United Irish leaders rallied behind him, Myles Byrne, for instance, stating that Emmet's 'powerful, persuasive language, and sound reason, all coming from the heart, left it impossible for any Irishman, impressed with a desire for his country's independence, to make any objection to his plans'.

The plans they made, for the capture of Dublin Castle, rousing the citizens to their cause, and capturing control of the government, were by no means as farcical as they are sometimes made to appear. Emmet and his followers manufactured large numbers of weapons, principally pikes, and developed their own explosives devices, all of which were carefully stockpiled, and even Hurling Clubs were established in order to provide cover for their drill-practice. But it all went horribly wrong, the result of a litany of mishaps and communications-breakdowns. When the rising did occur, on 23 July 1803, it amounted to little more that some street disturbances in Dublin, during which several government officials were killed. Emmet was later captured, hanged, drawn, and quartered, but not before making a moving speech from the dock which famously concluded: 'When my country takes her place among the nations of the earth, then, and not till then, let my epitaph be written'.

Life Under the Union
When the alarm caused by Emmet's rebellion receded, Irish politics returned to the vacuum they had assumed in the aftermath of the Union. And in the course of time, the inadequacy of that union as an answer to England's Irish problem became apparent. One of the weaknesses inherent from the start was the fact of the continued existence of the Irish government and the full apparatus of the Dublin Castle administration (unlike, for instance, the situation in Scotland after 1707 whereby its government ceased to have a separate existence when Scotland's parliament had been united with that of England). After 1801, therefore, Ireland's legislature was merged with that of Britain, but not its executive: it still had a Viceroy and a Chief Secretary and a raft of other officials answerable to Whitehall but functioning in Dublin. The result, apart from anything else, was that those who thought the extinction of the Irish parliament would bring an end too to the Protestant ascendancy were to be disappointed, because the same sort of people monopolised power after 1801 as had done so before.

The Union, therefore, came to be seen more and more as a bulwark of the

Ascendancy, as the only guarantee against the threat allegedly posed by the country's large Roman Catholic majority. Protestants, while in day-to-day charge of the Dublin administration, no longer had control over their long-term destiny but were instead dependent on Westminster to maintain their position of supremacy. Hence, almost by accident, they found themselves playing the role of a loyal 'garrison' surrounded by a largely hostile 'native' enemy. The irony was that many Catholics had been sympathetic to union because they hoped for better treatment at the hands of Westminster, and Pitt and others had hinted that Emancipation would shortly follow, but instead they too soon saw what the Union had brought. Since union with Great Britain was prolonging the Protestant Ascendancy, it was in the Catholic interest to seek to end it.

Thus, the Union polarised opinion along religious lines: by and large, Protestantism became synonymous with Unionism, and Catholicism with a desire to smash it. How different might the later history of Ireland have been if the Union had quickly delivered their 'emancipation' to Catholics and had religion not come to play such a prominent role in determining views with regard to it: the Catholics and Protestants of Ireland might have been at one in seeking to make the Union work for the benefit of both, or at one in seeking to end it and to pursue a united goal of national independence.

O'Connell and Emancipation

There were, of course, Irish Protestants who wholeheartedly supported the idea of Catholic Emancipation, none more so than Henry Grattan himself: coming out of retirement, he became a member of the British House of Commons in 1805 and devoted the rest of his life, until his death in 1820, to the struggle for Emancipation. But one of the obstacles in the way of its achievement was the conservatism and the fear of rocking the boat that existed among the upper-class spokesmen for the Catholics themselves. It was only when the increasingly more vocal middle-class lawyers and merchants began to make their presence felt that the campaign gained momentum.

By far the most charismatic among their number was Daniel O'Connell, a member of a Catholic landed family in Kerry who had managed to hold on to their estates and had later profited as merchants and indeed smugglers. O'Connell received part of his education in St Omer in France and it is often thought that his lifelong aversion to violence was a product of his experience of its revolution at first hand. Having studied for the bar, he was one of the first batch of Irish Catholics permitted to practise law and, even as a young man in the late 1790s, was one of a limited number of Catholics prominent in their opposition to Castlereagh's plan for a Union.

What really propelled O'Connell on to the national and international stage, however, was his establishment in May 1823 of a new Catholic Association. This might have gone the way of its predecessors had O'Connell not devised, with the support of the parochial clergy, a method whereby it would have a truly popular appeal: while membership was confined to those wealthy enough to afford a guinea a year, the public at large could become associate members by subscribing a penny a month. This became known as the 'Catholic Rent' and was virtually an instantaneous success: from £8 in its first week, within a year it was taking in over £1,000 a week.

Irrespective of the amount collected, the Catholic Rent is significant because it gave its contributors for the first time a real sense of 'ownership' of a political movement, and O'Connell's Catholic Association must rank as one of the most remarkable vehicles of popular politicisation hitherto seen in Europe, let alone Ireland. The fact that its immediate goal, the admission of Roman Catholics to parliament, was a moderate one, likely to benefit only an elite, did not appear to matter. To the Catholics of Ireland their exclusion from parliament, even the British parliament, was a symbol of their exclusion from power and from the determination of their own destiny, and securing 'emancipation' even to this modest extent stood for something much more than that in the popular mind. A deep sense of grievance, a yearning for equality and justice, existed among them. And it is this which Daniel O'Connell managed to tap so brilliantly, using his boundless energy, apparently large-than-life physique, and magnificent oratorical skills to spectacular effect at the mass popular meetings which he began to hold at this point.

The British government, of course, was alarmed by the rapid success of the Catholic Association and tried to prosecute O'Connell and to ban his movement, but their charges were thrown out of court, the Association simply changed its name, and the campaign went on. At the general election of 1826 the voters known as 'forty-shilling freeholders', inspired by O'Connell and backed by the Catholic clergy, withstood the usual pressure from their landlords and elected MPs sympathetic to their cause. Two years later, at a by-election in Clare, O'Connell took the campaign one step further: he gambled on standing for election himself, and won. As a Catholic, he could not take the Oath of Supremacy and the government of Wellington and Robert Peel had little choice but accede to a change in the law. In April 1829 the Catholic Emancipation Act became law; Catholics were allowed to enter parliament and made eligible for all but the most senior offices of state, and Daniel O'Connell was truly, in the eyes of the Catholics of Ireland and of many similarly disenfranchised people throughout the world, the 'Liberator'.

The Aftermath of Emancipation

In some respects the winning of Catholic Emancipation had long-term consequences as important as the passing of the Act of Union itself. One of its consequences arose from the grudging way in which Emancipation was granted – it was accompanied, for instance, by an Act taking the vote away from the forty-shilling freeholders – so that Irish Catholics regarded it as the product of their own agitation rather than the action of a government in which they could place their trust. It had been wrung from an unwilling British government by the power of mass popular agitation, and the message was not lost on future gener-ations: parliamentary politics alone would not yield results unless backed up by extra-parliamen-tary activity. O'Connell knew better than anyone the power of mass popular action and now set his sights on a far more ambitious goal: the repeal of the Act of Union.

What O'Connell sought was not Irish independ-ence and ending the link with Great Britain, but simply the restoration of an Irish parliament, and he was firmly opposed to the use of physical force in its attainment. His vast following shared his goal to varying degrees, but many of them cared not a whit about the restoration of a Dublin par-liament because their day-to-day grievances were far more pressing, and neither did they all have his qualms about the use of violence. The success of the Emancipation campaign had raised expecta-tions that these grievances would be remedied, and when this did not happen – despite O'Connell's best efforts in the House of Commons to obtain reforms for Ireland – there was widespread disap-pointment and anger.

Daniel O'Connell (1775–1847), the nephew and heir of a Catholic landowner in Kerry, first came to note as being one of the few Catholics prominent in opposing the Union in 1800. His skills as a political leader were his oratory, organisational ability and sheer brinkmanship, the last being perhaps his downfall. A hero of moderate Irish nationalists because of his loathing of violence, he was hailed throughout the world in his lifetime as a champion of anti-Semitism and the abolition of slavery.

One of the things the Catholic peasantry felt strongest about was the fact that they were forced to pay 'tithes' for the upkeep of the Protestant clergy. Beginning in Leinster in 1830, and spreading rapidly over much of the country, a campaign of non-payment began, which became known as the Tithe War. Agrarian secret societies – most notably the Whiteboys and Ribbonmen – which O'Connell had kept silent during the Emancipation campaign, resorted to their traditional anti-landlord activities, leading to an explosion in rural crime. The government sought to quell this with a repressive Coercion Act, one effect of which, since public meetings were suppressed, was to limit O'Connell's capacity to mobilise the populace. Therefore, although his slogan during the general election of 1835 had been 'Repeal, sink or swim', O'Connell now embarked on a period of co-operation with the new Whig government in Britain.

The alliance between the O'Connellite MPs and the Whigs, known as the Lichfield House Compact, won some benefits for Ireland, including reform of the police and the magistracy, and the appointment of Catholics to prominent civic offices previously dominated exclusively by Protestants. The sectarian

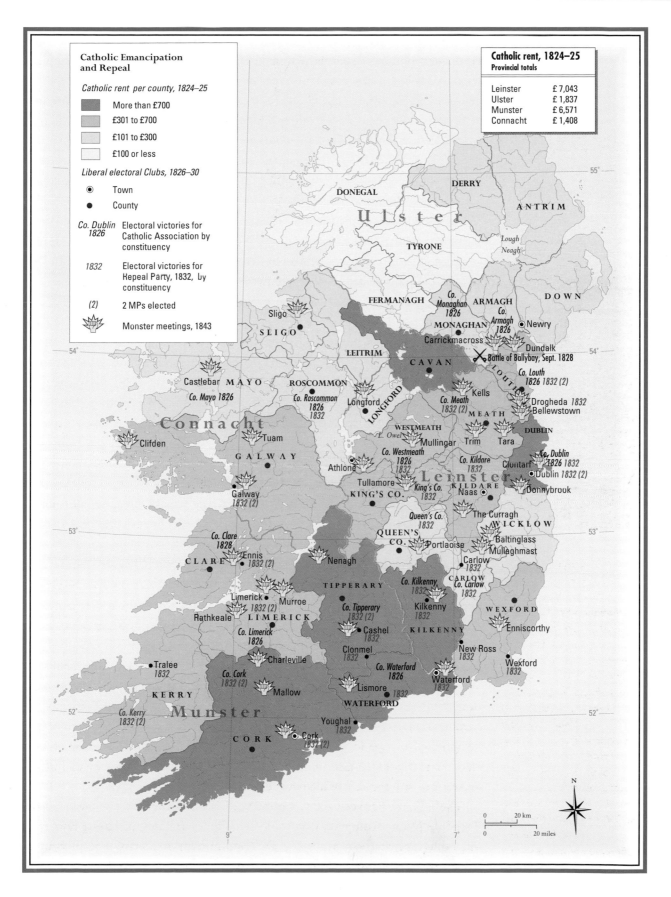

Catholic Emancipation and Repeal

Catholic rent per county, 1824–25

- More than £700
- £301 to £700
- £101 to £300
- £100 or less

Liberal electoral Clubs, 1826–30

- ◉ Town
- ● County

Co. Dublin 1826 — Electoral victories for Catholic Association by constituency

1832 — Electoral victories for Repeal Party, 1832, by constituency

(2) — 2 MPs elected

Monster meetings, 1843

Catholic rent, 1824–25
Provincial totals

Leinster	£ 7,043
Ulster	£ 1,837
Munster	£ 6,571
Connacht	£ 1,408

activities of the Orange Order were also the subject of government intervention: their marches were banned, magistrates with known Orange links were removed, and its influence for the next half-century was greatly reduced, until its revival at the time of the Home Rule campaigns of the 1880s. The question of tithe was also dealt with, and although it was not abolished and the minority established Church of Ireland continued to be maintained by those of other religions, it became less of a cause of complaint. A system of Poor Law was also introduced, far from adequate of course, but it provided some degree of relief for the destitute. Finally, local government was reformed and under the Municipal Corporations Act of 1840 more democratically-accountable elected councils were established: one of the first fruits of it was the election of Daniel O'Connell as Lord Mayor of Dublin, the first Catholic to hold the office in over 150 years.

O'Connell and Repeal

All of these reforms were, however, half-hearted and by no stretch of the imagination could they be considered as evidence that the Union was working. O'Connell's disillusionment with the limited results from his parliamentary alliance increased his conviction that the Act should be repealed, and in April 1840 he founded the National Repeal Association. He won the support of the influential archbishop of Tuam, John MacHale, and as the clergy rallied behind him the people followed. In the short term, his cause was done no harm at all by the establishment in October 1842 of a newspaper known as *The Nation*, which soon had a readership of perhaps 250,000, run by a remarkable group of romantic young Protestant and Catholic radicals who called themselves 'Young Ireland'. Their leaders included Mayo-born John Blake Dillon and Charles Gavan Duffy from Monaghan, but by far the most talented, energetic and idealistic among them was Thomas Davis, born in Mallow, Co. Cork in 1814. Davis, partly because of the popularity of his ballads, most notably 'A Nation Once Again', and partly, no doubt, because of his early death (in 1845 at the age of thirty-one), soon joined Tone and Emmet as the inspiration for this and for later generations of Irish nationalists. To begin with, they backed O'Connell, and his 'Repeal Rent' modelled on the earlier 'Catholic Rent' was soon providing ample funds for a massive campaign to secure Repeal. But this was a much more ambitious task than the campaign for Emancipation and the prospects were not as favourable. For one thing, the forty-shilling freeholders who had earlier helped elect his supporters were now denied the vote. Furthermore, many liberal Protestants had backed the cause of Catholic Emancipation but, with few exceptions, they were anything but enthusiastic about Repeal. Even middle-class Catholics were worried by some of the forces which the Repeal campaign unleashed: they had no objection to the restoration to Ireland of a parliament in which they could participate, but that was probably the extent of their desire to tamper with the status quo, and the ever more militant demands of agrarian 'Ribbonmen' and urban radicals undoubtedly frightened some of them. But the most difficult hurdle O'Connell faced lay, not in Ireland, but in Britain, where public opinion was almost entirely opposed to the break-up of the United Kingdom which Repeal entailed.

O'Connell's tactic was to pressurise the government by holding 'monster meetings' throughout 1843, which he perhaps unwisely declared 'Repeal Year', with the object of demonstrating to the government the strength of his support. Hundreds of thousands gathered to hear him and national and international opinion was largely on his side. But the government of Peel was unyielding. O'Connell used ever more inflammatory language but was still committed to non-violence, and all that the government needed to do was to hold firm and, in effect, call his bluff. This it did on the occasion of his last planned monster meeting of the year, due to be held, quite deliberately, on the site of Brian Boru's great victory at Clontarf, outside Dublin. On the eve of the meeting, which was intended to be the largest yet, the government banned it, and O'Connell, true to his constitutional principles, cancelled the meeting. It was the turning-point in his career.

The Young Irelanders

In a sense, the O'Connell bubble was burst. Those of his followers for whom he had an almost messianic appeal and who regarded him as invincible saw his action in calling off the Clontarf meeting as surrender. His vast popular prestige began to seep away. It was only a matter of time before the Repeal Association would begin to fracture, and the crunch issue came over religion. When in 1845 the government proposed the establishment of a new University in Ireland with constituent colleges at Belfast, Cork and Galway, O'Connell opposed the legislation because the Queen's Colleges were to be secular institutions. He, along with Archbishop MacHale and others, condemned them as 'Godless Colleges' but the Young Irelanders, who included Protestants and Catholics in their ranks, favoured the Colleges for this very reason, since they believed that sectarianism was damaging to the cause of national unity, and fundamentally disagreed with the tendency of O'Connell to identify the cause of Ireland with that of Catholicism.

These differences between the Young Irelanders and O'Connell were very real. Daniel O'Connell was, first and foremost, a Roman Catholic and in many respects he did lasting damage to Ireland's cause by being content to confine his appeal to Catholics. He was a pragmatic politician who pursued legislative and governmental reform, but the compromises that this involved and the co-operation with government which was part and parcel of O'Connell's *modus operandi*, were suspect in the eyes of youthful idealists like Thomas Davis and his associates. Above all else, though, O'Connell was not a doctrinaire nationalist and valued the connection with the Crown, while Young Ireland, on the other hand, was committed to the cause of Irish independence. And here lay the crux, because national independence, they believed, might have to be fought for. *The Nation* newspaper was effused with a pride in those who had earlier fought and died for Irish freedom, and implicit in this was the belief that it was justified. This view is well captured in perhaps the greatest song of the age, 'The Memory of the Dead', written by John Kells Ingram, later Vice-Provost of Trinity College and President of the Royal Irish Academy, which was published in *The Nation* in 1843:

> *Who fears to speak of Ninety-eight, who blushes at the name?*
> *When cowards mock the patriot's fate, who hangs his head for shame?*
> *He's all a knave or half a slave, who slights his country thus;*
> *But a true man, like you, man, will fill your glass with us.*
>
> *We drink the memory of the brave, the faithful and the few;*
> *Some lie far off beyond the wave, some sleep in Ireland, too;*
> *All, all are gone; but still lives on the fame of those who died;*
> *All true men, like you, men, remember them with pride.*

When, in the summer of 1846, O'Connell moved a resolution committing the Repeal Association to the view that violence could never be justified in pursuit of national freedom, a split with the Young Irelanders was inevitable. They had as yet no plans for a rising, but refused to rule it out in all circumstances, and withdrew from the Association. In January 1847 they set up a rival body, the Irish Confederation, under the leadership (since Thomas Davis was now dead) of a Protestant landlord MP, William Smith O'Brien. A month later in the House of Commons O'Connell made his last speech in favour of Repeal and, knowing that he was close to death, set off for Rome, but died at Genoa on 15 May. Whatever his faults, his life was devoted to the service of his country, he was a man of quite the most extraordinary ability, and it is doubtful if any other single individual has had as great an impact on modern Irish history.

The 1848 Rebellion

O'Connell's death marked the end of an era, and this was highlighted by the decision of the Young Irelanders to defy his non-violent policy and return to the methods of the men of '98: it is significant, too, that when the most radical of their number, the Ulster Presbyterian John Mitchel, founded a new journal in 1848 he chose to name it *The United Irishman*. Mitchel called on the people 'to strike for a republic...to raise the Irish tricolour, orange, white and green, over a forest of Irish pikes'. When revolution broke out that same year in France the Young Irelanders sent a delegation to Paris to seek the support of the new revolutionary régime for their cause. The British government responded by sentencing Mitchel to transportation and prohibiting membership of the Confederation, so that the leadership decided to gamble on a rebellion before it was too late. But their preparations were woefully inadequate and conditions in the country far from suitable for an insurrection. What became know as the 'cabbage patch' rebellion fizzled out in the Widow McCormack's cottage in Ballingarry, Co. Tipperary, and Ireland's 1848 revolution was at an end.

The events of '48 did have long-term effects. The Young Ireland leaders were either transported or fled overseas. Some became remarkably successful in

public life elsewhere, others were later to feature prominently in what became the Fenian movement. The latter, in their new homes, principally in North America, kept alive the hatred of British rule and the dream of ending it by a more successful military strike and by the propagation of the doctrine of revolutionary republicanism. In the New World, their condemnation of British injustice in Ireland found a ready audience because, when, in 1848, they had donned their uniforms for their desperate rebellion, they did so against the almost surreal backdrop of a national catastrophe, a famine which forced literally millions of their compatriots into the grave or the emigrant ship. It truly was, in the words of the contemporary author of 'The Wearing of the Green', 'the most distressful country that ever yet was seen'.

This is McArt's Fort overlooking Belfast Lough as painted by Andrew Nicholls (d. 1886). It was chosen by the United Irishmen as their meeting place because of its ancient legendary associations.

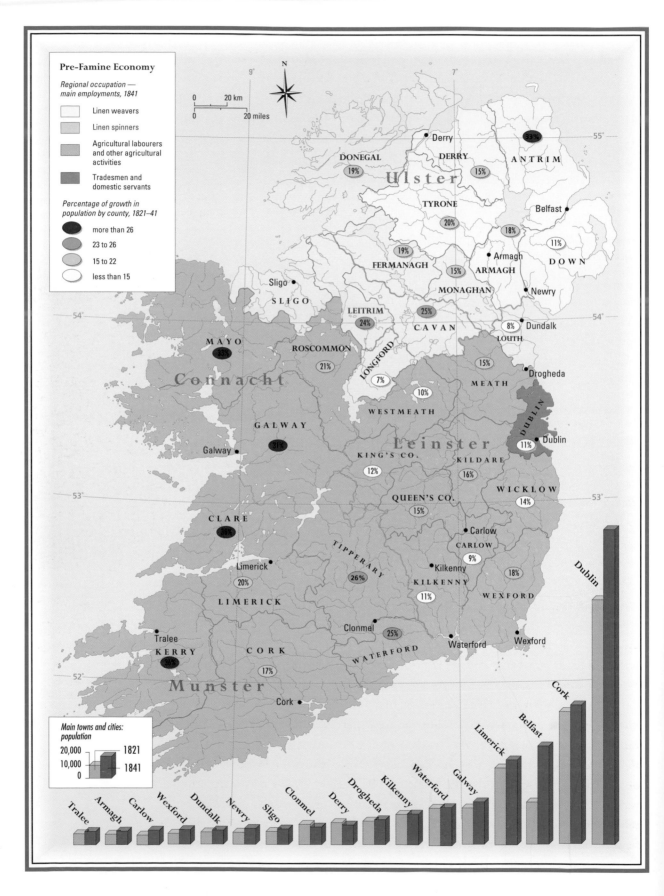

Pre-Famine Economy

*Regional occupation —
main employments, 1841*

Linen weavers

Linen spinners

Agricultural labourers
and other agricultural
activities

Tradesmen and
domestic servants

*Percentage of growth in
population by county, 1821–41*

more than 26

23 to 26

15 to 22

less than 15

N

9°   7°

0   20 km
0   20 miles

55°

Derry

DONEGAL
19%

DERRY
15%

ANTRIM
33%

U l s t e r

Belfast

TYRONE
20%

18%

11%

FERMANAGH
19%

ARMAGH
15%

Armagh

D O W N

MONAGHAN
15%

Newry

Sligo

SLIGO

LEITRIM
24%

CAVAN
25%

8% Dundalk

54°

54°

LOUTH

MAYO
33%

ROSCOMMON
21%

LONGFORD
7%

15%

Drogheda

M E A T H

DUBLIN
11%

WESTMEATH
10%

GALWAY
31%

C o n n a c h t

L e i n s t e r

Dublin

Galway

KING'S CO.
12%

KILDARE
16%

WICKLOW
14%

53°

53°

QUEEN'S CO.
15%

CLARE
40%

Carlow

CARLOW
9%

Dublin

Limerick

TIPPERARY
26%

Kilkenny

KILKENNY
11%

WEXFORD
18%

LIMERICK
20%

Clonmel
25%

Tralee

KERRY
36%

CORK
17%

WATERFORD

Waterford

Wexford

Cork

M u n s t e r

52°

Cork

Belfast

Limerick

Galway

*Main towns and cities:
population*

20,000
10,000
0

1821
1841

Tralee
Armagh
Carlow
Wexford
Dundalk
Newry
Sligo
Clonmel
Derry
Drogheda
Kilkenny
Waterford

CHAPTER VII

FROM FAMINE TO FREEDOM

The great potato famine of 1845–49 is generally regarded, and not without reason, as one of the most significant watersheds in Irish history. It is true that many of the processes which it so rapidly and so horrifically accelerated were already in train before the blight struck, and that crop failures, food shortages and mass emigration were not new to the Ireland of the 1840s. But the scale of the catastrophe that was the Great Famine had not hitherto been felt. Economic historians differ in their analyses of cause and effect, but none can deny the centrality of Ireland's over-reliance on the potato.

The Potato Failure

A stranger to the Old World until the discovery of the New, the potato gained a remarkable grip on Irish dietary patterns by the eighteenth century which has remained unchallenged until recent decades. The reason is a combination of its nutritional value (which meant that the poor could live on virtually potatoes alone), its storage-life (the crop harvested in late summer was still edible and nutritious into and beyond the following spring), and its

In the period from 1300 to 1900 there were up to 30 severe famines in Ireland, about a dozen in the period 1290–1400 alone, and another dozen between 1500 and 1750. After 1750 there were several serious regional famines, culminating in the great national famine of 1845–49.

prolific fertility (which made it cheap and meant that one small landholding could produce enough to feed a large family for almost an entire year). Problems only arose when the crop failed. Potato-failure was a factor as far back as the severe famine of 1740–41, and it failed either partially or totally in 14 out of the 27 seasons between 1816 and 1842.

Many contemporaries were extremely concerned about over-reliance on such a volatile staple and warnings of impending danger grew ever more frequent. But what brought disaster in the end was attack by a fungal disease, *phytophthora infestans*, hitherto new to Ireland. It thrived on the mild, moist conditions of the Irish climate and although its first strike in 1845 was by no means universal, it was the return of the blight in the following year that had such horrendous consequences. Even when it failed to appear in 1847 it made little difference to many people because there had been a lack of seed potatoes for planting and the crop was therefore low. The blight returned with a vengeance

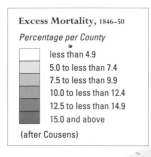

Excess Mortality, 1846–50

Percentage per County

	less than 4.9
	5.0 to less than 7.4
	7.5 to less than 9.9
	10.0 to less than 12.4
	12.5 to less than 14.9
	15.0 and above

(after Cousens)

in 1848, and struck again to a lesser extent in 1849, but by 1850 had all but run its course. The result was that throughout the latter half of the 1840s, over vast tracts of the country where dependence on the potato was near-total, Ireland experienced a crisis of cataclysmic proportions.

The Government's Response

Arguably, no nineteenth-century government was capable of handling such a disaster, and certainly not one imbued with contemporary notions of 'political economy', usually summed up in the callous phrase *laissez-faire*, which discouraged large-scale state intervention. To be fair, though, the response of the government of Sir Robert Peel to the outbreak of famine in Ireland was quite prompt: in November 1845 he ordered the purchase of £100,000-worth of Indian corn in the United States for shipment to Cork – but not to feed the hungry, rather to keep food prices down. A Relief Commission was set up at the same time, with the task of establishing local Relief Committees, run by magistrates, clergy, and well-to-do ratepayers, who would raise funds and distribute food. The third measure introduced was the provision of employment by having the Board of Works construct new roads.

The man given the task of overseeing this programme was Charles Trevelyan, Assistant Secretary to the British Treasury, who, in common with prevailing civil service opinion, did not believe in 'handouts', and considered that compelling those in need of assistance to build a

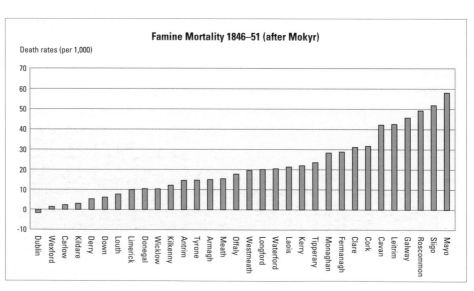

Famine Mortality 1846–51 (after Mokyr)

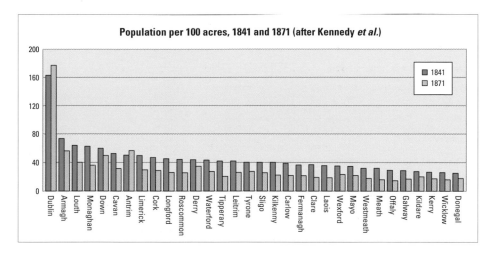

road going nowhere, or a wall encircling nothing, or a pier where no boats could land, in return for meagre pay, was preferable to feeding them. He has tended to be singled out for opprobrium when, in fact, his views were commonplace. Nevertheless, it is hard to see much in the way of a humanitarian streak in the man. At the height of the Famine, Trevelyan wrote an anonymous piece entitled 'The Irish Crisis' in which he sought to justify the continued export of food from Ireland, criticised those who thought that 'the government

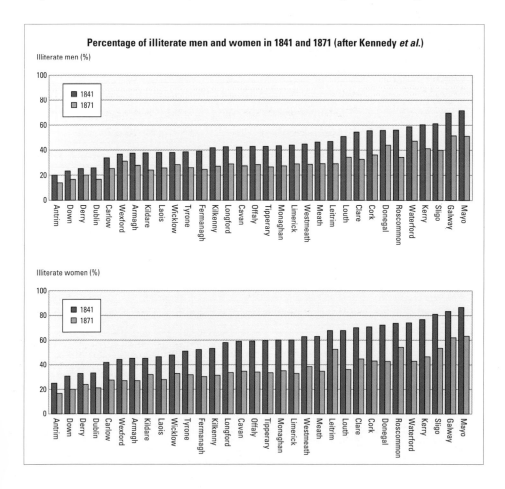

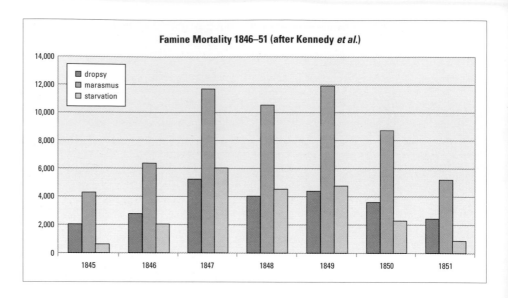

Famine Mortality 1846–51 (after Kennedy *et al.*)

should be made to support the people, instead of the people the government', and implied that famine was simply God's way of relieving over-population.

In July 1846, Peel was replaced as Prime Minister by Lord John Russell, but within a matter of days it became clear that the potato crop had again failed in Ireland and that this failure was far more widespread than the previous year. The crisis facing the population is captured in the contemporary words of Fr Theobald Mathew, the remarkable leader of Ireland's Temperance movement: 'On the 27th of last month [July] I passed from Cork to Dublin, and this doomed plant bloomed in all the luxuriance of an abundant harvest. Returning on the 3rd instant [August], I beheld with sorrow one wide waste of putrefying vegetation. In many places the wretched people were seated on the fences of their decaying gardens, wringing their hands, and wailing bitterly the destruction that had left them foodless'.

The government's response? It was not its job to feed the masses; that was to

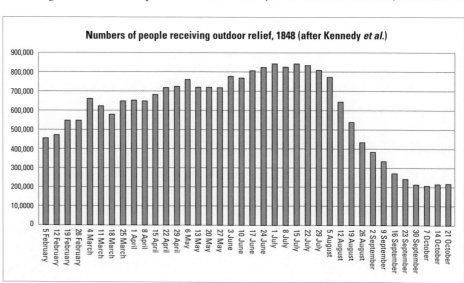

Numbers of people receiving outdoor relief, 1848 (after Kennedy *et al.*)

This illustration shows the soup kitchen run by the Cork Society of Friends and published as part of a report on conditions in Ireland in The Illustrated London News *on 16 January 1847. In addition to food, the Society was to the fore in providing cooking equipment, clothing, money and seeds.*

be left to private charity, and landlords should take responsibility for their own tenants. The problem was that landlords whose tenants were unable to pay their rents were themselves facing bankruptcy; others took the opportunity of their tenants' misfortune to clear their estates by mass eviction. Private charity did Trojan work to keep as many as possible alive. Some benevolent landlords were to the fore but most fondly remembered are the soup-kitchens of the Society of Friends (Quakers). Unlike some other denominations they did not offer help in return for a conversion from Catholicism, the phenomenon known as 'souperism'; although its presence has no doubt been exaggerated, the tactic was indeed employed and the insult of having 'taken the soup' had a potent force for generations to come.

Total Numbers in Workhouses, 1844–53 (after Nicholls)

Year	Number of Workhouses in Operation	Total No. of Persons Relieved During the Year
1844	113	105,358
1845	123	114,205
1846	130	243,933
1847	130	417,139
1848	131	610,463
1849	131	932,284
1850	163	805,702
1851	163	707,443
1852	163	504,864
1853	163	396,438

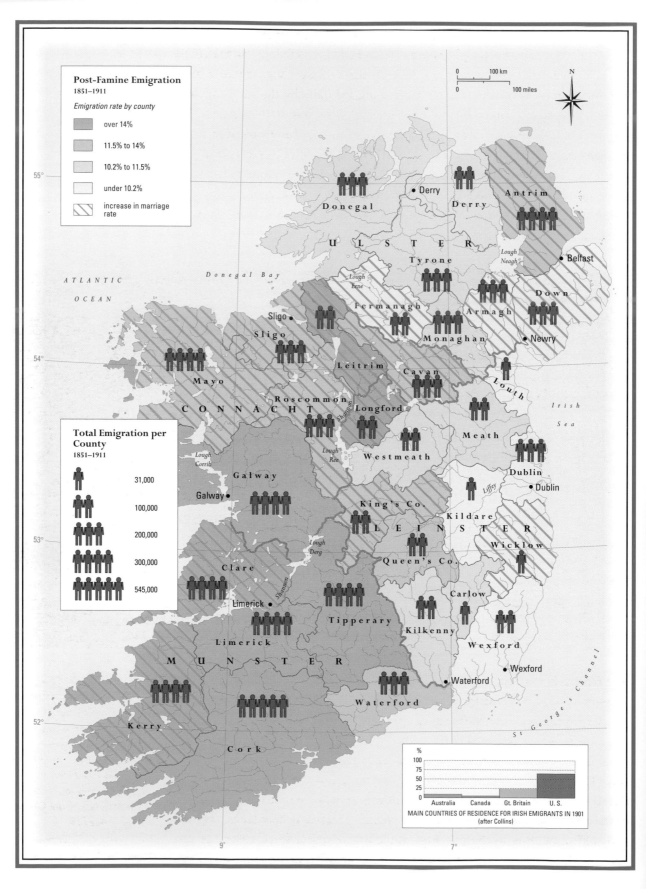

Post-Famine Emigration
1851–1911

Emigration rate by county

- over 14%
- 11.5% to 14%
- 10.2% to 11.5%
- under 10.2%
- increase in marriage rate

Total Emigration per County
1851–1911

- 31,000
- 100,000
- 200,000
- 300,000
- 545,000

MAIN COUNTRIES OF RESIDENCE FOR IRISH EMIGRANTS IN 1901
(after Collins)

By the early weeks of 1847 even the new Whig government realised it would have to change tack: the people would have to be fed, and fed out of the public purse. The change in policy was slow to take effect, but by August 1847 almost half the population of the country were being fed daily by the state. By now, though, disease was rampant, and 'poor-houses', fever hospitals, and local dispensaries could not cope with the vast hordes of human beings reduced to little more than skeletons who thronged to them; apart from anything else, the Poor Law dictated that they be turned away if they possessed more than a quarter of an acre of land. Those who failed to meet this criterion either sought salvation in exile or immured themselves in their infested cabins and rotted to death before winter's end.

The Effects of the Famine

Those parts of the country most affected by the Famine were those where subsistence farming on tiny holdings was prevalent, primarily the west (especially Mayo, Sligo, Roscommon, Galway and Clare) and south-west (especially Cork), while Cos. Cavan and Leitrim were also badly hit. In south-east Leinster (especially Cos. Dublin, Kildare, Carlow and Wexford) and north-east Ulster, where the economy was more diversified, the effects were far less severe. Even in the towns and cities, however, mortality was significant, partly because of the ease with which the fever (including cholera, typhus, relapsing fever, dysentery and scurvy), which accompanied the food shortage, spread in an urban environment.

This photograph of so-called 'lazy beds' (potato cultivation ridges) on Djouce Mountain high above sea level in the Wicklow Mountains shows the extent to which Ireland's over-population in the period before the Great Famine forced the exploitation of hitherto inhospitable landscapes.

This illustration of the famine-stricken village of Tullig appeared in The Illustrated London News *on 15 December 1849, but by then the generosity of the British public had been blunted by repetition of the tragic conditions of the masses. Besides, Great Britain had itself suffered a severe economic recession in 1847, and its sympathy for Ireland's problems had waned following the return of 36 Irish MPs in the general election of that year committed to Repeal of the Act of Union. This smacked of ingratitude in the eyes of the British public, a view compounded by the Young Ireland rebellion of 1848.*

Those who suffered most severely were the labouring classes, followed by very small-scale farmers. It is difficult to be accurate, but it seems that the population of Ireland stood at about 8,200,000 on the eve of the Famine (making it one of the most densely-populated countries in Europe), and that between 1845 and 1851 this was reduced by about 2,250,000. Of these, perhaps 1,500,000 emigrated: in 1851 alone, as many as a quarter of a million fled the country. The exodus continued, of course, so that throughout the twentieth century the population remained at not much more than half its pre-Famine level. It is harder to calculate the number of deaths, but they amounted to at least a million, more of them from disease than actual starvation.

After the Famine there was a large reduction in the number of tiny holdings: in 1831 as much as 45 per cent of the land of Ireland may have been made up of 'farms' of five acres or less; by 1851, this figure stood at 15 per cent. In the same period, the number of farms of thirty acres or more increased from 17 to 26 per cent. And among the latter group, the rearing of livestock increased. The practice of land-division between sons was abandoned, and one son succeeded to the whole farm: he often had a long wait, however, and this may have contributed to the noticeable rise in the age at which people married and an increasing tendency not to marry at all. In terms of religion, it seems likely that the Famine strengthened the practice and power of Catholicism: there was one priest for every 3,000 of the population in 1840, but thirty years later the ratio was halved. The Famine also drastically hastened the abandonment of the Irish language, all the more so since the language had been strongest in those areas most heavily affected.

The Political Fallout

In the political sphere, the Famine could not but increase anti-English feeling in the country and among Irish emigrants, while hatred of the landlord-system also inevitably increased. In 1849 alone at least 16,000 families were evicted from their holdings and in October a Tenant Protection Society was founded in

Callan, Co. Kilkenny, with the aim of having rents independently fixed, and getting the agreement of farmers not to take up the lands of evicted tenants. Within a year at least 20,000 more families were evicted and perhaps twenty similar tenant societies had sprung up throughout the country, which were combined together in Dublin in August 1850 in the Tenant League. Its aims were to get lower rents, and more secure tenure, and to establish on a legal footing the custom known as the Ulster tenant-right (which gave northern tenants security against eviction so long as they paid their rent).

Among the leaders of the Tenant League was the former Young Irelander, Gavan Duffy, who advocated that they pursue their agenda by forming an independent Irish party in parliament, and in the election of 1852 their supporters numbered 48 out of the total of 105 Irish MPs at Westminster. But this attempt to establish an independent Irish party, which would act as a constant opposition in parliament, pledged to securing its demands, was a dismal failure, and both it and the Tenant League had collapsed within a few years, partly because of the opposition of the Archbishop of Dublin, Paul Cullen, who was suspicious of Duffy's involvement in view of his past history. Many of its members defected to the government side, many failed to get re-elected because of the

The revolutionary movement popularly known as Fenianism originated in the hugely expanding Irish immigrant community in the USA, whose attention remained focused on Ireland as a result of their difficulties in integrating and the prejudice they experienced. While in theory a secret society it quickly attracted police attention when it put itself on a national footing, and its rising was a dismal failure, though the government's handling of it helped mobilise nationalist opinion in a way the Fenians themselves had never managed.

1865 would perhaps have been the optimum year for a Fenian rising, since the movement had established a strong urban base and recruited successfully among the British army and the Irish community in Britain. But a pre-emptive swoop by the authorities in that year led to the arrest and imprisonment of many of the leaders and thereafter the organisation was very much on the defensive and lacking in direction. After the failure of the rising held two years later the large-scale imprisonment and ill-treatment of many of the participants did, ironically, produce benefits for the organisation through public agitation for an amnesty for the prisoners.

sheer expense involved, but most damaging of all was their failure to realise, as O'Connell before them and Parnell and Davitt after them proved so effectively, that parliamentary activity on its own was not enough, unless backed by a powerful mass movement at home. The result, by the early 1860s, was disillusionment with constitutional methods and a renewed faith in the potential of armed rebellion.

Fenianism

The natural successor to the Young Ireland movement was Fenianism. Many of the Young Ireland leaders found succour abroad, mostly in North America and Britain, but several of them, most notably James Stephens, Michael Doheny and John O'Mahony, began their exile as refugees in Paris. Stephens later moved to America and in 1856 returned to Ireland where, on St Patrick's Day, he founded a new organisation 'to make Ireland an independent democratic republic'. It was a secret society (at least in theory), so much so that it began with no name and only later became known as the IRB, or Irish Republican Brotherhood. It was John O'Mahony's love of Ireland's literary and mythological past that gave the movement their more familiar name, the Fenians – after Fionn Mac Cumhaill's legendary warrior-band, Na Fianna – a term which still has potent resonances today.

In Ireland, Stephens was aided by Thomas Clarke Luby, and soon made contact with Jeremiah O'Donovan Rossa, who had recently founded his own 'Phoenix Society' in Skibbereen, Co. Cork. From 1858 onwards the movement spread rapidly, intent upon an early insurrection. In order to spread the word, Stephens founded a newspaper called *The Irish People*, which provided a forum for the work of the Tipperarymen Charles Kickham, author of the famous novel, *Knocknagow*, and the indefatigable John O'Leary, inspiration of Yeats's famous line 'Romantic Ireland's dead and gone, it's with O'Leary in the grave'. However, the efforts of Kickham and O'Leary were often diverted from the business of spreading the Fenian message to defending themselves from the Catholic Church's opposition, since, as a secret oath-bound society, they were suspected of being atheist and socialist, and were consistently condemned by Cardinal Cullen, and most memorably by Bishop Moriarty of Kerry who thought that 'eternity is not long enough, nor hell hot enough' to punish them for their sins! One consequence, though, of the clerical opposition to Fenianism, and the Fenian insistence that the church keep out of politics, was that it perpetuated an Irish republicanism in the tradition of Tone and Davis, and averted the equation of nation and Catholicism which had been such a feature of O'Connellite politics.

The Fenian Rising

The efforts of the Fenians to put their ideals into practice were delivered a hammer-blow in September 1865 when the government raided the offices of *The Irish People*, and arrested most of the leaders. Real leadership of the organisation was now taken over by a young Kildareman and former member of the French Foreign Legion, John Devoy. He embarked on a risky scheme of swearing into the Brotherhood Irish soldiers based in British regiments around the country, especially in the Dublin garrison. But the technical head of the movement was still James Stephens and, for whatever reason, he refused to authorise a rising and instead left for America, while Devoy was himself captured in February 1866, and it seemed that the optimum moment had passed.

Nevertheless, in America Stephens encountered many Irishmen who had fought in the recently-ended Civil War, trained soldiers, eager for revenge on the enemy back home. The question was: how best to go about this? Some favoured a rebellion in Ireland, but another wing believed what, with hindsight, seems a bizarre notion, that the Fenian cause could best be promoted by an invasion of Canada! The hope was that this might provoke an outbreak of hostilities between the United States and Britain which they could then capitalise upon; they tried it, not once but three times, in 1866, 1870 and 1871, but on each occasion it was, as one might expect, a rather pathetic failure. Stephens favoured direct intervention in Ireland, but his aims were stymied by a personal animosity between himself and the head of the American Fenians, John O'Mahony. The other major difficulty that was becoming apparent was that

A complex character, the British Prime Minister William Ewart Gladstone (1809–98) developed an interest in Ireland for a number of reasons: one was a sense of moral responsibility, another a genuine belief that Ireland was a separate nation which needed distinct treatment, and a third a conviction that the preservation of the United Kingdom depended on constitutional reform.

this so-called secret society was riddled with informers.

Nevertheless, a rising was at length attempted. On the night of 5 March 1867 – as ill-luck would have it, a night of heavy snow – groups of Fenians answered the call to arms in seven counties: in Cork, there may have been up to 4,000 rebels, in Dublin perhaps half that number, and smaller groups in Limerick, Tipperary, Clare, Waterford and Louth. But, especially in view of the prevailing weather conditions, it was a hopeless case. Many were arrested and, although none were sentenced to death, long imprisonments and harsh treatment were meted out to them, so that – as happened in the case of the execution of the 1916 leaders – public opinion soon turned in their favour.

Some months later this became all the more the case when one of the leaders of the rising, Thomas J. Kelly, was arrested in Manchester. Three of his comrades – Allen, Larkin and O'Brien – accidentally killed a police-guard in rescuing him, and were executed. Soon they became known as the 'Manchester Martyrs' and the effect of their death, combined with the growing sympathy for the other Fenian rebels who had been prepared to give their lives for this cause, was to reinforce the power of the 'physical force tradition' in Ireland, and to convince future generations of the nobility of fighting for Irish freedom.

There was one other by-product of 1867. Later that year, some Fenians attempted to blow up the wall of Clerkenwell prison in London, but killed several innocent people. In general, English public opinion was understandably outraged by this, but it seems to have prompted others to ponder what motivated the perpetrators, and to think in terms, not of repression and revenge, but rather of trying to remove the causes of such violence. The most influential of those was William Ewart Gladstone.

Gladstone and Ireland

Mid-Victorian England was dominated by two great political parties each in turn dominated by two outstanding leaders, the Conservatives under Disraeli and Gladstone's Liberals. Both had an interest in Ireland but in the end it was Gladstone's conscience which prompted action. He believed that Irish violence was a product of Irish grievance and famously stated in the year of the Fenian Rising that those grievances needed to be addressed, so that 'instead of hearing in every corner of Europe the most painful commentaries on the policy of England towards Ireland we may be able to look our fellow Europeans in the face'. When swept to power in the following year he began by turning his attention to the question of disestablishing the Church of Ireland. The need to address the issue had been made patently clear by the publication of the results of the 1861 census, which showed that out of a population of 5.75 million, 4.5 were Catholics, and members of the established Church amounted to no more than 700,000. When Gladstone himself steered the Irish Church Act (1869) through parliament, breaking the official connection between Church and State in Ireland, it marked the beginning of the end of the Protestant Ascendancy.

Gladstone next turned his attention to securing a fairer relationship between landlords and tenants, and in 1870 passed the first of a series of Land Acts which were to revolutionise the tenure of land in Ireland. In order to protect the rights of tenant farmers, Gladstone sought to give legal status to the so-called Ulster 'custom' whereby tenants had security of tenure so long as their paid their rent (of course, a landlord who wanted rid of a tenant had merely to raise his rent to a level the latter could not afford, and then evict him). Under the Act, some tenants without the benefit of the custom could be compensated for disturbance and for improvements they had made to their holding, if evicted in spite of having paid their rent. Finally, tenants could borrow money from the government towards the cost of buying their holdings, though the terms were severe and few could afford to do so. Nevertheless, it was a first step on the road to solving 'the Land Question'.

The Origins of 'Home Rule'

Land, however, was only part of England's 'Irish problem'. As might be expected, the failure of the Fenian rising gave a spur to advocates of peaceful methods of securing constitutional reform for Ireland. The Home Rule movement was initially the creation of one man, Isaac Butt, a lawyer who from conservative beginnings earned the respect of Irish nationalists

Charles Stewart Parnell (1846–91) established his political power through leadership of the Land War, and by portraying an image of himself that appealed to both moderates and extremists alike. His great achievement was in obtaining land reform, especially the 1881 Land Act, and bringing Irish Home Rule to the centre of British politics through a disciplined and independent parliamentary party and an alliance with Gladstonian Liberalism.

for defending Young Irelanders and Fenians, and for campaigning for an amnesty for the latter. In May 1870 he established in Dublin the Home Government Association, in order to mobilise opinion behind his demand for a federal solution to the government of Ireland. This differed from O'Connell's Repeal idea in only one major respect: Butt too sought the return of a parliament to Ireland, but, unlike the majority of Irish nationalists, he believed that Ireland should continue to be represented at Westminster.

In 1873 Butt set up a new body, the Home Rule League, and the cause of Home Rule was helped greatly by the Electoral Reform Act of the previous year which had introduced for the first time the free ballot and had greatly extended the vote among less wealthy sections of the population. The result was that in the ensuing elections, 59 Irish MPs were returned on a Home Rule ticket. They were not a political party as such and their capacity to deliver on their election promises was severely hampered by Gladstone's loss of power to Disraeli and the Conservatives. The British government could perhaps have been compelled to deal with Irish reform but it was Butt's view that the only way self-government could be obtained for Ireland was if Irish MPs showed themselves deserving of it, and that meant behaving like gentlemen and not rocking the boat.

Other Home Rulers, however, were impatient with this conciliatory and moderate approach, and the most active proponent of a more aggressive stance in parliament was the remarkable Belfast merchant, Joseph Biggar. Elected to parliament in 1874, he was on the Supreme Council of the IRB within a year, and, having little regard for the niceties of British party politics and House of Commons procedure, embarked on a campaign of obstruction in the House designed to force attention to Irish affairs, much to the disgust of Butt. Biggar, however, had not the dynamism or, to be honest, the family background essential for leadership in that age, and only the success in a by-election in Meath in April 1875 of a young man called Charles Stewart Parnell brought hope of a vigorous new approach.

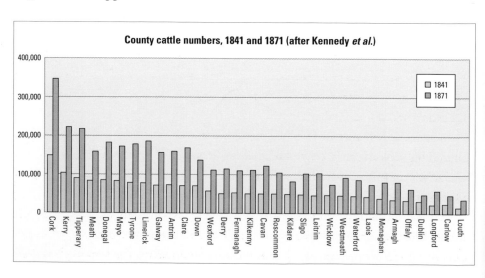

The Rise of Parnell

Charles Stewart Parnell was an Irish Protestant landlord. His mother, Delia Stewart, was, however, an American who was strongly anti-English, while his Parnell antecedents had opposed the Act of Union and supported Catholic Emancipation. He himself later recalled that it was Fenianism which first attracted him to politics, along with stories of the 1798 rebellion heard during his childhood on the family estate at Avondale in Co. Wicklow. He seems to have inherited his mother's Anglophobia, though personal experience of English condescension during his aborted studies at Cambridge may also have played a part.

Upon entering parliament Parnell strongly supported the obstructionist tactics employed by Biggar, and it was this rather than his early, faltering oratorical skills, that caught the attention of leading Fenians. The prominent activist J.J. O'Kelly met with Parnell in Paris in the summer of 1877 and wrote back to John Devoy, one of the leaders of the powerful Irish-American Fenian society, Clan na Gael, describing him simply as 'cool – extremely so – and resolute'. When the breach with Butt finally came within days, Parnell replaced him as president of the Home Rule Confederation of Great Britain, and as Butt's stature and health declined (he died in 1879), Parnell's star rose. What ensured his widespread support was his ability to be all things to all men, the product of the ambivalence of his language on the question of politics versus violence, parliamentary agitation or national revolution. All that was needed was an issue around which he could marshal a nationwide campaign.

The 'New Departure'

From the mid-1870s there had been an agricultural depression in Ireland which resulted in many tenants, unable to pay their rents, being evicted. There was also a widespread potato-failure, particularly in Connacht, the poorest of the provinces, and famine was imminent. In the spring of 1879 a young emigrant named Michael Davitt, who had grown up in Lancashire when his family had been evicted in the Great Famine, returned to his native Mayo and saw the misery afflicting the tenantry. Though previously active as an IRB man, and having served a long sentence for gun-running, his Mayo visit, and participation in April in a tenants' protest meeting at Irishtown, convinced him that the Land Question should take priority.

In June, Davitt met in Dublin with Parnell and John Devoy, both of whom shared his view of the need to improve the tenants' lot. Devoy, furthermore, had a plan for what he called a New Departure, whereby Home Rule and the Land Question would be pursued simultaneously, with the ultimate goal of securing Irish freedom and peasant proprietorship, with or without the use of armed force. Whether or not Davitt and Parnell shared Devoy's view is a subject of debate, though Devoy certainly thought they did: Davitt, the tenant's son, was

The Land War, in origin a campaign of agrarian protest, succeeded in developing a rhetoric which challenged the legitimacy of the very system of landlordism in Ireland and equating it with the British connection. It became a massive nationalist mobilisation which provided the basis for Parnell's political triumphs.

certainly won over (soon, to the exclusion of all else) to solving the land question but turned his back on political revolution; for Parnell, the landlord, on the other hand, the land issue was more of a tactic – though he was certainly moved by the tenants' plight – and legislative independence remained the ultimate goal.

The Land War

In any case, there was enough agreement between them for Parnell to accept the position of President of a new organisation called the Irish National Land League, founded by Davitt in October 1879. Its aims were to protect tenants from rack-renting landlords and unjust eviction, but ultimately, as its slogan – 'the land of Ireland for the people of Ireland' – emphatically made clear, to make them owners of their own farms. It was a mass movement which sought to employ moral as opposed to physical force, though the latter, from the start, was an unhappy feature of what soon became known as the Land War. The League organised popular demonstrations against evictions, and campaigned with spectacular success against those tempted to take over the holdings of the evicted. Any man who did so was ostracised by his neighbours, shunned, as Parnell put it, 'as if he were a leper of old', and when the policy was extended from their fellow tenant-farmers to a landlord's agent, Captain Boycott, it gave a new word to the English language.

The Land League's short-term demands were largely met by a Land Act introduced by Gladstone in 1881, which conceded what were known as 'the 3 Fs': fair rents, fixity of tenure, and free sale. The first would be decided by judicial arbitration by a new Land Commission, and it was hoped that so long as the tenant paid the agreed amount he would be secure from eviction and could get a fair price for any improvements he had made should he decide to vacate his holding. It was a half-hearted measure designed to restore calm in Ireland and it certainly took much of the wind out of the Land League's sails. Parnell was faced with a difficult choice in deciding whether to support it, and lose his more radical followers, or reject it and forfeit moderate opinion. As ever, he performed a high-wire balancing act on the subject and at the appropriate moment conveniently got himself thrown into Kilmainham jail, from which he wrote to his mistress, Katharine O'Shea: 'Politically it is a fortunate thing for me that I have been arrested, as the movement is breaking fast and all will be quiet in a few months, when I shall be released'.

What had happened was that the 1881 Land Act had broken the unity of the Land League. Its leaders, like Parnell, were now in prison under the terms of new draconian coercion laws, agrarian violence having replaced the earlier mass peaceful agitation. But Parnell was the only political figure capable of restoring order in the country and Gladstone now released him in May 1882 under the terms of the so-called Kilmainham 'Treaty'. This brought some amendments to the provisions of the Land Act and an end to coercion, in return for Parnell's promise of support for future Liberal reforms and disavowal of agrarian unrest. Such a compromise was bound to lose Parnell his radical backing and the coalition of Land Leaguers, Home Rulers and Fenians was doomed. The collapse of the movement was, however, delayed by the assassination at that very point, in the Phoenix Park, of the new Chief

Parnell's beloved Avondale, near Rathdrum, Co. Wicklow, was built in 1779 for Samuel Hayes, an amateur architect who may have designed it himself. It passed to William Parnell-Hayes, grandfather of the great nationalist leader, who was actually born in the house and lived there for most of his life with his mother and older brother. He is said to have panned for gold in the Avonmore River which runs through the estate, from which he had a ring made for his future wife, Katharine O'Shea.

Secretary for Ireland and his Under-Secretary. The British government reacted by reintroducing coercion, opposition to which helped paper over the cracks in the movement, but when the storm abated the Parnell who emerged was one committed, not to land agitation, but to political reform.

Parnellism and Home Rule

By the end of 1882 the Land League was replaced with the Irish National

In 1887 a series of letters appeared in The Times *entitled 'Parnellism and Crime' suggesting Parnell's involvement in the assassination in the Phoenix Park five years earlier of the Irish Chief Secretary and Under-Secretary. A commission established to investigate the matter proved that the letters were forged and vindicated Parnell's reputation.*

League, on whose agenda land came second to Home Rule, and which was dominated by Parnell's parliamentary party. When further electoral reform trebled the Irish electorate in 1884, Parnell's party swept the boards in the election held in the following year, winning every seat in the country outside east Ulster and Trinity College. Its 85 members were a tightly-knit and disciplined party of the modern type, pledged to taking the party line and voting as instructed on every issue, and in June 1885 they used their position of influence to join forces with the Conservatives in bringing the Liberal government down. The new Conservative government under Lord Salisbury introduced the Ashbourne Act, which provided funds for Irish tenants to buy their farms, to be repaid over a period of 49 years.

But the Conservatives were no advocates of Home Rule whereas Gladstone was won around to support for it at this point and was returned to government thanks to the balance of power Parnell's Irish party held in the House of Commons. He drafted a Bill making modest provision for Irish Home Rule, but it was opposed by dissidents within his own party such as Joseph Chamberlain, and by the Conservatives, principally Lord Randolph Churchill. The latter argued that Home Rule could not be foisted on the Unionist population of Ireland, and in 1886 threatened that 'Ulster will fight and Ulster will be right'. Others opposed Home Rule because they feared the break-up of the Empire and could quote in support of their stance Parnell's recently-uttered declaration to the effect that 'No man has a right to fix the boundary to the march of a nation. No man has a right to say to his country: "Thus far shalt thou go and no further." We have never attempted to fix the *Ne plus ultra* to the progress of Ireland's nationhood, and we never shall'. A third group within the British political establishment believed, quite simply, that the Irish were incapable of governing themselves.

The Plan of Campaign

The result was that Gladstone's 1886 Home Rule Bill was defeated by a margin of thirty votes and he felt compelled to resign. The Conservatives came back to power and Parnell's supporters turned their attention for the time being to the renewed land crisis and depression. They devised a 'Plan of Campaign' which they put into operation in the period 1886–90, and which involved tenants combining, in the manner of trade unions, against unfair rent demands by refusing to pay unless the landlord agreed to reduce his demands.

The Plan proved very successful in certain areas such as Kerry, Limerick and Tipperary, but the new Conservative government used very repressive tactics to counter the agitation. Police brutality was combined with newspaper articles in *The Times* newspaper trying to implicate Parnell in support for violence, including letters purportedly written by Parnell subsequently exposed as forgeries. In fact, Parnell did not support the Plan of Campaign as he was busy trying to reconstruct an alliance with Gladstone to bring about Home Rule. However, his career came crashing down about him when a certain Captain W. H. O'Shea filed for divorce in December 1889.

The Fall of Parnell

Parnell had had a love affair with Captain O'Shea's wife, Katharine, since they first met in the summer of 1880. In 1882 she had given birth to a first child by him (who died soon afterwards), and to two others in the years following, and they were living as a married couple in all but name by 1886. But it was only when the divorce case came to court in 1890, and the full details of the affair were revealed, that it became public knowledge. The scandal that ensued saw Gladstone pressurised into breaking his connection with his discredited Irish ally and calling privately for Parnell's withdrawal from public life. The members of the Irish parliamentary party were, in effect, forced to make a choice between their beloved leader Parnell and Gladstone, the only British political leader capable of delivering their objective of Home Rule.

Parnell's response was to issue a public 'Manifesto to the Irish People', ignoring the divorce scandal entirely, accusing some within his own party of having become too closely aligned to the Liberals, and challenging Gladstone's commitment to Home Rule. The effect of this was to force his critics within the party out into the open and to lose all Liberal support, but by ignoring his affair with a married woman he angered Catholic opinion, and the bishops in particular. After a week of heated debate in the infamous Committee Room Fifteen in Westminster, the party split in two: 45 went with the Vice-Chairman, Justin McCarthy, 27 stayed with Parnell. He returned to Ireland where his support remained strong among those devoted to him in Dublin and other towns, but the anti-Parnellite ground-swell had begun.

In three hotly-contested by-elections the Parnellite candidates were heavily defeated. Yet his self-belief remained strong and he resolved to fight on. His language became ever more militant, securing him the continued backing of the Fenians at home and abroad. But his pride as a leader spurned by his following led him to increasingly heated assaults on his former friends, and his outrage at the public insults to Katharine O'Shea (whom he married in June 1891) added to his immoderation. He began to appear ever more desperate, and his health, which had been poor for several years, deteriorated rapidly. He died in Brighton in the arms of his new wife on 6 October 1891, aged only forty-five.

Politics after Parnell

Parnell had overseen a revolution in the Irish land question – it was not yet fully resolved, but well on its way to resolution. He had brought the subject of Home Rule from a peripheral pipe-dream to the centre stage of British politics. And he had done both by a combination of mass popular agitation and extraordinary parliamentary manoeuvring. He fashioned a great modern-style parliamentary party, complete with a network of constituency organisations at home on the ground, and had shown that Ireland was indeed ready for self-rule and modern democratic government.

The Parnellite split was, therefore, extremely damaging. Yet in deposing their titanic leader the party had shown that it was bigger than any one man and that it operated on the principle of majority rule rather than hero-worship or benign dictatorship. In fact, in 1893, after Parnell's death, the cause of Home Rule was still very much alive when Gladstone, in his last throw of the dice, introduced his second Home Rule Bill; this time it made its way successfully through the House of Commons but was predictably dealt a fatal blow in the Lords. With Gladstone's passing, it is true, the subject was removed for the medium term at least from the British government's agenda, but, when the bitterness of the split receded, the Irish Parliamentary Party re-emerged as a potent force committed to, and skillful in employing, the methods of parliamentary politics, and the cause of Irish Home Rule once more came to dominate British politics.

Killing Home Rule with Kindness

When the Conservatives took power after Gladstone's demise their Irish policy was led by the belief that Irish nationalism could be smothered by improving the social condition of the country. The Chief Secretary for Ireland, Arthur Balfour, pushed ahead with further land reform, in the belief that the best way of producing a stable countryside in Ireland was if the peasant farmer had a real stake in the land – this would turn him, it was hoped, into a conservative force rather than an advocate of any kind of political revolution. A new agency was set up called the Congested Districts Board, with the task of easing social conditions in those parts of the country considered over-populated: it would promote local agriculture, industry and education, try to increase the size of farms by amalgamating small holdings into larger units, and encourage inhabitants in 'congested' areas to move to these new larger holdings.

The Congested Districts Board did very valuable work in improving the physical infrastructure of the West (not just roads and bridges but even a light rail system), encouraging cottage industries, improving agricultural methods and the fishing industry, and redistributing land bought from landlords. Individuals also began to work to improve the farmers' lot; principal among whom was Sir Horace Plunkett, son of Lord Dunsany, who saw that, since the landlord-tenant situation was well on the way to resolution, future progress would depend largely on farmers' own efforts, and this should come in the form of 'co-operation'. In 1894 he founded the Irish Agricultural Organisation Society, which would act as a non-political umbrella-group for the local farmers' co-operative societies and creameries, the establishment of which he had been encouraging for some years, and within ten years of its foundation the IAOS counted 876 farmers' 'co-ops' on its books, which had helped to improve the quantity and quality of agricultural production, the profits of which were shared among members.

The major obstacle still standing in the way of 'killing Home Rule with kindness', as it became known, was the denial to Ireland of a proper system of local government on English lines, and this came with the passing of the Irish Local Government Act (1898). This established county councils, urban district councils, and rural district councils, elected bodies, in which for the first time women had the vote. The effect of this measure was to produce a minor revolution in Irish life, the last vestige of real power in the localities shifting permanently from the landlord class to the new power in the land – the Catholic farmer, the shopkeeper, the publican, and so forth. This was followed in 1899 by an Act establishing the Department of Agriculture and Technical Instruction. The culmination of these initiatives came with the Wyndham Land Act of 1903, which went so far as to get landlords to sell, not simply small holdings to individual tenants, but their entire estates: by 1920, ten million acres of land had changed hands as a result.

The Cultural Awakening

Perhaps the greatest social change to take place in Ireland in the nineteenth century was the all-but-extinction of the country's native language. There were bodies which sought to preserve the records of a Gaelic civilisation on the brink of the abyss, but their interests were predominantly antiquarian, motivated by a desire to gather the fossils of a lost world rather than to breathe new life into it. The first signs of real enthusiasm to keep the Gaelic past alive were the rapid successes that greeted the foundation in Thurles in Co. Tipperary, on 1 November 1884, of an organisation called the Gaelic Athletic Association. The driving force behind it was a Clareman, Michael Cusack, and it was dedicated to preserving and codifying the exclusively Irish game of hurling, and Irish varieties of other field sports, primarily Gaelic football.

Ostensibly an entirely sporting organisation, at least four of the seven founders of the GAA were Fenians, which is a good indication of the way in which a love of things Irish so often overlapped with activity in the political sphere. The ban which the organisation imposed on participation in what it termed 'foreign' games had a strong Anglophobic aspect to it, but in another respect it proved remarkably successful in kindling local community spirit and national pride. Those involved in Gaelic games understood too the importance

Illuminated Address presented to Douglas Hyde by a New York branch of Conradh na Gaeilge on 26 November 1905. This document was designed by Éoin S. Ua Liaigh.

of the national language and the most significant development in the awakening of interest in its revival came with the foundation in 1893 of the Gaelic League, Conradh na Gaeilge.

The League's founders were a mixed lot: Fr Eugene O'Growney was Professor of Irish at the Catholic seminary at Maynooth; Eoin Mac Neill was an Antrim Catholic, a gifted young scholar whose great love was the history and literature of early Ireland; and Douglas Hyde was the son of an Anglican clergyman who grew up in Frenchpark in Co. Roscommon, who had developed a love of Irish from the people of the surrounding countryside and then joined the short-lived Society for the Preservation of the Irish Language (founded in 1877) as a student in Trinity. In a public lecture delivered by him in Dublin in November 1892, entitled 'The Necessity for de-Anglicising Ireland', he commented on how the Irish public 'continues to apparently hate the English, and at the same time continues to imitate them; how it continues to clamour for recognition as a distinct nationality, and at the same time throws away with both hands what would make it so'. This prompted the suggestion by Mac Neill that a new society be formed to promote the speaking of Irish and of modern literature in Irish, and Hyde was appointed its first president.

From the start, the Gaelic League was declaredly non-political, and Hyde was anxious to keep it that way, but it was hard to keep politics far at bay from such a society for long. Apart from the fact that Irish nationalists tended to be the very people most interested in fostering the language, trying to pressurise the government into introducing the teaching of Irish in national (i.e., primary) and secondary schools was of its nature a political act, at which the League was very successful, to the extent that when the National University of Ireland was established in 1909, the League succeeded in making Irish a compulsory subject for matriculation.

Arthur Griffith and Sinn Féin

With the cultural resurgence of the 1880s and 1890s came a sharpened national consciousness, intensified at the end of the century by the centenary commemorations of the 1798 rebellion. A remarkable Dublin printer and journalist by the name of Arthur Griffith became editor at this point of a new newspaper called, not coincidentally, *The United Irishman*, which had as potent an effect on contemporaries as *The Nation* had for its readers a half-century earlier. Griffith has remained something of an enigma, and his significance has been overshadowed by other more flamboyant characters, but few ever cast doubt on his commitment to his country. It is beautifully summed up in the words of a contemporary, H.E. Kenny ('Sean-Ghall'), one of the few who broke through Griffith's rather protective exterior:

> *To die daily, even hourly, for your country; to dwell in the slums when you might have lived in the light laughing places of the world; to go clad as the very poor are clad when purple and fine linen might have been yours; to eat dry bread, and not much of that, when you might have feasted full; to act thus not for one year nor for ten, but for more than a generation – that is a heroism of which few but God's Great are capable, and that was the heroism of Arthur Griffith.*

Griffith sought to help Irishmen recover their self-respect, to love their native language and history, and to develop home-grown industry, but, above all, to stop looking to England for their inspiration. In his book *The Resurrection of*

The Ulster Volunteer Force, created in January 1913, was intended to co-ordinate the paramilitary activity of Ulster Unionists. It was led largely by retired British Army officers and grew to about 90,000 strong, but even after the Larne gun-running of April 1914 it remained imperfectly equipped. Many of its members did subsequently assume full soldier status, serving in the Great War in the 36th (Ulster) Division.

Hungary (1904) he developed his ideas for a strategy of Irish self-government which he called 'the Hungarian policy': by this he meant that Irish parliamentarians should follow the example set by their Hungarian counterparts of 1867 when they withdrew from Vienna and established a separate parliament in Budapest, while at the same time remaining subject to the Austrian Emperor.

It was a complex notion which had little appeal to the general public, but not so Griffith's other scheme. If Irish independence was to be meaningful, he argued, it had to be both political and economic, and for it to be the latter Ireland's dependence on British manufactures must end. This viewpoint became known as 'the *Sinn Féin* policy', an Irish phrase which means 'We ourselves' (often translated 'Ourselves alone'), which was coined for Griffith by Máire Butler, a cousin of none other than Edward Carson, the hero of Unionism! By 1908 it had become the name of an amalgam of organisations attracted by Griffith's ideas, which defined its goal quite simply as 'the re-establishment of the independence of Ireland'. But Sinn Féin had a slow start, and its early prospects were not helped by the fact that in 1909 the powers of the British House of Lords were curtailed: this meant that the great obstacle to the passage through parliament of a Home Rule Bill was removed, and, after many years in abeyance, Home Rule once more became a live issue in British politics.

Home Rule: The Final Push

The Irish parliamentary party finally recovered from the damaging Parnellite split in 1900, under the leadership of John Redmond, a fine orator and a Wicklow country gent in the mould of Parnell, of whom he had remained an adherent. In the general election of that year they won 80 seats, but it was to be a decade later before they were in a position to exploit the balance of power in the Commons to persuade the Liberal Prime Minister, Asquith, to reconsider the question of Home Rule. He had little choice but to accede to their pressure if he was to stay in power, and in April 1912 unveiled the Home Rule Bill before the House of Commons. The new curtailed House of Lords could only veto the passage of the Bill for two years, so with the majority in the Commons secure, it seemed that Irish Home Rule was at last to become a reality.

The problem was that there was a very considerable number of people in Ireland, overwhelmingly, though by no means exclusively, Ulster Protestants, for whom Home Rule was a dreaded prospect. They found a voice in a remarkable and successful lawyer named Sir Edward Carson. The Unionists of Ulster in particular rallied around his compelling, not to say theatrical, oratory, and his mass-rallies were formidable events, especially that held in Belfast in September 1912 when vast numbers gathered to sign what was called the Solemn League and Covenant. Carson, though, was a died-in-the-wool southern Unionist, born, reared, and educated in Dublin, and his goal was not that Ulster alone be saved from the introduction of Home Rule, but all Ireland. The man who best typified the resistance of Ulster to the prospect of being coerced into even a partially independent Ireland was the wealthy Belfast-born MP, James Craig, a man willing to resist that prospect by force of arms if necessary. Both men were joined in their opposition by the new leader of the Conservative Party in Britain, the Canadian-born Andrew Bonar Law, whose ancestors came from Ulster, a heritage he took very seriously indeed. It was he, in fact, who stated that even if the Home Rule Bill passed through the Commons, 'there are things stronger than parliamentary majorities', an extraordinary remark from a candidate for prime ministerial office, adding with regard to Ulster Protestants that 'if an attempt were made to deprive these men of their birthright ... they

The Nationalist response to the UVF: John Redmond inspecting Irish Volunteers, August 1914.

would be justified in resisting by all means in their power, including force … I can imagine no length of resistance to which Ulster can go in which I should not be prepared to support them'. Evidently, Home Rule was heading for a crisis.

The Home Rule Crisis

In January 1913 the Ulster Unionist Council set up the Ulster Volunteer Force, a military organisation dedicated to opposing the introduction of Home Rule. They drilled openly, admittedly with wooden rifles, and though many considered it an elaborate bluff, the government had intelligence reports of the secret importation of arms into Ulster at an increasing rate, and was made even more aware of the volatile situation when the so-called Curragh 'mutiny' occurred, whereby senior officers of the British army in Ireland announced their decision to resign rather than be party to any attempt to 'coerce' Ulster out of the Union. The government therefore began negotiations to determine if it might be possible to secure the exclusion of some at least of the traditional nine counties of Ulster from the new arrangements.

John Redmond declared that 'Irish nationalists can never be consenting parties to the mutilation of the Irish nation', but the Liberal government persisted, arguing that partition need only be temporary. In response, in November, the prominent academic and Gaelic Leaguer, Eoin Mac Neill, published in that organisation's journal, *An Claidheamh Soluis*, an article entitled 'The north began', which became the impetus for the formation by nationalists of the Irish Volunteers, whose aim was precisely the opposite of their Ulster opponents. This in retrospect can be seen to have been a defining moment, because the existence of such an extra-parliamentary force was bound to weaken Redmond's freedom of manoeuvre and, once established, unlikely to fade away. Redmond might claim nominal leadership of the Force, but in reality power was beginning to slip from his hands.

When a vast shipment of arms was landed at Larne and elsewhere on the coast of east Ulster, in April 1914, their southern counterparts responded in late July with the equally famous Howth gun-running. The prospect of civil war was drawing ever closer, but at that precise moment the outbreak of the Great War brought a stark change of mood. Asquith did indeed introduce and pass his Government of Ireland Act, but with two provisos: it would not come into force until, one, the war had ended and, two, some special provision had been made for Ulster. Redmond, in a speech at Woodenbridge in Co. Wicklow, urged the Irish Volunteers to do as their Ulster counterparts had, and join Britain in the war. The result was a momentous split: the great majority, about 170,000, stayed with Redmond, renamed themselves the National Volunteers, and served bravely and in many cases with their lives in the war that followed; the remainder, not many more than 10,000, who could not bring themselves to fight for a country whose rule they were seeking to overthrow, regrouped.

1916: The Assault on the GPO

The new Central Executive of the Irish Volunteers had as its Chief of Staff Eoin Mac Neill, Bulmer Hobson was Quartermaster, and The O'Rahilly was Director of Arms. But when the crunch came it was three other officers who took the lead: Patrick Pearse (Director of Military Organisation), Thomas MacDonagh (Director of Training), and Joseph Mary Plunkett (Director of Military Operations). All three were IRB men: the old Fenian secret society had penetrated to the core of the public movement. All three were also poets, Gaelic language enthusiasts, and consumed with a romantic attachment to winning Ireland's freedom through bloody revolution.

That revolution was a long time in preparation and the prelude was a mass of confusion and misadventure, but at noon on Easter Monday, 24 April 1916, a group of Volunteers left Liberty Hall and marched on the General Post Office. An hour later the Irish tricolour was raised over the building and Patrick Pearse went outside to read, to bemused passers by, a Proclamation from 'the Provisional Government of the Irish Republic to the people of Ireland'. The fight for Irish freedom had begun.

One of the most famous documents in Irish history, the 1916 Proclamation was written largely by Patrick Pearse and approved by the Military Council of the IRB. 2,500 copies were printed in Liberty Hall early on Easter Sunday morning for circulation throughout the country.

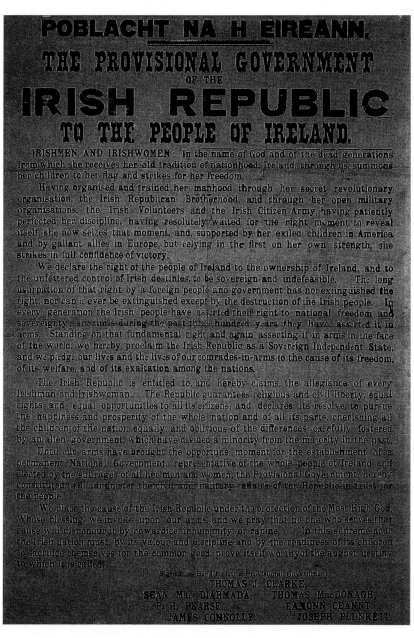

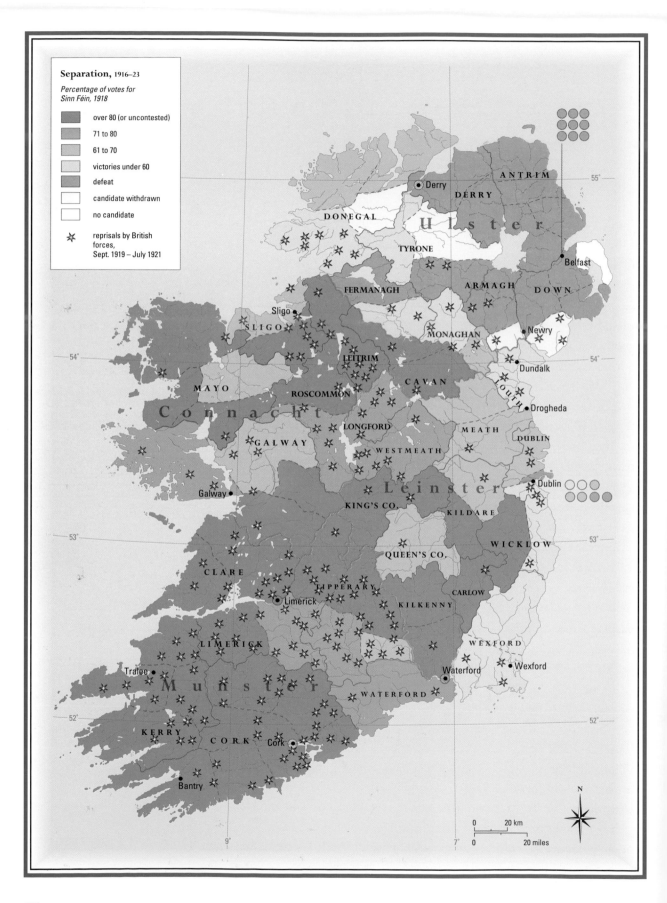

Separation, 1916–23

*Percentage of votes for
Sinn Féin, 1918*

- over 80 (or uncontested)
- 71 to 80
- 61 to 70
- victories under 60
- defeat
- candidate withdrawn
- no candidate

✴ reprisals by British
forces,
Sept. 1919 – July 1921

CHAPTER VIII

THE WRITING OF EMMET'S EPITAPH

The origins of the 1916 Rising are as complex as its impact. For all the attention Dublin has grabbed in connection with it, Belfast provided much of the impetus. Here, a younger generation had grown impatient at the sluggishness of the old IRB leadership, and men like the remarkable organiser Bulmer Hobson (a middle-class Quaker) and the Belfast publican's son Denis McCullough joined forces as early as 1905 to found the Dungannon Club, taking its name from the Volunteers of the late eighteenth century, soon to be joined by Leitrim-born Seán Mac Diarmada (MacDermott). Their newspaper *The Republic* made clear their goal, in the first issue of which Hobson stated that 'We stand for an Irish republic because we see that no compromise with England, no repeal of the Union, no concession of Home Rule, or Devolution, will satisfy the national aspirations of the Irish people'. Their tactics involved intensified recruitment into the IRB and the active discouragement of enlistment into the British army.

By 1908 Hobson and Mac Diarmada had moved to Dublin and merged their organisation with

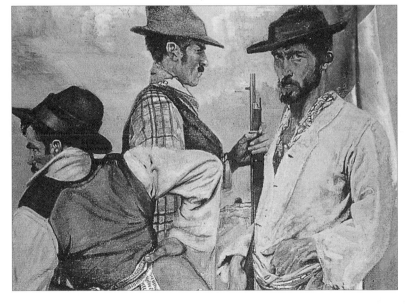

Seán Keating painted Men of the West *in the year before the 1916 Rising, and it offers a romanticised image of the fighting Irishman. Though the Rising when it transpired was a largely urban affair, the men with their steely stare, their commitment to the Republic made plain by the tricolour in the background, are dressed in western 'peasant' costume to link the Gaelic world of the West of Ireland with the new Ireland that they would shortly forge by force of arms.*

Griffith's Sinn Féin. There, an earlier Belfast-based scheme of Hobson's, the formation of a youth movement called Na Fianna Éireann, was revived nationally and spearheaded by the flamboyant Constance Gore-Booth of Lissadell in Co. Sligo, by now Countess Markievicz (having married a Polish count). It was Hobson's intention that its members' study of Ireland's history and language and military drilling would form a good apprenticeship for future IRB membership, but first the old guard in the latter organisation needed replacement. At this point, the young Turks found an ally many years their senior in Tom Clarke, recently released from prison after fifteen years of penal servitude for the Fenian bombing campaign; he was now co-opted on to the IRB's Supreme Council, which, through his support, the younger generation soon came to dominate.

The Howth Gun-running

They seized the opportunity provided by the formation of the Irish Volunteers, initiated by Eoin Mac Neill, to infiltrate the new paramilitary force, and before long, although its chairmanship was still in the hands of the moderate Mac Neill, Bulmer Hobson had become secretary and his ally, M.J. Rahilly (known as The O'Rahilly), was treasurer. They needed money with which to buy arms, and this was supplied through the fund-raising efforts of the remarkable humanitarian activist and historian Alice Stopford Green, author of *The Making of Ireland and its Undoing*, under encouragement from one of the most widely-respected contemporary campaigners for human rights, Sir Roger Casement.

Born in Sandycove, Co. Dublin and raised in Co. Antrim, Casement was formerly a high-ranking British Foreign Office official, but had become disquieted at the manner in which British governments allowed the playing of the 'Orange Card' to retard the progress of Home Rule, and was now a member of the Provisional Committee of the Irish Volunteers. It was another former British civil servant, with a similar proud Anglo-Irish pedigree, Erskine Childers, author of the famous spy-novel *The Riddle of the Sands*, whose yachting skills and whose boat, *The Asgard*, provided a means of bringing into Ireland the arms purchased in Germany with Mrs Green's funds. In a spectacular publicity stunt, the guns and ammunition were successfully landed at Howth, though by day's end British soldiers had killed three civilian supporters of the operation on Bachelor's Walk in the city.

The Emergence of Patrick Pearse

In the aftermath of the arms-landing, the split in the Volunteers on the issue of John Redmond's support for Britain's war-effort meant that the rump who broke with him were, of their nature, its most radical wing. Eoin Mac Neill was still in command, assisted by Hobson and The O'Rahilly, but others now started to take the lead. The young and romantic (though, by now, seriously ill) Joseph Plunkett, a member of that well-known Irish family, was very keen on military action, as was his teacher of Irish, Tipperaryman Thomas McDonagh, who since 1911, had been a lecturer in English in University College, Dublin. He shared his poetic talents and interest in Irish with Patrick Pearse, born in Dublin in the same year as McDonagh, 1879, a barrister by profession, an educationalist at heart. His love of the Irish language was so precocious that he had founded a society to promote it when he was only seventeen. And we get an early insight into his thinking from his presidential address to his Society in 1897 when he described the destiny of the Gael as 'to become the saviour of idealism in modern intellectual and social life'.

No word better sums up Pearse's life than idealism. His criticism of the Dickensian vestiges of the contemporary education system led to his writing

Joseph Mary Plunkett (1887–1916) though born in Dublin was forced by ill-health to live abroad for much of his life, in southern Europe and Algiers. He learned Irish from Thomas MacDonagh who steered his first poetry-collection The Circle and the Sword *(1911) through the press and with whom he formed the Irish Theatre in Hardwicke Street to perform Irish plays and major foreign works. His poetry is very intense and rhapsodic and almost liturgical in style.*

of the damning and still powerful pamphlet *The Murder Machine*, and the foundation by him of his own school, Scoil Éanna (St Enda's), in which he could put his modern ideas into practice. Irish was the language of the school, Pearse being until 1909 editor of the Gaelic League's journal *An Claidheamh Soluis*, and the school had an avowed nationalist ethos, though his conversion to extreme republicanism came quite late in the day. When chosen to deliver the oration at the annual Wolfe Tone commemoration in 1913, the militant language he employed – calling on Irishmen 'to follow only the far, faint call that leads them into battle or to the harder death at the foot of a gibbet' – caught the attention of the IRB, who enthusiastically paved his way to their inner ranks.

Preparations for a Rising

Pearse's language throughout 1914 and beyond became ever more violent, the theme of bloodshed and blood sacrifice becoming dominant, his goal being the organisation of an armed insurrection. When he spoke at the graveside of the old Fenian father-figure, O'Donovan Rossa, in August 1915, he stated that 'life springs from death, and from the graves of patriot men and women spring living nations'. The panegyric is best remembered today for Pearse's marvellous rhetorical flourish in which he said that the British 'think that they have pacified Ireland … The fools, the fools, the fools! They have left us our Fenian dead, and while Ireland holds these graves, Ireland unfree shall never be at peace'.

In May 1915 the IRB set up a Military Council, whose first members were Pearse, Plunkett, and Galway-born Éamonn Ceannt; later joined by Seán Mac Diarmada, Tom Clarke, Thomas MacDonagh, and the Socialist leader James Connolly, editor of *The Irish Worker*, who had his own small force of men and women volunteers, known as the Irish Citizen Army, and whose priority was social revolution. These were the men who would later sign the 1916 Proclamation of Independence. By the end of 1915 they had selected the following Easter as the date of the rising, though it was kept a closely-guarded secret.

With the outbreak of the First World War, Sir Roger Casement, who had long believed that a war between Britain and Germany would provide the best opportunity for an Irish rebellion, went to Germany with the aim of enlisting

The role of the 1916 rebels in seeking German support, in particular the secret shipment to Ireland of German arms, was, in the eyes of the British government at war with Germany, the most serious indictment of their actions. Here Roger Casement is pictured (top centre) aboard a German submarine.

their support, especially in the form of arms. He eventually persuaded them to supply arms aboard a steamer named the *Aud*, which arrived on the Kerry coast from Lübeck on Holy Thursday, 20 April 1916, three days before the planned outbreak of the insurrection on Easter Sunday. There, however, they were intercepted by British warships and its captain scuttled the *Aud* rather than lose its valuable cargo to the enemy. Meanwhile, a German submarine put Casement ashore nearby in Ballyheige Bay on the morning of Good Friday, but he was captured and brought to London to be tried and subsequently executed for treason. The loss of the German arms was a severe body-blow to those who had hoped for military success in the insurrection, and only the very optimistic or those, like Pearse, who believed in the long-term worth of their own blood sacrifice (hence, perhaps, the choice of an Easter Rising) could contemplate continuing.

Eoin Mac Neill had long suspected that extreme elements in the Volunteers were intent on a rising irrespective of its prospects, but had been, for all intents and purposes, deceived by Pearse into thinking that this was

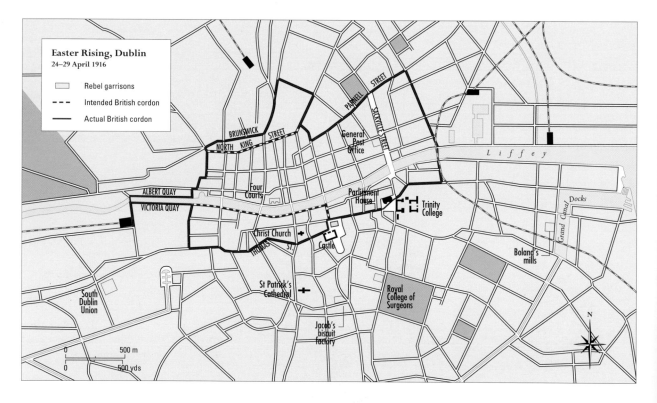

Easter Rising, Dublin
24–29 April 1916

☐ Rebel garrisons
- - - Intended British cordon
—— Actual British cordon

The position of rebel garrisons and the British cordons. The northern cordon was intended to run along North King Street but never did, due to rebel activity (after Killeen).

not the case. But when he confronted Pearse on the subject late on Holy Thursday night, Pearse admitted their plans and Mac Neill, still Chief of Staff, set about countermanding the orders that had secretly gone out at Pearse's direction, including the placing of a notice in the *Sunday Independent* newspaper prohibiting all Volunteer movements on that day. On

Sunday morning Pearse, Connolly and their comrades met at Liberty Hall, and decided to push ahead with the Rising, but at noon the next day. However, the outcome of the confused series of orders and counter-orders was that numbers of Volunteers ready for action were heavily depleted and, with few exceptions, it was only in Dublin where news could travel more quickly that numbers came out in any force – even here, though, perhaps as few as 1,600 answered the call.

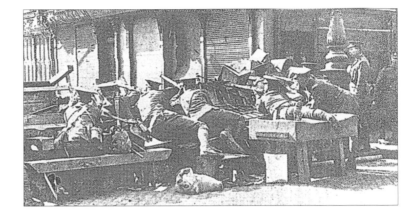

British troops man a makeshift barricade in a side street off Sackville Street (now O'Connell Street), disrupting contact with the rebel headquarters in the GPO.

The Easter Rising

The plan was to seize certain key buildings and hold them for as long as possible, and to use the occasion of the protest, however long it might last, to declare an independent Irish republic. The General Post Office was the headquarters, with other garrisons in the Four Courts, City Hall, the South Dublin Union, the Mendicity Institution, Jacob's biscuit factory, Boland's mills and the College of Surgeons. Patrick Pearse was commander-in-chief and head of the Provisional Government of the Irish Republic, and so it was he who proclaimed its establishment to the crowds in Sackville (now O'Connell) Street: 'We declare the right of the people of Ireland to the ownership of Ireland and to the unfettered control of Irish destinies, to be sovereign and indefeasible. The long usurpation of

The greatest part of the damage to Sackville Street, previously regarded as one of the most elegant thoroughfares in Europe, was done by British shelling of rebel positions, especially in the aftermath of the docking opposite the Custom House of the fisheries patrol boat, the Helga.

One of the most flamboyant of the rebel leaders was Countess Markievicz who, ironically, was a member of one of the most notable Anglo-Irish aristocratic families and had been presented at court to Queen Victoria at the age of 19 as 'the new Irish beauty'.

that right by a foreign people and government has not extinguished the right, nor can it ever be extinguished except by the destruction of the Irish people. In every generation the Irish people have asserted their right to national freedom and sovereignty; six times during the past three hundred years they have asserted it in arms. Standing on that fundamental right and again asserting it in arms in the face of the world, we hereby proclaim the Irish Republic as a Sovereign Independent State, and we pledge our lives and the lives of our comrades in arms to the cause of its freedom, of its welfare and of its exaltation among the nations'.

To begin with, the rebels were outnumbered by perhaps as much as three to one, and that numerical inferiority increased massively as British reinforcements arrived with each passing day. The static insurgent garrisons suffered more and more heavily from British artillery bombardment, especially with the deployment on the Liffey of the gunboat *Helga*. Fighting continued for a week, normal life in the city was brought to a standstill, and damage to buildings was immense, especially in the previously splendid Sackville Street. By Friday evening the position of the rebel leaders in the GPO had become untenable; they abandoned it and made for the Four Courts along Henry Street, but came against a military barricade in Moore Street, where The O'Rahilly led a brave but futile charge against the enemy only to suffer an heroic death, whereupon the others were forced to seek refuge in neighbouring houses. Connolly was already gravely wounded and Pearse, who was no longer willing to risk further loss of either civilian or rebels' lives, eventually agreed to an unconditional ceasefire. By the night of Sunday 30 April the Rising was at an end: 450 people were dead – 116 were military and another 16 police, while the rest, 318, were rebels and civilians.

The Bloody Aftermath

Major-General Sir John Maxwell had been given absolute powers to deal with the insurrection, and proclaimed martial law throughout the country. Nearly 2,000 people were interned in camps in England, though the great majority of them were home by Christmas. However, a further 170 people, including one woman, Countess Markievicz, were convicted by courts martial. There were those in and out of government, including Irish MPs at Westminster, who urged moderation in their treatment. Their view was that the Rising had patently failed and its instigators were unpopular, since they were held responsible by the people of Dublin for the destruction of their city and, for many, their loss of jobs or income. These people argued against doing anything which might alter the public mood. But their appeals to General Maxwell for restraint fell on deaf ears, and the courts martial which followed changed everything. It is true that most of those who initially received sentences of death saw them reduced to penal servitude for life, such as Countess Markievicz (because she was a woman, at which this life-long suffragette took grave offense) and Éamon de Valera, the leader of the Boland's mills garrison (probably because he was American by birth). But fifteen were executed between May 3 and 12, an agonisingly long period in terms of public opinion.

The public knew that Joseph Plunkett was terminally ill even before the Rising began, and marriage to his sweetheart Grace Gifford hours before his execution turned the traitor's death which the authorities had planned into that of a romantic hero. It was perhaps inevitable that General Maxwell would insist on Pearse's execution, but the gentle Willie Pearse, who was by no means a rebel leader, simply a younger brother devoted to his better-known sibling, was executed a day later, and this smacked of gross injustice. As for James Connolly, he had been severely wounded, and when it was revealed that he was shot by firing-squad while tied to a chair it seemed the act of an inhumane government. Finally, in August Sir Roger Casement was hanged in Pentonville Prison in England, a man whose motives were viewed throughout the world as noble, and who had, for that matter, been at one with Eoin Mac Neill in seeking to call off the Rising at the last minute.

The Change of Public Mood

The effect, together with that of the many arrests and deportations, was to change the popular mood in Ireland, and to make heroes of the dead and deported. Public masses were frequently held commemorating those who died, who were rapidly acquiring cult-like status, and these were turning into large public demonstrations of solidarity for the bereaved families. When hundreds of internees arrived home at Christmas 1916 they were if anything more hardened in their commitment to the achievement of the republican ideal, and looking for a new avenue in which to channel their political energies. The perception existed – quite unfounded – that the rebellion had been organised by Sinn Féin, probably because the activities of the latter were well known, whereas the IRB remained intensely publicity-shy. And so when, in January 1917, there was a by-election in North Roscommon, supporters of the Rising put forward as their candidate, standing against a member of Redmond's Home Rule Parliamentary Party, Joseph Plunkett's father, a papal count. He was in everything but name a Sinn Féin candidate and won easily, but when he announced that he would not take his seat in Westminster the Irish political landscape changed dramatically.

Éamon de Valera, little-known before 1916, nevertheless was chosen to serve as commander of the rebel garrison in Boland's Mills and went on to dominate Irish political life throughout the first half of the twentieth century.

Count Plunkett's victory represented only one by-election defeat for the Irish Parliamentary Party, but it was clear to all that its days were numbered, and that the public were no longer content to pursue their political goals by what seemed the failed tactics of dependence on Westminster parliamentary mathematics. Sinn Féin won three other by-elections in the summer of 1917, the last of which, in East Clare, saw the election for the first time of the most senior of the surviving leaders of the Rising, Éamon de Valera, just recently released from prison, whose manifesto was the 1916 Proclamation. A vote for him was a vote for 1916 and marked another nail in the coffin of Home Rule. It also marked the emergence from obscurity of this extraordinary individual.

The Rise of de Valera and Collins

De Valera's unusual name was acquired from his Spanish father whom his mother had met in New York, where Éamon was born in 1882, though he grew up with her family in Bruree, Co. Limerick. By means of a scholarship he studied at Blackrock College in Dublin and then at the forerunner of University College Dublin, and became a teacher of mathematics. His nationalism, as with so many of his generation, was acquired through love of the Irish language and involvement in the Gaelic League, but although he had sufficient status to be appointed commander of the Boland's mills garrison during the Rising, he had a low public profile, partly because of his rather aloof, not to say brooding, image, and his real leadership qualities only emerged in the various prisons in which he and his fellow rebels were afterwards incarcerated. It was his capacity to intellectualise the revolution, and give authoritative guidance to young men who had become swept up in the movement for a multitude of sometimes conflicting reasons, that made a leader out of de Valera, and earned him the extraordinary loyalty with which his followers repaid him in the years that followed.

The rise of Sinn Féin was facilitated by the folly of the British government led by David Lloyd George, which persisted throughout 1917 with provocative coercive measures and the detention of prominent critics. When they sent Thomas Ashe, one of the heroes of the Rising, to Mountjoy Jail he embarked on a hunger-strike and died as a result of the authorities' bungled attempts at force-feeding. His funeral became a mass demonstration of nationalist anger and the oration at his graveside consisted of two sentences uttered, after a volley of shots, by a largely unknown veteran of the GPO, though still only 27, named Michael Collins: 'Nothing additional remains to be said. The volley which we have just heard is the only speech which it is proper to make above the grave of a dead Fenian'.

Born in Clonakilty, Co. Cork, Collins had emigrated to London at the age of sixteen to work as a Post Office (and later a bank) clerk, and was an activist in the GAA and the Gaelic League. But it was his recruitment into the IRB in 1909 that mattered, because, although he spoke at Thomas Ashe's funeral in the uniform of an Irish Volunteer, he spoke on behalf of the IRB, who were now the secret driving force behind the gathering revolution. Collins, on the surface a rough, tough country lad with a contempt for sentiment and romantic idealism, had an equal disdain for inefficiency, even unpunctuality, boundless courage and physical energy; all of this, though, concealed a complex intellect and a ruthless conspiratorial streak. The phrase 'a born leader' might have been coined to describe him, as he possessed an immediate physical dynamism that inspired devotion in men and women alike.

The problem in 1917, however, was that there were by-elections taking place with candidates standing for Sinn Féin, there were groups of men and women marching in the uniform of the Irish Volunteers, and then, at the back of it all, this secret organisation to which Collins belonged, the IRB. The potential for chaos and disagreement was great, but it was resolved, for the moment, in October when all bodies assembled a convention or Árd-fheis organised under the aegis of Sinn Féin, where de Valera was elected unopposed as president of the movement, Arthur Griffith having magnanimously stood aside in the interests of unity. De Valera's formula for a new constitution for Sinn Féin was likewise accepted, which would reconcile the radical republicans and the more moderate elements, in the following words: 'Sinn Féin aims at securing the international recognition of Ireland as an independent Irish Republic', followed, though, by the qualification that 'Having achieved that status the Irish people may by referendum freely choose their own form of government'. Immediately afterwards, de Valera was also elected President of the Volunteers, bringing both bodies into line.

The Road to Revolution

Unity in nationalist Ireland was consolidated further by Lloyd George's intention to force conscription on Ireland to counter the 1918 German offensive, and by the arrest of almost all the Sinn Féin leaders whom the military authorities accused of being involved in a 'German plot'. The organisation was banned and thus driven underground, but Michael Collins was one of the few leaders who escaped arrest, and now emerged as a leading figure in the independence movement. As its Director of Organisation he built up a very effective

Arthur Griffith was born in Dublin in 1871 and was a printer by trade, but most of his life was given to journalism and political activism. Although he joined the Irish Volunteers and actually participated in the Howth gun-running, he rejected the use of force to establish an Irish Republic and did not participate in the 1916 Rising. It was the British authorities' mistaken belief that his organisation, Sinn Féin, was responsible that revived the latter's fortunes, transformed it into a Republican organisation, and propelled Griffith to a position of responsibility which no doubt hastened his death.

The first Dáil met on 19 January 1919 and lasted until May 1921, consisting of the 73 Sinn Féin candidates elected in the 1918 general election. As this photograph shows, many of its younger and more active members were necessarily absent from its proceedings because of their imprisonment.

intelligence service to forewarn them of government plans. Meanwhile, military training and tactics were in the hands of the indefatigable Cathal Brugha, no admirer of Collins, and his deputy Richard Mulcahy, along with the likes of Rory O'Connor and the energetic Dubliner, Harry Boland. Still, though, their plans involved no more than preparation to resist by force of arms, if necessary, the compulsory conscription into the British army of members of an unwilling Irish public: the view was that the imposition of conscription would be an act of war which the Irish people would be justified in resisting by war.

However, even when the Great War ended in November 1918, which should have caused this anti-conscription ground-swell to subside, it failed to do so; and it failed because the political goals of nationalist Ireland had advanced greatly since the Rising. Sinn Féin fought the election which soon followed on a platform calling for the withdrawal of Irish MPs from Westminster and the establishment of a national assembly in Ireland, appealing to the Versailles Peace Conference to recognise Ireland's right to independence, and declaring their intention to use 'any and every means available to render impotent the power of England to hold Ireland in subjection by military force or otherwise'. Before the November 1918 election, the last time in the twentieth century in which a parliamentary election took place in all of Ireland on the same day, Sinn Féin had seven seats, the Unionists 18, and the Irish Party and others 78. After it, the Unionists had increased somewhat to 26, and Sinn Féin to 73, while the Home Rule Party was reduced to six MPs (and four of these were in constituencies where Sinn Féin had not run in case a split vote would see a Unionist elected). The days of the once great Irish Parliamentary Party were at an end, Irish politics had been transformed, and the point of no return had been reached.

The First Dáil

True to their word, the Sinn Féin MPs did not take their seats in Westminster and (those, that is, who were not actually in prison) began preparations for establishing an independent Irish parliament. It was called the 'Assembly of Ireland' or Dáil Éireann in Irish, and it held its first session on 21 January 1919. Of course, the Unionist and other non-Sinn Féin MPs boycotted it. A Declaration of Independence was passed which begins 'Whereas the Irish people is by right a free people, and whereas for seven hundred years the Irish people has never ceased to repudiate and has repeatedly protested in arms against foreign usurpation, and whereas English rule in this country is, and always has been, based upon force and fraud and maintained by military occupation against the declared will of the people ... we, the elected representatives of the ancient Irish people in national parliament assembled, do in the name of the Irish nation, ratify the establishment

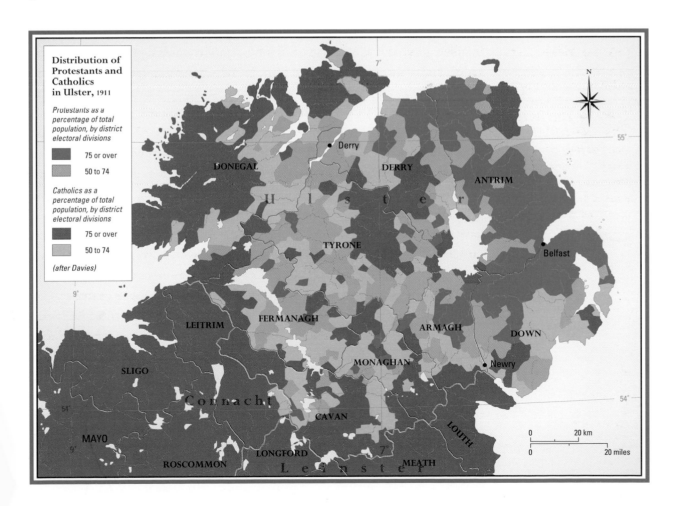

of the Irish Republic and pledge ourselves and our people to make this declaration effective by every means at our command'.

The Dáil proceeded to appoint three delegates – Arthur Griffith, Éamon de Valera and Count Plunkett – hopefully to represent Ireland at the Versailles Peace Conference, though this aim was never realised. Before concluding its business, the First Dáil also passed what it called the 'Democratic Programme', a radical document drawing on the writings of Pearse and Connolly which, though it declared the first duty of the 'Government of the Republic' to be 'to make provision for the physical, mental and spiritual well-being of the children, to secure that no child shall suffer hunger or cold from lack of food, clothing or shelter, but that all shall be provided with the means and facilities requisite for their proper education and training as Citizens of a Free and Gaelic Ireland', was tall on aspirations and short on specific measures for securing their implementation.

The next session of the First Dáil was on 1 April 1919, by which time more of its members had been released from prison, and at which de Valera was elected President of the Dáil, and chose as his government Griffith (Home Affairs), Collins (Finance), Cathal Brugha (Defence), Count Plunkett (Foreign Affairs), Eoin Mac Neill (Industry), Countess Markievicz (Labour), W. T. Cosgrave (Local Government), and Robert Barton (Agriculture). It was to be their job to convince the people of Ireland that they should turn their back on the Dublin Castle régime, and allow them to assume the role of an alternative government. Of course, normal parliamentary work for the Dáil was impossible, since many of its members were 'on the run' avoiding arrest, and the new ministers operated in secret, having no formal offices or departments as such.

Yet, some of them proved remarkably successful. Collins, in Finance, managed to raise a 'National Loan' of over a third of a million pounds. W. T. Cosgrave, assisted by the young Kevin O'Higgins, linked up with local councils, Sinn Féin performed spectacularly in the local elections of 1920, and they persuaded many of them to break away from the British-appointed Local Government Board. Barton set up a Land Bank which provided small loans to farmers to purchase land, and a Land Commission to oversee the redistribution of landed estates. Finally, 'Dáil Courts' were established at parish, district, 'circuit court', and Supreme Court level, and they worked tolerably well, representing a real challenge to the established processes for the administration of justice.

The Anglo-Irish War

The British authorities, of course, did everything in their power to bring down this threat to its rule, and an armed struggle between the two was almost unavoidable. In fact, the first shots in that conflict were fired on the very day that the Dáil first met, 21 January 1919: at Soloheadbeg in Co. Tipperary a group of Volunteers, led by Dan Breen, Sean Treacy and Seumas Robinson, killed two members of the Royal Irish Constabulary who were escorting a cart-load of explosives to a quarry. They might not have set out with the intention of killing the policemen, but the net effect was that a deadly guerrilla war had begun. These Volunteers were acting in the name of the new government of the Irish Republic and so became known as the Irish Republican Army, the IRA.

For the first year of the War of Independence, the IRA generally directed its operations against the RIC, and the targets were, therefore, usually fellow Irishmen, albeit in the service, nationalists argued, of an enemy government. The IRA was less successful in forcing the police out of their barracks – only a small number in isolated areas were evacuated – than they were in discouraging recruitment to the force, and thereby depleting its manpower. It was only in

This photograph shows a bombed bridge near Bandon, Co. Cork, at the height of the Anglo-Irish War in 1921. By this period the insurgents had perfected the structure of the 'flying column', a body of IRA men permanently under arms of the kind led by Tom Barry in Co. Cork, the particular specialism of which was the ambush.

the winter of 1919–20 that the campaign intensified and the IRA exploits became ever more daring. Michael Collins established a 'Squad' whose task was to eliminate the detectives attached to the Dublin Metropolitan Police, known as G-men, and they proved remarkably successful in their methodical, if cold-blooded, task. The retaliatory murder in his own house of the Lord Mayor of Cork, Tomás Mac Curtain, who was also Commandant of the IRA's Cork No. 1 Brigade, was widely regarded as an act of government terrorism, and served only to solidify IRA support.

The Ulster Question

- Counties with Catholic majority, 1911 census
- Counties with Protestant majority, 1911 census
- Limit of Northern Ireland, Government of Ireland Act, 1920
- Limit of historic Ulster province

Partition

Lloyd George's response was the usual one of coercion combined with proposed reform. In 1920 he passed the Government of Ireland Act, intended to set up two Home Rule-style parliaments in Ireland, one Dublin-based, the other to cater for six – Antrim, Down, Armagh, Fermanagh, Tyrone and Derry – out of the nine Ulster counties where Unionist opposition to Home Rule had been strongest. The new parliaments' powers would be limited, but they would link together in a Council of Ireland, the few real powers of which might increase if both parliaments assented, and the partition of the country would end only when both parliaments agreed that it be so. For southern nationalists, of course, it was too little too late, but Ulster Unionist opponents of Home Rule accepted Home Rule for this north-eastern enclave as the best way of retaining a link of some sort with Great Britain. The partition of Ireland had begun.

Sir Edward Carson, a southern Unionist of course, could not accept this, and retired from politics, but James Craig became the first Prime Minister of the new north eastern statelet, now Northern Ireland, the 'parliament' of which was inaugurated by King George V on 22 June 1921. But there were two very fundamental obstacles facing this statelet from the start. The first was that it involved abandoning all those Unionists who lived beyond its quite arbitrary boundaries. Unionists in the other three Ulster counties and elsewhere in Ireland would now be a tiny minority in whatever new political arrangement emerged from the war being waged around them: they were almost exclusively Protestant, but the new nationalist state, whatever shape it took, would be a Catholic-dominated affair and their ethos would be severely challenged. Before long, some of them were physically forced out of the new southern state; others left for a multiplicity of reasons, but those who chose to remain came in time to play a full role in its affairs. The parents' Unionism and sense of Britishness may have remained with them, but their children and grandchildren found in time that the new state was one to which they could give their loyalty and in the affairs of which they eventually came to play a full and equal part.

The other problem with the new northern statelet has proved more intractable. From the start, it was a state the boundaries of which were selected so as to guarantee permanent Protestant/Unionist dominance over the Catholics/Nationalists. It catered for the needs of a minority in Ireland, but had within its own boundaries a very substantial minority of its own who wanted nothing to do with it. At the time of its inception, Counties Fermanagh and Tyrone had clear nationalist majorities, as had the southern part of two more of the six counties, Armagh and Down; its second city, Derry, had the same, and even Belfast, especially the Falls district, had a significant nationalist population. To begin with, the new statelet had a

From January 1920 the Royal Irish Constabulary was reinforced by the recruitment of British ex-soldiers and sailors, and by November 1921 almost 10,000 of them were in the country. Issued on their arrival with khaki army trousers and dark green police uniforms they quickly became dubbed the Black and Tans. Their reputation for brutality only served to alienate the public more from the RIC.

Catholic/nationalist population of 34 per cent, and this continued to grow, so that by the 1990s even Belfast had a nationalist majority, Sinn Féin being the largest party on its city Council. With hindsight, the only surprise is that it managed to get off the ground at all and to survive for as long as it did before its descent, in the late 1960s, into turmoil.

The Black and Tans

In 1920, however, even though religious/political riots were rampant throughout the north, the focus lay elsewhere. In the spring the British government began recruiting in Britain former soldiers, soon known (because of the odd assortment of uniforms supplied to them) as the Black and Tans, who were sent to Ireland to reinforce the RIC. They quickly earned a reputation for ruthlessness and sheer contempt for the law. By the summer the 'Tans' were joined by the 'Auxies', an Auxiliary Division of the RIC, equally notorious as a result of their indiscriminate and callous treatment of armed opponents and civilian population alike. Between troops and police they may have amounted to as many as 40,000 men, against an IRA force of at most 5,000 at any one time.

The war was therefore one of guerrilla activity by the latter, followed by ever more alarming reprisals. Anyone suspected of Sinn Féin associations was imprisoned without trial (if not gunned down in cold blood), and wholesale destruction of property was a hallmark of Black and Tan reprisals against whole communities suspected of harbouring IRA men.

They were not free from danger themselves, of course, as when a group of Volunteers in plain clothes opened fire and killed several soldiers in Dublin: one of the Volunteers was an eighteen-year-old youth, Kevin Barry, whose hanging in Mountjoy Jail produced scenes of enormous emotion in the capital. Similar emotions were then sweeping Cork at news of the death on hunger strike of its Lord Mayor, Terence MacSwiney. This, the latter part of 1920, was the bloodiest period of the conflict, which climaxed on 21 November when Collins's hit-squad assassinated eleven suspected British intelligence officers on a Sunday morning, only to see the Black and Tans arrive at Croke Park in the afternoon and open fire on the crowd attending a football match, killing twelve innocent spectators. This vicious circle of attack, reprisal and counter-reprisal continued for more than another six months, its most horrendous scene being perhaps the unleashing on Cork of the Tans and Auxiliaries who proceeded to burn much of the city centre, in revenge for a successful ambush by the 'flying-column' of the redoubtable Tom Barry.

The Path to Peace

De Valera had spent most of the Anglo-Irish War in America, arguing the case for recognition of Ireland's independence and raising funds by which the war could be prosecuted. It was in 1921, after he had returned to Ireland, that Lloyd George, conscious of the extent to which Britain's reputation had been damaged by unfavourable publicity abroad, began to make moves to securing a truce. The negotiations got nowhere at first because of his insistence on the IRA disarming in advance of a settlement, which was utterly unacceptable. Lloyd George also insisted on Craig being present at the negotiations to represent the new 'Northern Ireland', but the Dáil, and its President, de Valera, could not accept the legitimacy of the new northern statelet and only agreed to a truce when the British dropped this insistence. The truce took effect on 11 July 1921, not a moment too soon for the by now over-stretched resources of the IRA, who badly needed a breathing-space. De Valera went to London along with Griffith and others and was offered the status of a Dominion within the Empire along the lines of Canada, but minus the six north eastern counties.

This, understandably, proved unacceptable to the Second Dáil which met in August, partly because it fell far short of the goal of an independent Republic and because it would copper fasten partition. De Valera then came up with the idea of 'external association': Ireland would be independent of the British Empire but associated with it by some external mechanism. On this basis, it

Michael Collins (front left), pictured here with Richard Mulcahy (front right), was perhaps the most charismatic of the Revolutionary leaders, though, unlike others who survived into old age, his early death denied posterity the opportunity to assess him in any mould other than that of the dashing young hero. He was certainly a gifted military commander and an inspirational leader of men, and had a good organisational mind, but it is impossible to say how he would have responded to the mundanities of day-to-day administration in a post-Revolutionary government lacking the resources to fulfil the objectives for which so many had fought and died.

was decided to resume negotiations in London, but de Valera, now no longer President of the Dáil but President of the Irish Republic, chose not to go in person, but rather to send an experienced delegation led by Arthur Griffith, and consisting of two other cabinet ministers, Collins (a most unwilling participant) and Robert Barton, and two lawyers, George Gavan Duffy and Eamon Duggan, with Erskine Childers as secretary. On the British side they faced among others Lloyd George, Winston Churchill, Austen Chamberlain and Lord Birkenhead.

The Treaty negotiations were tense and protracted and came to place a severe mental and physical strain on the Irish side. They knew full well that they would not come home with the cherished republic, and would instead end up with a compromise which some of those who had refused to participate in the negotiations – Cathal Brugha, for instance, and Austin Stack – would reject as unacceptable. Three things were at issue: the precise sort of Irish state that would emerge and its relationship with Britain; the northern question; and, of keen interest in British strategic thinking, the safeguards that would be built in to protect Britain's security in time of war. The solution to the latter problem was a provision in the eventual treaty for Britain to retain control over a small number of Irish naval bases (Cobh, Berehaven, Lough Swilly and Belfast). A solution to the other two problems remained more elusive. The first to be over-come was the northern question because, although the Irish were determined not to concede to partition, Lloyd George came up with the idea of a Boundary Commission which led them to believe that the frontier between north and south would be adjusted so drastically in favour of the latter that 'Northern Ireland' would no longer be a viable entity.

The Irish delegation to the Treaty negotiations in London in 1921 was a peculiar mix of conflicting characters and barely concealed dislikes. They were by no means a cohesive negotiating team and their British counterparts seem to have been able to play upon their mutual mistrusts and suspicions.

That left one sticking point: would the new Ireland be inside or outside the British Commonwealth? More specifically, what role would the British Crown play? The British insisted on an Oath of Allegiance to the Crown and much of the ensuing debate – on both sides of the Irish Sea – was on the precise word-ing of such an oath. Lloyd George, a tough and unscrupulous negotiator, pro-duced an arbitrary deadline by which the treaty must be agreed, and, under threat of an immediate return to war, one by one the weary delegates signed up for it. Although they were officially styled plenipotentiaries, they had under-taken to consult with President de Valera before agreeing to any proposed treaty, but, for whatever reason, they failed to do so, and by 2.10 AM on 6 December 1921 the entire delegation had signed the Articles of Agreement establishing 'the Irish Free State'.

The Treaty Split

Under the terms of the treaty the Free State, Saorstát Éireann, was established as a Dominion within the British Empire, acknowledging the British monarch as sovereign. To Griffith, Collins and the other signatories it represented, as the latter put it, not freedom, but freedom to win freedom, though it certainly fell far short of the Republic declared at Easter 1916. In the Dáil debates that ran from 14 December 1921 to 7 January 1922, President de Valera rejected it outright, arguing that dominion status allowed for too much British influence. Although this issue and that of the Oath of Allegiance, rather than partition, took up much of the debate, many of those who joined de Valera on the anti-Treaty side could not bring themselves to accept the six counties remaining part of the United Kingdom (though some of them were willing to accept a Belfast parliament, so long as it was subject to Dublin rather than London), and there were those, like Sean MacEntee, who forecast the difficulties that lay ahead.

Sure enough, throughout 1922 Belfast was in the grip of violence as nationalists vented their sense of betrayal and full-scale pogroms were perpetrated on their communities; by the end of May 236 people were dead as well as 11 members of the 'security' forces and 73 Protestants. The new government of Sir James Craig passed the Special Powers Act which remained in force for decades thereafter and allowed for detention without trial. They also established the Royal Ulster Constabulary, to take the place of the RIC. Although it was intended that one-third of its membership would be Catholic this never materialised. As an armed force, backed up by 16,000 part-time 'B specials' recruited from Protestant vigilante groups which had emerged during the War of Independence, the nationalist community never came to view it as anything other than an armed militia serving Unionist interests.

The Treaty Debate was one of the most fractious and damaging clashes of principle in Ireland's history, but when the vote was taken, it was passed by the Dáil by a margin of 64 votes to 57. De Valera resigned as President (to be replaced by Griffith) and led his supporters from the Dáil, including Cathal Brugha, Liam Mellows and Rory O'Connor. Collins was appointed Chairman of the Provisional Government and on 16 January 1922 the historic nature of the agreement they had wrested from the British – however circumscribed – was given public expression when the forces of the new Free State took command of Dublin Castle, bastion of British rule. But it was only a matter of time before conflict broke out between the now fatally divided former comrades. Rory O'Connor was the first to test the new régime when, in an echo of 1916, he seized possession of the Four Courts. Elections in June showed a pro-Treaty majority which emboldened the new government to act, and, under encouragement from the British who supplied them with artillery, they bombarded the Four Courts, destroying the national archives in the process, and forced the garrison to surrender within two days. Civil War had begun.

The Civil War

The open violence of the Civil War was an almost inevitable consequence of the violent language which the debate on the Treaty had brought forth. The sadness and madness of the affair was heightened by the fact that, not only were both sides fighting for what they believed was in their country's interest, but both had until recently stood shoulder to shoulder through many months of dire struggle against a common enemy, and many had been the closest of friends, now driven to inflict death and injury on each other over an issue of abstract principle. A generation who had shown enormous talent and patriotic commitment met their end in the Civil War, to add to the toll since 1916. Cathal Brugha met his death as he would have wished: leading anti-Treaty troops (known as 'Irregulars') in O'Connell Street in July 1922, while Liam Mellows and Rory O'Connor were executed by their former comrades-in-arms in December: scarcely a year earlier O'Connor had been best man at the wedding of the man who ordered his execution, Kevin O'Higgins.

Opposite: The majority of the IRA were opposed to the Treaty, becoming known as the Irregulars, and included among their ranks some of the most experienced and strongest units from the South-West and from Dublin. But the long delay before the Treaty Split erupted into violence allowed Collins to build up a new Free State army, ironically with the aid of his formerly virulent enemies, the British government, so that by the time hostilities finally broke out the initial numerical superiority of the Irregulars was lost.

As for the Pro-Treaty leaders, though technically the result of a brain haemorrhage, few doubted that Arthur Griffith's heart was broken when he too died in August; he seemed by then an old man, though he had scarcely turned fifty. As for Michael Collins, it was a similarly aged 31-year-old who met his death in an ambush at Béal na mBláth, Co. Cork, just ten days later, a catastrophe that stunned an already traumatised nation. How prophetic the words he had written to a friend on the very day he signed the Treaty: 'When you have sweated, toiled, had mad dreams, hopeless nightmares, you find yourself in London's streets, cold and dank in the night air. Think – what have I got for Ireland? Something she has wanted these past seven hundred years. Will anyone be satisfied at the bargain? Will anyone? I tell you this: early this morning I signed my death warrant. I thought at the time how odd, how ridiculous – a bullet may just as well have done the job five years ago'.

Charge of the Free State government was now taken by W. T. Cosgrave and Kevin O'Higgins, while command of its forces devolved on General Richard Mulcahy. It was only when Liam Lynch, the resolute Commander-in-Chief of the Anti-Treatyites, met his death in the following April that his followers became convinced that the war was unwinnable, and by May hostilities had ceased, though certainly not the bitterness which continued to divide family from family in succeeding generations. All told, perhaps as many as 4,000 met their deaths.

The Boundary Commission Collapse

To compound the misery of the Civil War nationalists were confronted in its aftermath with the cruel reality that Lloyd George had sold them a pup in his much-vaunted provision of the 1921 Treaty allowing for the establishment of a Boundary Commission. Griffith and Collins had been won over to signing the Treaty in the expectation, which he fed, that such a Commission would make the northern enclave unviable. It set to work in 1924 under the chairmanship of the South African jurist, Richard Feetham, the Free State representative being Eoin Mac Neill, with the newspaper editor, J. R. Fisher, representing the north. Nationalists expected the wholesale transference to them of counties, cities and

towns with nationalist majorities, but the Commission's chairman took a min-imalist approach, proposing that small Catholic enclaves like Crossmaglen in south Co. Armagh should go to the Free State while Protestant east Donegal, for instance, should come under the jurisdiction of Belfast.

When these proposals were leaked to the press the resulting furore was enough to sink the entire enterprise, and the border remained unchanged. To make matters worse, Prime Minister Craig soon replaced the proportional representational voting system, which favoured minorities and independents, with the British first-past-the-post one, which favoured majorities. The result was a permanent Unionist majority in the magnificent, if almost ludicrously ostentatious, new parliament building which he began constructing at Stormont, outside Belfast. This Unionist Party monopoly on government, with Craig himself as premier from 1921 until his death in 1940, and only limited nationalist opposition as many of the latter refused to take their seats, led to a malaise in government. The long continuation of one-party rule is unhealthy in any society, in one so polarised as that in this six-county statelet it was ultimately disastrous: a Unionist/Protestant government would rule uninterrupted and the substantial Nationalist/Catholic minority could have no hope of a share in that government, unless by some miracle of demographics they themselves became the majority. Stormont was truly, in the words of Craig himself, 'a Protestant parliament for a Protestant people'.

Life in a Free State

One of the greatest tragedies of the period from 1916 to 1923, as we have seen, was that so much of the nation's talent was lost. The President of the Executive Council of the new Free State was not therefore a giant of the stature of Collins or a visionary in the mould of Pearse or Connolly, but the modest, cautious and conservative W. T. Cosgrave, who, though only 43 when he took over the reins of government, seemed a generation older. Charisma and leadership skills he may have lacked, but his patriotism was never in doubt, and, as different times call for different types, perhaps he was just the stabilising 'chairman' figure that the Free State government needed. In 1923 he established a new party in Cumann na nGaedheal, which later became Fine Gael, and he brought the new ship of state safely through several crises, including the so-called army mutiny of 1924 and the assassination of his highly-talented right-hand man, Kevin O'Higgins, in 1927.

The Official Handbook of the Free State. The cover, by Art O'Murnaghan, is in the traditional style of Celtic manuscript illumination.

The Cumann na nGaedheal government provided the basis of the modern impartial civil service by the Civil Service Regulation Act (1923) and of the departmental system of government under the Ministers and Secretaries Act (1924); it took the brave step of making the new police service, An Garda Síochána, an unarmed force; the courts were revamped under the Courts of

Justice Act (1924); the Local Government Act (1925) remodelled the system at council level and introduced County Boards of Health, County Homes for the elderly and invalided, and County and District Hospitals for the sick. This was, in a sense, a conservative programme since it built upon rather than sought to overturn the basic structures inherited from the British. But the government showed its tolerant and libertarian credentials in sticking by Proportional Representation for Dáil elections, and it nominated a considerable number of southern Unionists to the Senate of the new state.

In economic affairs, caution was the name of the game. The Cumann na nGaedheal government believed that the well-being of the state depended on

Seán Keating witnessed at first hand perhaps the single greatest capital project undertaken by the government of W.T. Cosgrave – the electrical revolution which resulted from the completion of the famous Shannon Scheme undertaken by the Electricity Supply Board after its foundation in 1927. Keating was commissioned by the ESB to record the work in progress, partly to give publicity to the scheme, partly to provide propaganda for the Free State. Night's Candles are Burnt Out *(1927) is his best-known painting of the Scheme in which the heroic gunmen of his earlier work are replaced by the technocrats and bureaucrats of the new state.*

agriculture and did its utmost to protect the latter, however sluggish it had become. They continued the policy of land purchase and the Land Acts (1923–25) were concerned with advancing further the process begun under Gladstone a half-century earlier of making proprietors out of tenants. The fiscal policy of the government was frugal, and as regards the public finances good book-keeping its watch-word. In spite of that, it did take some extraordinary steps. In 1927 it set up the Agricultural Credit Corporation (ACC) and the Electricity Supply Board (ESB), the latter administering the Ardnacrusha hydroelectric generation plant on the Shannon, by far the greatest single piece

The financial resources of the Free State government were so limited that it was normal practice simply to replace the red paint of the post-boxes of the old regime with a new coat of green. Here, one of the few newly-commissioned ones bears the state's initials 'SÉ', for Saorstát Éireann.

of public investment by the new state and a symbol of its optimism that the days of Civil War and disturbance were over.

Coming in from the Cold

By 1926 Éamon de Valera realised that Sinn Féin's policy of non-participation in the new state structures was doomed to sterility, and that he would need to re-enter the political domain. The problem was the Oath of Allegiance to the British monarch which members of the Dáil were required to make upon taking their seats. When Sinn Féin refused to budge on this issue de Valera broke away from them and formed his own party, Fianna Fáil, which eclipsed Sinn Féin in the general elections of 1927, and, calling the oath 'an empty formula', he and those elected with him overcame the obstacle by the simple device of covering over the offending words of the oath before signing the book! But it was not until the 1932 election that de Valera got his first chance at government, in coalition with Labour, when Cumann na nGaedheal fell from power partly because of the country's disillusionment at the slow pace of change and its failure to combat poverty and unemployment, and partly no doubt because of the more immediate impact of the Great Depression unleashed by the Wall Street crash.

De Valera's entry into government was one of the most important turning points in modern Irish history for a multitude of reasons. Less than a decade earlier his supporters had lost a bitter Civil War to the government he was preparing to oust: some among the latter, fearing victimisation, might have been forgiven for contemplating a refusal to hand over the reins of government to such an enemy. And yet the transfer of power ran smoothly – democracy had already taken strong roots. The Fianna Fáil philosophy was very much more radical than that of the outgoing government, not only in constitutional affairs but in economic matters, and it was clear that the Free State was due for an enormous shake-up. In truth, no one quite know what lay in store.

Fianna Fáil in Power

Fianna Fáil policy was a combination of cultural nationalism (especially the attempt to revive the ailing Irish language), economic nationalism (with the emphasis on making the state self-sufficient), and political nationalism (expressed in the attempt, begun almost immediately, to overcome the limitations set by the 1921 Treaty). One of de Valera's first acts on assuming power was to suspend what were called 'land annuities', the repayments made by Irish farmers to the British government for the loans with which they had purchased their farms from their former landlords. These were widely resented on political grounds and, since they represented 18 per cent of government spending at a time of enormous poverty, the action was a popular one in Ireland. However, the British retaliated by imposing duty of 20 per cent on imports from Ireland, the great majority of which were farm products. De Valera responded with duties on British coal, cement, iron, steel and other products, culminating in what contemporaries called the Economic War.

This, of course, damaged the Free State a great deal more than it did Britain, especially the small farmer sector who were the backbone of Fianna Fáil. The cattle industry was the lifeblood of the economy and whereas in 1929 more than three-quarters of a million were exported, almost all to Britain, by 1934 this had fallen to half a million. If this protectionist dispute had continued much longer it would have spelled ruin for the economy, and so an honourable

For many, the decision by de Valera to 'opt into' the system was worrying, particularly since the fear, as later bluntly admitted by one of his lieutenants, Seán Lemass, was that Fianna Fáil was still only 'a slightly constitutional party'. This election poster captures well the Cumann na nGaedheal tactic of playing on such fears.

settlement was finally reached in 1938, the Irish government making a once-off payment in lieu of outstanding annuities, the British returning the 'Treaty ports'. Although it was one of the goals of Fianna Fáil and de Valera to make Ireland more self-sufficient, one of the effects of the Economic War was to act as a reminder of the degree to which the country remained dependent on Britain, and, of course, to make the border more tangible since customs posts had to be erected there too.

The early Fianna Fáil governments were more successful in ridding the Free State of some of the more offensive provisions of the Treaty. De Valera first removed the Oath of Allegiance and then the office of Governor-General, and by the mid-1930s was working flat-out on a new constitution, very much his own creation. Bunreacht na hÉireann came into effect in December 1937, approved in a referendum by 685,105 votes compared with 526,945 against. In

Despite neutrality, the Free State's territory suffered some 160 crashed and forced landings by aircraft from Britain and Germany. Above, an HE-111 bomber of the Luftwaffe has crashed near Bonmahon in Co. Waterford.

the context of a Europe where democracy was coming under fire it is noteworthy for its adherence to democratic principles, albeit heavily influenced by Roman Catholic social teaching, the special position of the Catholic Church being recognised and divorce prohibited (though both of the latter articles have subsequently been deleted or amended). Its first article changed the name of the state from Saorstát Éireann to Éire (the Irish for Ireland), but the later widespread misuse of this word to mean the 26-county state, whereas the constitution intended it to apply to the entire country, and its pejorative use by London and Belfast, has meant that most Irish people have, ironically, tended to favour the English-language designation of their country.

The second article stated the boundaries of Éire as being the entire island, though this was qualified in Article Three which confined the working jurisdiction of the state to the 26 counties 'pending the reintegration of the national territory'. This latter remained unchanged until the Belfast Agreement of 1998. One of the most surprising aspects of the 1937 constitution was the lack of any reference to a Republic, even though the Head of State was to be a President, Uachtarán na hÉireann (the Prime Minister being entitled An Taoiseach): de Valera may have held back on this point to allow room for flexibility when the 'reintegration of the national territory' would come about. If anything, though, the deliberate distancing of the southern state from the British Empire had the effect of deepening the constitutional partition of Ireland.

Ireland and the Second World War

The growing institutional partition between north and south was exacerbated by the outbreak of war between Britain and Germany in September 1939. De Valera was determined that the southern state would remain neutral, but not out of mere anti-Britishness on his part. In fact, although Ireland remained neutral throughout the war, it was 'neutral' on the Allied side, and covert assistance was given to the British and later the Americans, especially in intelligence matters. De Valera steadfastly refused to allow the Allies use of the 'Treaty ports', but the Allies were allowed to overfly Irish air-space, and no attempt was made to discourage the recruitment of Irish citizens into the British armed forces.

The fact is that formal neutrality was deemed necessary for both practical and political reasons. Ireland was a small, impoverished state which had not yet recovered from the Revolution and Civil War it had left behind a mere 16 years earlier, let alone the 'Economic War' with Britain from which it was just emerging. At the outbreak of World War II – the 'Emergency' as it was termed by the government – it had a regular army of 7,000 men, who were hopelessly ill-equipped, and could not possibly offer effective resistance to Hitler's Axis forces if Ireland chose to follow Britain into war against them.

At a political level also, circumstances were not yet such that Ireland could ally

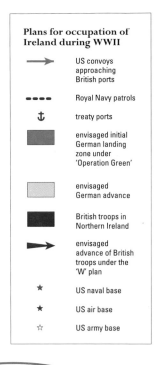

Plans for occupation of Ireland during WWII

→ US convoys approaching British ports

---- Royal Navy patrols

⚓ treaty ports

envisaged initial German landing zone under 'Operation Green'

envisaged German advance

British troops in Northern Ireland

➤ envisaged advance of British troops under the 'W' plan

★ US naval base

★ US air base

☆ US army base

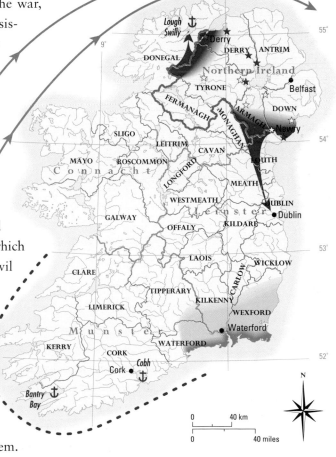

Though neutral throughout the Second World War – the Emergency as it was termed by the Dublin government – Ireland suffered the same food and fuel shortages as the combatant nations, and rationing of certain items remained in force for years afterwards, retarding economic and commercial life until the early 1960s.

itself with a country with which it had 'unfinished business': for Éamon de Valera to do so, whose primary political objective remained the ending of British-enforced partition, would have been an act of political suicide.

Churchill, of course, never forgave de Valera for his stance, while the northern state, by comparison, had proved invaluable to the British war effort, at a strategic level in providing bases from which to fight the Battle of the Atlantic, and in terms of war-production: Harland and Wolff built three aircraft-carriers but also specialised in the construction of convoy escort vessels; Short's aircraft factory helped produce 1,200 Stirling bombers; Mackie's Foundry manufactured some 75 million artillery shells; while the shirt factories of Derry were converted to the mass-production of uniforms.

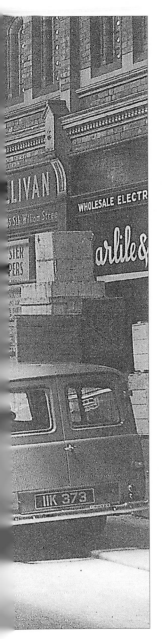

The Post-War Years

It is not surprising that in the aftermath of the war the northern state could rest assured of British support even from a Labour government and, under its new Prime Minister, Sir Basil Brooke (later Lord Brookeborough), it continued to work towards cementing the Union with Britain. Brooke, a Fermanagh landowner infamous among nationalists for his call for loyalists 'to employ only Protestant lads and lasses', was determined to prevent the Unionist monolith splitting: one of the threats to it was class politics, whereby working-class Protestants might turn away from the cause of Unionism in favour of a left-wing alliance with their fellow Catholic socialists. To counteract this, Brooke worked to bring the benefits of the British welfare state to the six counties: by catering for the immediate needs of the working classes he sought to smother any division within Unionist ranks based on class divide.

The south, on the other hand, emerged from the war with few friends in Britain or elsewhere. By this stage de Valera had been in power a decade and a half, Fianna Fáil had disappointed much of its Republican and small-farmer constituency, and there was a widespread feeling that it was time for a change. A new party emerged, known as Clann na Poblachta, which threatened to eat into the Fianna Fáil support-base, especially as it was led by Seán Mac Bride, a former Chief-of-Staff of the IRA, son of one of the executed leaders of 1916 and of the fiery Maud Gonne.

The First Inter-Party Government

In the election of 1948, Clann na Poblachta was able to keep Fianna Fáil out of government by forming an unlikely inter-party alliance with Fine Gael, Labour, the farmers' party (Clann na Talmhan), and independents.

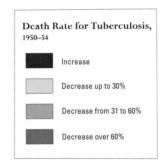

Death Rate for Tuberculosis, 1950–54

- ■ Increase
- □ Decrease up to 30%
- ▨ Decrease from 31 to 60%
- ▨ Decrease over 60%

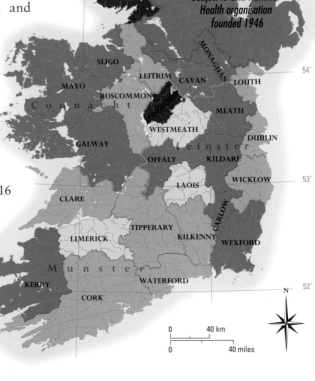

Northern Ireland
Subject to U.K. National Health organisation founded 1946

Mac Bride was made Minister of External Affairs but the new Taoiseach was John A. Costello of Fine Gael, who surprised the world in September 1948, while on a visit to Canada, by announcing that Ireland was to become a Republic and would be withdrawing from the British Commonwealth. This extraordinary development, which has given us the Republic of Ireland, has left the merest trace on the public consciousness, and its anniversary, for instance, is not regarded as an occasion for celebration, the reason being, perhaps, that in practical terms it made little difference.

We see a further development in Seán Keating's attitude to life in the Free State in his Economic Pressure (1930) which shows the graphic impact of emigration in spite of the earnest efforts of its government to improve Ireland's self-reliance. It is, for all intents and purposes, an indictment of the new state's performance to date.

Nevertheless, the declaration of a Republic had the effect of clarifying the southern state's constitutional position, and must rank as one of the most significant landmark actions of the first Inter-Party government. The others have stamped on them the name of the cabinet's young Minister for Health, Dr Noel Browne. Browne was a member of Clann na Poblachta, though his leanings were socialist rather than republican. His parents and two of his siblings had died of tuberculosis, from which he himself had suffered, and having qualified as a medical doctor, the eradication of the scourge of TB (which in the late 1940s was still killing between 3,000 and 4,000 Irish people a year) was a burning goal. Elected to the Dáil on his first attempt and appointed as a cabinet minister on his first day in the Dáil, the Health portfolio was ready-made for him. By a programme of vaccination for TB prevention, mass radiography for its early detection, and the building of new sanatoria where modern methods of treatment were available, Browne achieved extraordinary results in a very short space of time, and it has been his enduring legacy.

Another of Noel Browne's schemes, however, caused his government's fall from power. The National Health Service introduced in Britain after the war had shown up the inadequacies in Irish health and social welfare provision. Fianna Fáil, before falling from office in 1948, had intended to introduce a new health and welfare system, the essentials of which Noel Browne now sought to implement. The scheme would make medical services available to all mothers and to children below the age of sixteen, irrespective of family income, and was immediately opposed by the medical profession largely because of the potential implications of a free scheme on their own incomes.

The other group most opposed to what became known as the Mother and Child Scheme – and who ultimately sealed its fate – was the Catholic Hierarchy. Their tendency in general was to suspect any attempt to transfer responsibility for the welfare of children from their parents to state authority, but in this specific instance they feared that a hint of proposals to educate women 'in respect of motherhood' was code for contraception if not abortion, and condemned outright the provision of sex education by anyone who might not share the same religion of the patient. Once the Catholic Church committed itself to opposition to the Scheme it was a dead letter, since Browne's more conservative cabinet colleagues quickly distanced themselves from the proposal, and in any case he had few friends around the cabinet table for more personal reasons, having proven himself something of a maverick and difficult to work with. The result was Browne's resignation from cabinet in April 1951, and the government itself collapsed a month later.

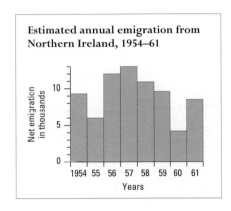

Estimated annual emigration from Northern Ireland, 1954–61

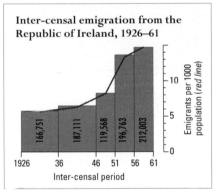

Inter-censal emigration from the Republic of Ireland, 1926–61

Few images capture the sense of stasis in the Republic in the 1950s better than those that deal with the chronic emigration of the period, which robbed the state of its most vital resource, its youth, many of whom left with bitterness in their hearts at the failure of their own government to provide for its people. The statistics from the north hide a considerably higher rate of Catholic as opposed to Protestant emigration which helped bolster the latter's rule by keeping the demographic gap intact.

The Stagnant Years

The abiding image of these years is one of economic and social stagnation, a state where government policy on everything from, as we have seen, health and education to such matters as what books one was allowed to read or what foreign films one was permitted to view, was dictated by edict – spoken and more often unspoken – of the Catholic Church. Although the state – and generations of Irish people in the years before they had a state – owed a great debt to church men and women who offered pastoral care and leadership in their

Éamon de Valera was by no means an extravagant man and certainly did not seek to use for his personal gain his position of power for so many years as leader of the Irish government, as others would later do. Nevertheless, the limited advances in the socio-economic conditions of the population at large in the decades that followed independence must be measured against the relative comfort that their leaders enjoyed. The photograph shows the fine house in Booterstown, Co. Dublin, in which Mr de Valera lived for many years before taking up residence in the even grander surroundings of Áras an Uachtaráin.

communities, a stabilising influence in times of calamity and crisis, and a sound education, by the mid-twentieth century the Church's influence was undoubtedly excessive. It had acquired something that was not far short of a stranglehold on Irish society, though it was only much later, in the mid- to late-1990s, that the worst excesses of this began to be fully explored. It must be said, for instance, that in an age when unemployment was endemic and opportunities for advancement few, the status afforded to clerics encouraged, and doubtless sometimes forced, individuals to join the priesthood or religious orders who were unsuited for a role as pastors and, indeed, as celibates. Thus, the enormously important role of such orders as the Irish Christian Brothers or the Sisters of Mercy, as educators of the nation's children and as custodians of orphans and those committed to state care, has been tarnished by the small minority in their ranks who used positions of unchallenged authority for their own sadistic or sexual gratification.

It is, of course, vital to bear in mind the contemporary context: this was a time when even the leader of the Irish Labour Party, Brendan Corish, could announce to the Dáil, as he did in 1953 that 'I am an Irishman second; I am a Catholic first'. It is hardly surprising that the only option for dissonant voices was emigration. Emigration also provided one of the few outlets for enterprise, and throughout the 1950s was running at levels which had not been witnessed since the 1880s, much of it to the industrial heartlands of the English Midlands. In truth, to those who looked back on the sacrifices made in the struggle for independence, the Irish state seemed at this point to have failed, at least in terms of its primary function of providing a reasonable quality of life and a basic standard of living for its citizens.

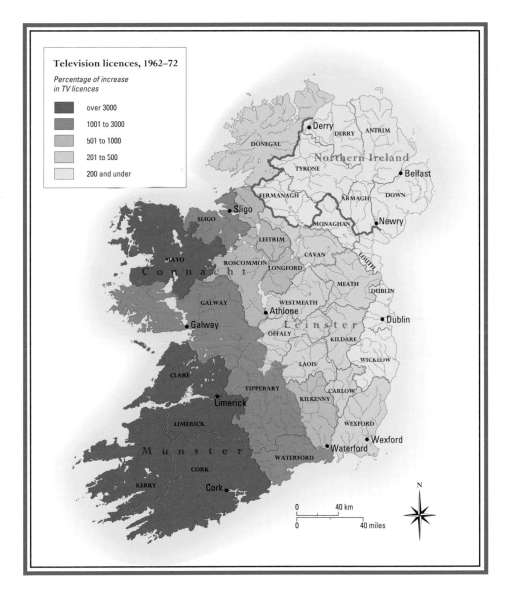

The Lemass Era

One of the reasons for the malaise at the heart of Irish society was undoubtedly the dead hand on the reins of government being wielded by what was now a generation of elder statesmen, whose revolutionary days were long since past. By 1957 when Éamon de Valera returned to government as Taoiseach after another brief Inter-Party interruption in Fianna Fáil rule, he was 75 years old

The entry of the Republic into the European Economic Community in 1973, along with Britain and Denmark, provided a long-awaited escape from dependence on the British market and economic stagnation. The referendum on the issue was passed by a majority of five to one in favour, the Common Agricultural Policy in particular acting as an enormous boost to Irish agriculture, because of the subsidies and higher prices it guaranteed for Irish farmers. Industry too gained from the diversification of markets and the inflow of funds from social and regional programmes.

but only his failing eyesight convinced him it was time to go (after which he served two seven-year terms as President). He chose as his successor another veteran of the War of Independence, Seán Lemass, who, however, differed from the 'Chief' in several important respects, most notably as regards the economy and, as we shall see, the north. It can rightfully be said that the modernisation of the Republic began under Lemass once he was elected Taoiseach in 1959.

The then Secretary of the Department of Finance was T. K. Whitaker who had been behind a report published in 1958 called the Programme for Economic Expansion (two more ambitious programmes were to follow). Whitaker concluded that the government's protectionist and self-sufficiency policies were retarding the expansion of the economy, and that free trade, while a risky strategy, was preferable to the doldrums produced by protectionism. No one could deny that the state remained over-dependent on the British market and that foreign investment should be encouraged which would help open up new markets for Irish exports. Europe at this juncture was undergoing a post-war economic revival and the new Irish expansionist policy produced rapid successes in terms of industrial output and employment (with a consequent fall in emigration), though the old-fashioned protected sector suffered badly.

The gains were so rapid that when President John F. Kennedy visited Ireland just months before his assassination, he paid tribute to the state's recent advances, in addressing a joint session of the Oireachtas (the Dáil and Irish Senate combined): 'You have modernised your economy, harnessed your rivers, diversified your industry, liberalised your trade, electrified your farms,

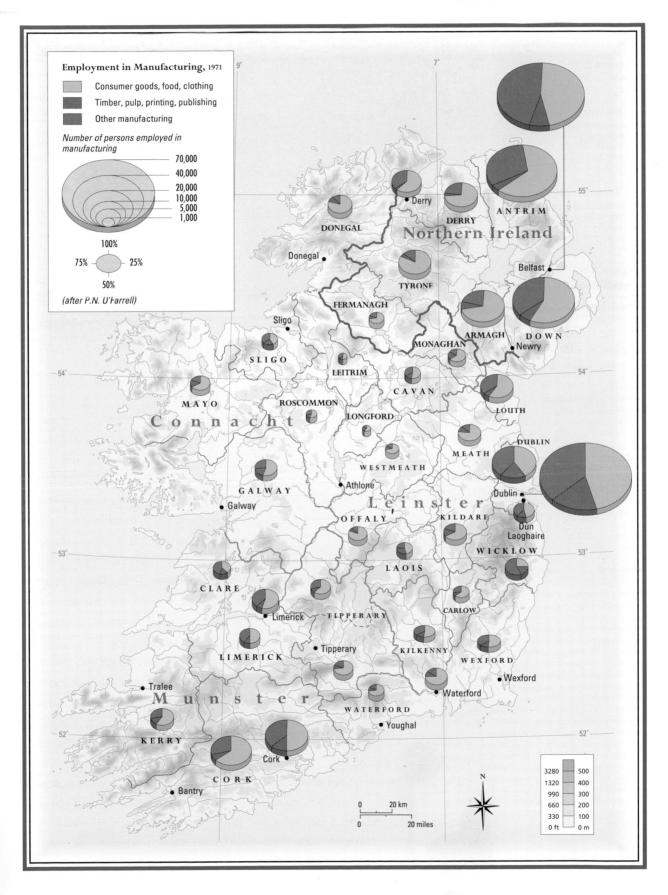

Employment in Manufacturing, 1971

Consumer goods, food, clothing

Timber, pulp, printing, publishing

Other manufacturing

Number of persons employed in manufacturing

70,000
40,000
20,000
10,000
5,000
1,000

100%

75%   25%

50%

(after P.N. U'Farrell)

accelerated your rate of growth and improved the living standards of your people'. The rural electrification to which he referred had, of course, been ongoing for many years, but its fruits were now being seen in terms of social development beyond the towns and cities. It meant that when the state had inaugurated a television service in 1961, it became – especially through its flagship Late Late Show, hosted by Gay Byrne (himself a newly returned emigrant) – a forum for public debate on social and political matters which had not hitherto been aired. When Pope John XXIII held the Second Vatican Council the Catholic Church too opened itself to radical change, the effects of which in Ireland cannot be overstated. The 'sixties had truly arrived, and they had the same radicalising effect in Ireland as they had throughout the western world.

Ireland's modernity is seen in an appetite abroad for things Irish, including its music, most successfully perhaps by the group U2, its dance, shown by the success of 'Riverdance', and even the enthusiasm in film and TV for works set in the country. The photograph shows the small bar in the village of Avoca, Co. Wicklow, which gained international fame through its quaint but still rather charming portrayal as the setting for the highly popular Ballykissangel TV series.

The Lemass Legacy

Seán Lemass did not spend long as Taoiseach, but he left a long shadow. The Lemass legacy manifested itself in various ways, not all, of course, as he would have wished. The overriding effect of the Lemass period in government and the ethos to which it gave rise was positive, but there was a price to be paid, as well as gains to be made. The Lemass era opened Ireland to economic growth, and inaugurated a period when government could at last look beyond its nearest neighbour for affiliation and inspiration. Ireland enthusiastically sought entry to the Common Market within a couple of years of Lemass's election as Taoiseach, but when Charles de Gaulle vetoed British membership in 1963, Irish admission foundered on the same rock.

However, general Irish enthusiasm for Europe never waned and its entry to the European Economic Community in 1973 was the beginning of an admittedly gradual realignment in the state's vital points of reference. Although coloured by being a net beneficiary of European funding programmes into the early years of the twenty-first century, Irish enthusiasm for the European 'ideal' has remained strong, and the Euro-scepticism that earned Great Britain so many enemies under its late-twentieth-century governments beginning with Margaret Thatcher was alien to the great mass of the Irish people and not a factor in state policy. By the end of the twentieth century, therefore, one of the positive contributions of the Lemass change of focus was to put Ireland, a small nation on its periphery, at the heart of Europe, and to foster a positive sense of European identity in the country.

From the Oil Crisis to the Celtic Tiger

Membership of the European Community brought very considerable benefits to Ireland in terms of the transference to it of very substantial 'structural' funds from wealthier members, as part of the process of 'cohesion' whereby poorer member-states would be aided to catch up economically on the larger

economies. This proved pivotal in transforming the agricultural sector in Ireland, so that while numbers dwelling on the land greatly diminished over time, the standard of living of those who remained was enormously enhanced.

Being part of the Common Market meant, however, that Ireland was not spared any of the hardship caused by the oil crisis of 1973 and the international recession that followed it. The coalition government led by Fine Gael under Liam Cosgrave (son of W. T.) struggled hard to counter this but, just as the new circumstances of membership of the Community left the country open to expansion, so too world recession was something from which the state could no

The government policy of seeking to attract foreign investment was for many years a near impossible task, and many false starts were made along the way. But the 1990s saw a shift towards computer-based and pharmaceutical industry which has led to spectacular growth.

longer find shelter. Lemass's successor, Jack Lynch, swept to victory in 1977, therefore, on a Keynesian expansionist manifesto which only succeeded in heightening the country's difficulties in terms of inflation, debt, and unemployment. When he was overthrown in 1979, in an internal Fianna Fáil coup, by Lemass's son-in-law Charles Haughey, crisis seemed on the point of being averted – especially when the latter appeared on a televised broadcast cautioning the nation against living beyond its means – but he too failed to live up to his early promise and the slide continued.

For much of the 1980s the Republic of Ireland lurched from crisis to crisis, some economic, some so extraordinary that when Charles Haughey, central to some at least of them, described them as 'grotesque, unbelievable, bizarre, unprecedented', an inveterate enemy, Conor Cruise O'Brien, coined an acronym for the period, 'GUBU', which has remained with it ever since. The 'eighties witnessed a see-saw pattern of government led in turns by Haughey and his long-standing Fine Gael opponent, Garret FitzGerald, the latter, though, unable to solve the economic catastrophe facing the state because of his reliance on Labour Party coalitionists unwilling to accept the budgetary cuts which alone could solve the state's frightening level of indebtedness. With it came rates of unemployment hitherto unknown in the country and the return of mass emigration on a scale not seen since the 1950s.

In the end, the corner was turned when the Haughey minority government elected in 1987, with a tough Finance Minister in Ray MacSharry, introduced stringent cuts in public expenditure, confident in the knowledge that the opposition would not out-vote them as long as the new Fine Gael leader, Alan Dukes, deemed them necessary in the country's interest. Dukes's 'Tallaght Strategy', arguably the most patriotic endeavour by any political leader in the history of the Republic – which in the end lost him his leadership of Fine Gael – won the state its freedom from financial crisis and set the scene for an unprecedented period of economic growth which turned the Republic from being the 'sick man' of Europe in the mid-1980s to the 'Celtic Tiger' of a decade later.

Why Ireland?

The precise 'trigger' of the Celtic Tiger remains a matter of speculation. European Union funding certainly helped, as did Ireland's keen participation in the development of a single European market, at a time when Great Britain under Margaret Thatcher and John Major was bringing down the shutters on Europe, and thereby losing friends and potential investors. One of the keys was the industrial peace heralded by the concept of 'social partnership' introduced under the later Haughey administrations. This brought together employers, trades unions, farmers, the voluntary sector and others, to negotiate a fixed 'programme' of pay rises, welfare provision, and so forth, and, by guaranteeing industrial harmony for the stated period of the agreement, set the foundation for stability. This stability extended beyond social partnership to government, so that although governments throughout the 1980s and 1990s came and went – including, by the late 1980s, Fianna Fáil 'partnership' governments with either the break-away Progressive Democrats or with Labour – the basic economic, industrial and fiscal strategy remained stable. Foreign investors could look to the future with a degree of confidence hitherto lacking.

Another factor was infrastructural development, such as the enormous telecommunications investment initiated by Albert Reynolds in the 1980s, which encouraged foreign investors to overlook Ireland's peripheral location. This infrastructure in place, state agencies charged with responsibility for targeting inward investment, shifted their focus from older-style heavy manufacturing, to the types of industries for which the technological infrastructure was best suited: these were lighter industries like the manufacture of pharmaceuticals and computers. Here, the ready availability of a well-educated English-

One of the key factors in the success of the 'Celtic Tiger' was the decision to seek to make Ireland a centre for international financial services, a gamble about which many were at first sceptical but which in time delivered enormous growth, especially by the early to mid-1990s. The photograph shows the Irish Financial Services Centre with its 18th-century equivalent, Gandon's magnificent Custom House, in the background.

speaking workforce was a big advantage: their computer-literacy meant that when the 'Information Age' dawned, the Republic of Ireland was well placed to serve it. Few sectors of the economy were to be so rapidly transformed by 'information technology' as that of financial services, and here another Haughey gamble paid off: the establishment in Dublin of the International Financial Services Centre, which struggled in its early years in spite of generous tax-incentives but did manage by the mid-1990s to turn Dublin into an important hub for European banking and investment services.

Less tangible, but perhaps no less important, in transforming the face of Ireland in the 1990s, were developments in the areas of sport, culture, music and literature which elevated Ireland's image abroad, produced a sense of national well-being – the 'feel good' factor – and led to a greater sense of belief in Ireland's potential. At its most visible and, perhaps, most joyous level, there was the albeit limited success of the Republic's international soccer team under Jack Charlton, the behaviour of Irish fans abroad contrasting markedly with that of other nations, and giving the impression, quite simply, that it was 'fun to be Irish'. There was the surprise election of Mary Robinson as President in 1990, a life-long champion of the rights of women and the oppressed, who revolutionised the rather moribund office of ceremonial head of state, turning it into one over which the people believed they had some 'ownership'. And there was the transformation of the Temple Bar area of Dublin – again, another Haughey brainchild – into the capital's 'cultural quarter', which went part of the way to making the city one of the most popular 'city break' destinations in Europe. These, and a multitude of other signposts, pointed the way to the Celtic Tiger.

The Downside

It was, unfortunately, another legacy of the Lemass era that rapid industrial, commercial and building development offered the potential for quick gain to those unscrupulous enough to seize it. Fianna Fáil, the party of the small farmer and the working man, came to be associated in the Lemass years with support for economic development, and, it must be said, so needy was the country for such 'advancement' that few questions were asked about the short-cuts taken to achieve it. The 'sixties became known as the era of the men in the mohair suits, a description which seemed to sum up the stock appearance of these young men in a hurry, who seized the opportunities then on offer, and, from humble backgrounds, gained riches overnight.

Nobody typified the breed more than Charles Haughey himself, a man born in poor circumstances, who benefited from a good Christian Brothers education, was the first of his family to attend university, where, at University College Dublin, he would meet the Taoiseach's daughter, Maureen Lemass, whom he was to marry. A career in politics beckoned, and that career gave him access to power, and, more importantly, to people who needed to be close to the centre of power if their get-rich-quick schemes were to be fulfilled. Overnight, it seemed, Haughey became an extremely wealthy man indeed and, although rumours about the source of his enormous wealth circulated all his political life, the real truth only surfaced under the scrutiny of judicial tribunals established in the late 1990s.

Like many others Charles Haughey invested heavily in land in the greater

Dublin area, and for many years in the latter decades of the century allegations circulated about corruption among local politicians and high-ranking public officials involved in the planning process. It was claimed that some of them were engaged in helping to have land which was part of the 'green belt' (preventing Dublin's sprawling suburbs from merging into one great concrete mass), or that had previously been zoned for agricultural use, redesignated for the purposes of housing. This, of course, vastly increased the value of the land, and it was alleged that they accepted bribes from property developers for voting for such rezoning. Again, only the 'planning' tribunals established in the dying years of the century managed to prove that some at least of these allegations were true. It seemed that the 'Celtic Tiger' had cubbed an ugly brood.

The Social Transformation

Every country which faces change faces challenges. It is fair to say that the Republic of Ireland in the late twentieth century failed in rising to meet many of the challenges that came with 'progress'. The social transformation was enormous. The solution to the rapid urban expansion of the 1960s, especially in Dublin, was to relocate whole communities from the inner city – converting it in places to a forgotten wasteland – and the ghettoisation of tens of

The summer of 1971 saw the deaths of two Catholics in Derry at the hands of British soldiers which caused the newly-founded SDLP to withdraw from the Stormont parliament when the authorities refused to hold an inquiry into the deaths. By 9 August internment without trial had been introduced, but nationalist outrage expressed on the streets led to a further 17 deaths within days.

thousands in vast, sprawling housing estates and flats complexes, communities on the margins of the city in every sense.

In deprived inner-city areas and suburban ghettos in the 1980s and 1990s, educational provision was poor and the prospects for employment negligible. As ever in such circumstances the nightmare of drug addiction gripped whole communities and the gang leaders who orchestrated the importation and distribution of drugs, heroin in particular, amassed fortunes out of the misery they inflicted, while the police made few inroads because of the inadequacy of the outmoded legal remedies at their disposal. Government and public alike were all too aware of the problem, since the activities of the gang leaders became more audacious, their flaunted lifestyles more flamboyant, and their contempt for the law ever more obvious. In fact, it was only when a prominent investigative newspaper journalist, Veronica Guerin, who had helped to highlight the problem, was murdered at the order of such a gangster in June 1996 that a stunned nation and government finally woke up to the danger the gangland problem posed, and stringent new laws were rushed through the Oireachtas which finally brought the problem under some degree of control.

The Northern State Challenged

If Seán Lemass can be said to have begun the 1960s social and economic transformation of Ireland, he played a critical role in yet another phase in Ireland's story. The election in 1962 of a new leader of Ulster Unionism, Captain Terence O'Neill, was significant in that he was intent on following the modernising economic policies that had worked well under Lemass in the Republic, and on making moderate gestures of accommodation to nationalists. O'Neill's most startling gesture in this regard was his invitation to Seán Lemass to visit Stormont in 1965, an innovation only rivalled by the latter's decision to accept (as did his successor, Jack Lynch, in December 1967). The significance of this first meeting between the leaders of the two administrations was that O'Neill was offering the hand of friendship to the head of a government of a state which denied the legitimacy of his own, while Lemass, in coming north, was conferring on the northern statelet a degree of de facto legitimacy.

The timing is also significant. It was inevitable that the worldwide radicalisation of the 'sixties would have profound consequences in the six counties. One of the great engines of social change in the Republic in the late 'sixties and after was

The Republic's Taoiseach, Jack Lynch, expressed as forcibly as he could the government's unwillingness 'to stand by' and watch its countrymen suffer the loss of their homes, and frequently life and limb, at the hands of Loyalist mobs. Others in the government, including Charles Haughey (seen here in the background) were accused of going beyond words and seeking to supply arms to the Nationalist community for their own defence.

the introduction of free second-level education by the then Minister, Donogh O'Malley, but the north was at that same point beginning to harvest the benefits of the 1944 Education Act which had opened the way to university for large numbers of working-class Catholics. These articulate and self-confident young men and women now started to make their presence felt, to air their frustrations and their aspirations, and they were no longer prepared to accept the second-class citizenship which had been their co-religionists' lot for generations.

Since 1953 the Nationalist Party at Stormont had been led by the moderate Derry constitutionalist Eddie McAteer, who ensured that the cause of Irish unity remained a live issue and the grievances of nationalists were heard. But the Nationalist Party was predominantly middle-class and rural and led from west of the Bann; working-class Belfast Catholics played little role in it. More

When the Stormont regime came under attack the Orange Order (seen here marching in Ballymena) sought to defend an institution it regarded as its own: all leaders of the Ulster Unionist Party had been members and between 1921 and 1969 all but three Unionist cabinet ministers had likewise been Orangemen.

extreme nationalists waged an armed campaign against Stormont beginning in 1956, but by 1962 the IRA announced its 'termination'. It was in the aftermath of this that the Lemass and Lynch visits to Stormont took place, and it must have been this hint of change in the air that unleashed the forces of loyalist reaction when, on 27 May 1966, a young Catholic named John Scullion was killed in a gun attack in Belfast, which was followed on 26 June by an attack on four Catholic barmen in a bar in Malvern Street, one of whom, Peter Ward, was killed. Responsibility for the murders was claimed by the recently formed Ulster Volunteer force (UVF).

Equally ominous at this point was the emergence from obscurity of an evangelical Protestant clergyman named Ian Paisley: the abiding goal of Rev.

Paisley's life was the protection of Protestantism from the threat which he believed Roman Catholicism represented, and the method by which he sought to achieve his goal was by resisting any developments which he viewed as undermining the Protestant basis of the northern state.

The Northern Eruption

Nothing short of a revolution began in the six counties in 1968. Its leadership was diverse, its objectives equally so, but it began from the premise that the power structures of the manufactured statelet of Northern Ireland deliberately marginalised a very sizeable minority of its population on the grounds of their religion and political allegiance: Stormont was an impregnable Protestant and Unionist citadel, which functioned through a civil service and a police service which were equally Protestant and Unionist. Eddie McAteer's Nationalist Party had argued for change, the IRA had ventured a more lethal solution, but to no avail. Meanwhile, a new, well-educated and vocal generation viewed on their television screens the progress of the black civil rights movement in the USA, the 'Prague Spring', the student riots in Paris in 1968, and saw what they themselves might achieve, through protest.

Apart from their exclusion from government they knew what it was like to suffer discrimination. Fermanagh was a county which had a Catholic majority, and yet, in the mid-sixties, only seven out of 75 school bus drivers were Catholic. Derry was a city with a Catholic majority: in 1967 there were 8,781 Unionist voters and 14,047 Nationalists, and yet the gerrymandering of seats on its council meant that it elected 12 Unionists and only 8 Nationalists. In the summer of 1968, in Caledon, Co. Tyrone, a strongly nationalist village with a severe housing shortage, a council-built house was given to a young, single Protestant woman, causing the Nationalist MP for the area, Austin Currie, to protest by squatting in the house until evicted by the RUC. The newly-formed Northern Ireland Civil Rights Association (NICRA) announced a civil rights march from Coalisland to Dungannon to protest against the case, though they were prohibited from entering the town centre: nevertheless, the publicity which the march attracted, and the way in which this helped to highlight the discrimination in housing allocation, served its purpose.

Derry had its own Housing Action Committee by this point, led by the life-long socialist activist, Eamon McCann, and on 5 October 1968 they organised a civil rights march which had been officially banned in advance by the Stormont Home Affairs Minister, William Craig, but this served only to attract further attention to the event. When the leaders – including McCann, Eddie McAteer, the Belfast socialist Gerry Fitt, and the young Derry schoolteacher and moderate nationalist John Hume – began to move the crowd forward, the police baton-charged them and then sought to disperse the crowd with water cannon. This event changed the course of the later history of the north, perhaps for one reason above all others: the police brutality was captured by television cameras and beamed around the world, where suddenly this place called Northern Ireland headline news.

This event was also important as marking the emergence of John Hume as a force in Irish politics, as the old Nationalist Party began to fade into history. He was one of the organisers of a massive march, over 15,000 strong, into Derry in early November after which O'Neill's government announced reforms in the local Derry administration. For Unionist extremists like Rev. Paisley and William Craig this was interpreted as a sign of weakness, but for civil rights activists it was, as always with such tinkering in the midst of a crisis, too little, too late. On New Year's Day 1969 a group of Queen's University students calling themselves People's Democracy began a march from Belfast to Derry. As they approached Derry on 4 January they were attacked by groups of loyalists at a place called Burntollet where many of them were badly injured. They claimed that the RUC had stood by while they were attacked and that among their assailants were off-duty members of the police's auxiliary wing, the B-Specials. There followed a night of rioting and police aggression in Derry's Bogside, where barricades were erected and the famous slogan 'You are now entering Free Derry' was painted on a

No single individual summed up the resistance of the Protestants of the six counties to admitting Nationalists to an equal role in government than Ian Paisley. He modelled himself consciously on Sir Edward Carson and his oratorical skills were put to effective use in marshalling support for his cause, a combination of loyalty to the British Crown and the assertion of Protestant supremacy, the latter usually, when it came to the crunch, being paramount.

gable wall. In the Stormont elections in February John Hume won at the expense of Eddie McAteer, while in a contest for a Westminster seat in April a young woman called Bernadette Devlin was elected MP for Mid-Ulster. Hume's forceful logic and Devlin's magnetic presence would further highlight the nationalist case.

By the summer of 1969 Terence O'Neill had been ousted by his critics within Unionism, and large-scale rioting in Derry – known ever since as the 'Battle of the Bogside' – had led to British troops being deployed on the streets. It was only a matter of time before the tinder-box that was Belfast burst into flame, and this it did on the night of 14 August. When rival crowds clashed in the streets between the Falls and the Shankill, a Protestant was shot dead: police in armoured cars opened fire with machine-guns and killed a nine-year-old

The Northern Crisis

1. October 1968: Civil Rights march conflicts with police
2. January 1969: march attacked
3. August 1969: British troops deployed
4. July 1970: Falls Road curfew
5. August 1971: Internment swoop
6. January 1972: 'Bloody Sunday'
7. July 1972: 'Bloody Friday'
8. May 1974: Loyalist car bomb
9. January 1976: 10 workmen shot dead
10. August 1976: Peace People movement starts
11. 1978: 'Dirty protest' by prisoners
12. August 1979: 18 paratroopers killed in explosion
13. August 1979: Lord Mountbatten assassinated
14. 1980–81: hunger strikes
15. 1982: 17 people killed in bombing
16. November 1985: Anglo-Irish Agreement signed
17. May 1987: 8 IRA members shot
18. November 1987: 11 killed at War Memorial bombing
19. January 1992: 8 killed in IRA bombing
20. October 1993: Shankill Road bombing
21. October 1993: Grey Steel shootings by Loyalists
22. 1995–2000: Orangemen march on Drumcree
23. August 1998: 31 killed in Omagh bombing

Seats Won at the General Election, 1997

- United Kingdom Unionist
- Ulster Unionist Party
- Social Democratic and Labour Party
- Democratic Unionist Party
- Sinn Féin

Catholic child in his own home. Rioting spread into the Catholic enclave of Ardoyne where the Catholics of Bombay Street were burned out of their houses by a Protestant mob. The violence was only quelled by the deployment of British troops in Belfast too, by which point eight people were dead and over 1,500 Catholic families had been driven from their homes. The drift into turmoil was beginning.

The Taoiseach, Jack Lynch, went on television to state that the Republic could not stand by and let its fellow countrymen suffer in this way, and two of his own cabinet – Neil Blaney and Charles Haughey – responded to the plight of northern nationalists by becoming embroiled in a plot to import arms for their defence, which led to the infamous 'Arms Crisis', during which they were sacked from government, tried and acquitted. In Britain, Labour Prime Minister Harold Wilson responded to the growing crisis by insisting on reforms, one of which included the disbandment of the notorious B-Specials. Ironically, loyalist rioting at this announcement caused the first death during the Troubles of an RUC man.

The Re-emergence of the IRA

During the rioting of the summer of '69 the IRA had been conspicuous by its absence, its initials being contemptuously reinterpreted as 'I Ran Away'. Its inactivity was partly the product of the prevailing ethos of the organisation which was strongly left-wing and in favour of moving away from traditional Republican tactics, including abstention from Stormont. Those opposed to this development broke from the main organisation at the party's Árd Fheis in Dublin in January 1970, forming a provisional executive and quickly becoming known as the Provisionals. Their immediate goal was the protection of nationalist areas, especially in Belfast and Derry, but they were equally committed to using the crisis in government to go on a new anti-partition offensive.

In addition to the formation of the Provisional IRA, 1970 also saw the Rev. Paisley get himself elected to both Stormont and Westminster and pose a growing threat to mainstream Unionism, while a cross-community group of moderate and largely middle-class Protestants and Catholics formed a new party called Alliance. This was followed in the same summer by the formation of another new party, calling itself the Social Democratic and Labour Party (SDLP), made up of constitutional nationalists and left-wingers from a nationalist background, and led by the Belfast-based Gerry Fitt, but the brainchild of John Hume.

The tensions of the marching season brought rioting to the streets again, this time with an IRA presence. In Derry, in late June, five people (including two young sisters) were killed when a bomb accidentally exploded under construction. After an Orange parade in Belfast on 27 June rioting broke out and

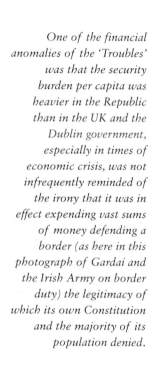

One of the financial anomalies of the 'Troubles' was that the security burden per capita was heavier in the Republic than in the UK and the Dublin government, especially in times of economic crisis, was not infrequently reminded of the irony that it was in effect expending vast sums of money defending a border (as here in this photograph of Gardaí and the Irish Army on border duty) the legitimacy of which its own Constitution and the majority of its population denied.

for the first time the Provisionals were deployed to protect the Catholic enclave of the Short Strand, as a result of which six people were killed. The result was the imposition of the 'Lower Falls Curfew', when 3,000 British troops were sent in to do house-to-house searches. Brought in to protect the nationalists of Belfast the army was now clearly their enemy; the IRA responded and a further five people died, though it was not until early in the following year, 6 February 1971, that the first British soldier was shot dead. Three weeks later, two RUC officers were killed, and a fortnight after that three off-duty soldiers were shot. The 'armed struggle' was well and truly under way.

The reaction within loyalism was the formation in October 1971 by Rev. Paisley of the Democratic Unionist Party (DUP), which had strong ties to his own Free Presbyterian Church. At about the same time Protestant vigilante groups in Belfast came together to form the Ulster Defence Association (UDA), a paramilitary organisation which, like Paisley, viewed everything that had happened since 1968 as a sustained Catholic/nationalist assault on their Protestant/loyalist state.

Internment and Bloody Sunday

To this point Belfast had been at the heart of Provisional IRA activity, but in July two innocent and unarmed Catholics were murdered by soldiers in Derry, and from this point onwards recruitment into the ranks of the 'Provos' swelled. If this wasn't enough, the new northern Prime Minister, Brian Faulkner, decided that he would become their recruiting sergeant by the introduction of large-scale internment without trial. It began in dawn swoops on 9 August 1971, several hundreds being forcibly detained, a great many of them totally innocent of any political involvement. The reaction against it was immediate: within the next three days 22 people were killed. For the rest

of 1971 the IRA was engaged on a massive bombing offensive against economic targets in Belfast and a gun offensive against the hated 'security' forces, during which 41 of the latter and 73 civilians lost their lives.

In 'Free Derry', the barricades were re-erected around the Bogside and the Creggan, and it was largely under IRA control. An anti-internment march on 30 January 1972 organised by the Northern Ireland Civil Rights Association (NICRA) was banned by Faulkner, but about 10,000 nevertheless assembled in the Creggan intent on marching to the city's Guildhall Square. A local RUC chief argued against interfering with the protesters but a decision was made further up the line to confine the marchers within the Bogside, and the Parachute Regiment was sent in. By evening they had killed or mortally wounded 14 men. None of them was armed, no arms were found, and there were no army casualties, yet the latter insisted that they acted only in response to firing.

Bloody Sunday was the most traumatic day in the Troubles to date, and one which few who lived through it could ever forget. It unleashed such an enraged frenzy throughout nationalist Ireland that even the British Embassy in Dublin was burned to the ground. And anger merely turned to contempt when the official report by Lord Widgery published in April seemed to exonerate those responsible and to blame the dead. Their families and nationalists in general continued to demand to know the full truth, but they had to wait an astonishing 28 years before the public hearings of the Bloody Sunday Enquiry, chaired by Lord Saville, began to reveal quite the extent of the atrocity which had been perpetrated against them.

The 1937 Constitution created a Presidential office with very restricted powers in order to ensure that its holder would act the role of a symbolic head of state only. Its early incumbents, including its architect Éamon de Valera, filled just such a role, but the election of Mary Robinson in 1990 breathed new life into the Presidency and she and her successor, Mary McAleese, worked skilfully within the narrow remit set by the Constitution to play a role of real value to the Republic's citizens at home and abroad.

The Fall of Stormont

In the aftermath of Bloody Sunday it became clear that the Stormont régime could not last. The Conservative government of Edward Heath had backed the introduction of internment in the hope that it might quell the unrest. It had sought too to end the affront to the state's authority which 'Free Derry' represented and which the protesters so loudly proclaimed when they pro-

The efforts to bring an end to the 'Troubles' had at their core a conviction that the time had come to 'remove the gun from Irish politics' forever. That meant, not simply the silencing of the weapons of the paramilitary groups on either side of the political and religious divide, but the reform and demilitarisation of the Royal Ulster Constabulary and the withdrawal to barracks and eventual removal from Irish soil of British troops, a complex jigsaw which has proved enormously difficult to assemble.

ceeded in holding marches which had been officially banned. But the awful aftermath of Bloody Sunday convinced Heath that Stormont must go. When Brian Faulkner rejected a package of reforms proposed by Downing Street in March 1972, Heath announced that the Stormont Parliament would be prorogued for one year. In fact, on 28 March 1972 Stormont's 50 years of one party rule ended for good.

With the collapse of Stormont, direct rule from Westminster was introduced as a temporary measure until a new power-sharing accommodation could be arrived at. Nobody at the time realised quite the journey that would have to be travelled to arrive at such a pass, a journey made necessary by, on the one hand, Unionism's refusal to recognise the validity of the nationalists' demand to have their Irish identity given formal constitutional expression and, on the other, the Republican refusal to accept that their ultimate goal of a re-united Ireland was not attainable in the prevailing circumstances.

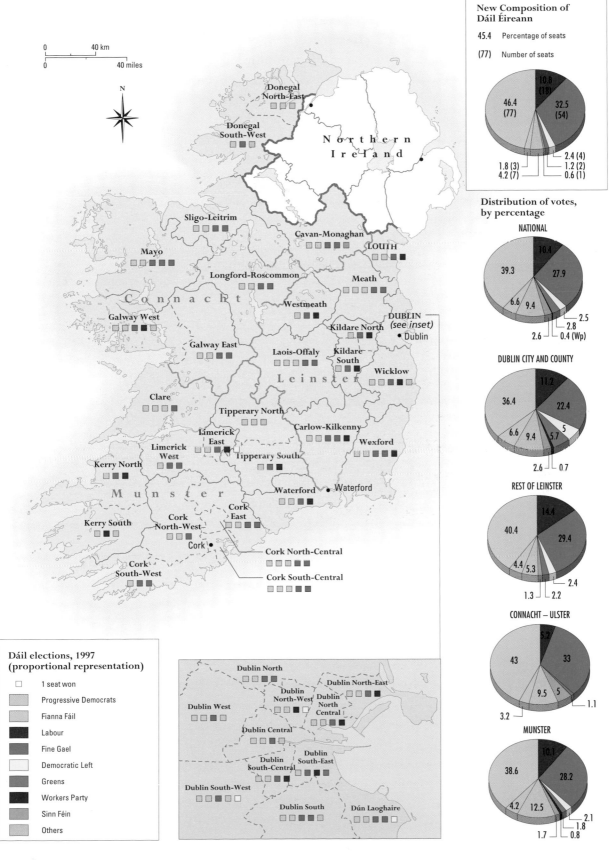

0   40 km
0   40 miles

N

Donegal
North-East

Donegal
South-West

Northern
Ireland

Sligo-Leitrim

Cavan-Monaghan

LOUTH

Mayo

Longford-Roscommon

Meath

C o n n a c h t

Westmeath

DUBLIN
(see inset)

Galway West

Kildare North

• Dublin

Galway East

Laois-Offaly

Kildare
South

Wicklow

L e i n s t e r

Clare

Tipperary North

Carlow-Kilkenny

Limerick
East

Wexford

Limerick
West

Tipperary South

Kerry North

M u n s t e r

Waterford   • Waterford

Kerry South

Cork
North-West

Cork
East

• Cork

Cork North-Central

Cork
South-West

Cork South-Central

**New Composition of
Dáil Éireann**

45.4   Percentage of seats
(77)   Number of seats

10.8
(18)
46.4
(77)
32.5
(54)
2.4 (4)
1.2 (2)
1.8 (3)
4.2 (7)
0.6 (1)

**Distribution of votes,
by percentage**

NATIONAL

10.4
39.3
27.9
6.6
9.4
2.5
2.8
2.6
0.4 (Wp)

DUBLIN CITY AND COUNTY

11.2
36.4
22.4
6.6
9.4
5.7
5
2.6
0.7

REST OF LEINSTER

14.4
40.4
29.4
4.4
5.3
2.4
1.3
2.2

CONNACHT – ULSTER

5.2
43
33
9.5
5
1.1
3.2

MUNSTER

10.1
38.6
28.2
4.2
12.5
2.1
1.8
1.7
0.8

**Dáil elections, 1997
(proportional representation)**

☐   1 seat won

Progressive Democrats

Fianna Fáil

Labour

Fine Gael

Democratic Left

Greens

Workers Party

Sinn Féin

Others

Dublin North

Dublin North-East

Dublin West

Dublin
North-West

Dublin
North
Central

Dublin Central

Dublin
South-East

Dublin
South-Central

Dublin South-West

Dublin South

Dún Laoghaire

The Long Road to Peace

It is hardly necessary to chronicle here the long and tragic story of the 25 years spent trying to find an agreement acceptable to all sides. In the aftermath of Stormont's fall the Sunningdale Conference of December 1973 sought a solution based on a power-sharing executive at Stormont and a Council of Ireland to give recognition to the Irish dimension. Successful for some months the executive sank on the rocks of loyalist objections to the all-Ireland Council and in the midst of a 'workers' strike' which was little short of a *coup d'état* which the British Labour government failed to face down. The rest of the '70s saw few signs of progress but the IRA hunger-strikes of 1981, and the perceived intransigence of the new British Prime Minister, Margaret Thatcher, succeeded in politicising a new generation of young nationalists. It was perhaps fear of the growing electoral success of Sinn Féin at the expense of the moderate SDLP that convinced her to conclude with the Republic's Taoiseach, Garret FitzGerald, the Anglo-Irish Agreement of 1985, giving the Republic for the first time the right to be consulted on matters of concern to do with the north.

This was by no means a solution, however. What really began the later peace process was the brave decision by John Hume, amidst widespread condemnation, to enter dialogue with the leader of Sinn Féin, Gerry Adams. This was successful in persuading the then British Secretary of State for Northern Ireland, Peter Brooke, to admit in November 1989 that the IRA could not be defeated militarily and to make a statement a year later to the effect that Britain no longer had any selfish economic or strategic reason for remaining in Ireland. These were important signals of good intent in the eyes of Republicans, but the Unionists were not yet ready to deal with them. Instead, abortive talks took place in 1991–92 between all parties except Sinn Féin, who were excluded because of the continued armed campaign, based on John Hume's three-strand formulation: Strand One dealt with possible arrangements for internal northern self-government; Strand Two with a possible north-south dimension to any new settlement; and Strand Three with east-west relations between all the inhabitants of Britain and Ireland.

This formula remained central to future negotiations but the missing link in the chain was Sinn Féin participation. Therefore, efforts behind the scenes focused on getting the IRA to agree to a cessation, efforts encouraged by John Hume's continuing dialogue, by the quiet mediation of the new Taoiseach, Albert Reynolds, and by leaders of Irish-American opinion, including President Clinton, who made Ireland one of his top foreign policy priorities. When Reynolds met the new British Prime Minister, John Major, in December 1993 they agreed a Joint Declaration by which the British formally agreed that it was for the people of 'the island of Ireland alone by agreement between the two parts respectively, to exercise their right of self-determination on the basis of consent freely given, North and South, to bring about a united Ireland, if that is their wish'.

All of these moves resulted in the declaration by the IRA on 31 August 1994 of 'a complete cessation of military operations'. By October, Loyalist paramilitaries had made a similar announcement. All the pieces required for political progress seemed to be in place, but not so. The fall from power of the Fianna Fáil Taoiseach and his replacement by Fine Gael's John Bruton was not a welcome development in Republican eyes, as he had shown little understanding of their concerns in the past. This was followed by the greatest bugbear of all to political advancement, the insistence by John Major on what he termed the 'decommissioning' of paramilitary weapons in advance of talks.

To make matters worse, the climate for compromise deteriorated when the issue of Orange parades through Catholic areas reached boiling point in the summer of 1995. It did so over one parade in particular, to Drumcree parish church outside Portadown, when the Orangemen insisted on their 'traditional right' to march home down the Garvaghy Road, even though it cut through a predominantly nationalist housing estate. After a stand-off the Orangemen forced their way through on 9 July 1995, led by Ian Paisley and the local Ulster Unionist MP, David Trimble, whose stance on behalf of the Orangemen helped win him the leadership of his party soon afterwards. Perceived as an uncompromising leader, Republican faith in the peace process was further undermined, and when John Major decided to hold

The Orange Order is a Protestant political society, founded in 1795, which has continued to provide an organisational resource for Ulster Unionism and has been a cause of sustained sectarian tensions in the north in particular for many generations. This early 19th-century hall in the sleepy Co. Down village of Grey Abbey, replete with red, white and blue kerbstones, has an innocuous appearance which belies the Order's more extreme tendencies.

elections to a new northern Forum in advance of any talks, their patience broke. On 9 February 1996 the IRA ended its 17-month ceasefire with a massive explosion at London's Canary Wharf, killing two people. Stalemate had returned.

The Good Friday Agreement

John Major's precarious hold on power prevented him from risking any move which might alienate the Unionist MPs on whom he relied for political survival. It took the Labour landslide on 1 May 1997 and the election of Tony Blair as British Prime Minister, with Mo Mowlam as his Northern Secretary, to produce movement. By 22 July the IRA had announced a new cessation. Negotiations began in the autumn under the chairmanship of the former American Senator, George Mitchell, though they were boycotted by Paisley's DUP because of Sinn Féin's participation. The talks were hard and fraught, and seemed many times on the brink of collapse, only to be rescued by Blair and his Irish counterpart Bertie Ahern, but an Agreement was eventually reached on Good Friday, 10 April 1998.

The Belfast Agreement stated that Northern Ireland would remain part of the United Kingdom unless a majority voted otherwise. A 108-member Assembly was to be established, elected by proportional representation, with cross-community consensus, ministries and membership of committees to be allocated on the basis of party strength. The Irish dimension critical to nationalist and Republican support was in the form of a North-South Ministerial Council, where the appropriate ministers from the Assembly and the Dáil would meet to co-operate on areas of mutual interest, and a number of 'Implementation Bodies' would be established to promote cross-border activities. The east-west aspect of the arrangement was a British-Irish Council with representatives of both sovereign governments and of the northern assembly, the Welsh Assembly, and the Scottish Parliament. Finally, the Republic's government agreed to hold a referendum to amend Articles 2 and 3 of its constitution which Unionists considered a belligerent claim on their territory.

It was a complex agreement which, although it had safeguards built in to protect the vital interests of all sides, could never hope to please the extremes. Nevertheless, in referenda held north and south on the same day, 2 May, the Good Friday Agreement was endorsed by 71.2 per cent in the north and over 90 per cent in the south. Assembly elections were held on 25 June where pro-Agreement parties fared well, though anti-Agreement Unionists were dangerously close to securing a majority within that community and thereby leaving the Assembly hamstrung since major decisions needed a cross-community majority. The leader of the Ulster Unionists, David Trimble, was elected First Minister with Seamus Mallon of the SDLP as his Deputy.

The euphoria which greeted the successful implementation of the Agreement was cruelly dashed on 15 August by the bomb left by a Republican splinter-group which killed 31 adults and children, two of them unborn. Omagh was the single greatest atrocity in the history of the Troubles. But, if anything, it served merely to strengthen the resolve of those committed to the Peace Process to overcome the odds, to prove wrong the doubters, and to consign to the past the divisions – political and sectarian – which had torn Ireland apart so often in previous generations as in this.

The Good Friday Agreement, like all products of human ingenuity, had its imperfections. It did not give Republicans the United Ireland they had fought so long to achieve, but the North-South Ministerial Council and Implementation Bodies put in place mechanisms whereby the partition between north and south could gradually be torn down. For Irish nation alists the time began to seem nearer when Robert Emmet's epitaph might be written, his country, more united than at any point in its earlier history, getting ready to take its rightful place among the nations of the world. Unionists, partly for this very reason, were and are lukewarm about the Agreement, but it has remained, as its supporters have so often reiterated, 'the only show in town'.

The parliament buildings at Stormont, outside Belfast, were erected to parade the dominance of what its first Prime Minister, James Craig, once proudly announced would be 'a Protestant Parliament for a Protestant people', but the road-sign beneath the statue of the father-figure of Unionism, Sir Edward Corson, seems to indicate that it may be time to yield ground to those of the other tradition.

CHRONOLOGY

8000 BC	First people arrive in Ireland, perhaps across the land bridge from Britain.
3000 BC	Arrival of New Stone Age people who built Newgrange.
c. 200 BC	Arrival of speakers of what develops into Gaelic.
AD 78–84	Roman Governor of Britain, Agricola, considers the invasion and conquest of Ireland.
c. 130–80	Ptolemy's account of Ireland.
367	Major offensive on Britain by the Irish, Picts and Saxons.
431	Pope sends Palladius as Bishop to Irish Christians.
432	St Patrick arrives to help convert pagan Gaelic kings to Christianity (traditional date).
c. 550–650	The growth of monasticism in Ireland.
563	Foundation of Iona by Columba.
575	Convention of Druim Ceat.
7th and 8th centuries	Ireland's Golden Age, *Book of Durrow*, *Book of Kells*, Ardagh Chalice.
c. 670–700	Tírechán and Muirchú produce hagiographical works on St Patrick.
697	Synod of Birr and the proclamation of the 'Law of the Innocents'.
c. 700	The Eóganacht become dominant in Munster.
721–42	Cathal mac Finguine King of Munster.
c. 725	Uí Briúin dynasty gain dominance in Connacht.
734	Abduction of Flaithbertach mac Loingsig. Cenél Conaill now excluded from Uí Néill Overkingship.
743	Clann Cholmáin first take the Overkingship of Uí Néill.
795	First Viking raid on Iona, Rathlin, Inishmurray and Inishbofin.
806	Vikings murder 68 members of Iona community.
820–47	Feidlimid MacCrimthainn King of Munster.
836	Viking raids penetrate deep inland.
837–42	Large Viking fleets appear and overwinter on the Boyne, the Liffey, Lough Neagh and in Dublin.
842	First reported Viking-Irish alliance.
845	Abbot of Armagh captured by Vikings.
846–62	The reign of Máel Sechnaill I, powerful Overking of Uí Néill.
914	The second wave of Viking raids.
975–1014	Brian Boru King of Munster.
980	Máel Sechnaill II becomes Overking of Uí Néill.
997	Brian Boru and Máel Sechnaill II divide Ireland.
999	Brian Boru defeats the Leinstermen and the Ostmen at Glenn Máma. Sitric Silkenbeard, King of Dublin, surrenders.
1002–14	Brian Boru King of Ireland.
1014	Death of Brian Boru at the Battle of Clontarf.
1142	Foundation of the first Cistercian house in Ireland.
1169	Arrival of English military leaders, fitz Stephen, FitzGerald and others.
1170–71	Arrival of 'Strongbow' in person. Strongbow becomes King of Leinster.

	Arrival of Henry II. Submission of most Irish Bishops and Irish Kings.
1175	Treaty of Windsor between Henry II and Rory O'Connor, High King of Ireland, who submits to rule unoccupied regions as a vassal.
1176	Death of Strongbow.
1177	Prince John made Lord of Ireland – first visit 1185.
c. 1200	Start of Classical Irish period in literature, lasting until 1600.
1210	King John's second visit. Confiscation of the Earldom of Ulster and Honor of Limerick – submission of some Irish kings.
1260	Battle of Down, death of Brian O'Neill.
1261	Battle of Callan.
1315	Invasion of Ireland by Edward Bruce. Proclaimed by Irish allies as King of Ireland.
1316	Rebellious Irish Chiefs defeated at Athenry.
1318	Battle of Dysert O'Dea. Battle of Fochart, Edward Bruce killed.
1333	Murder of Earl of Ulster, William de Burgh. Crown loses control of Anglo-Norman Connacht and the Irish Chiefs in Ulster.
1366	Statutes of Kilkenny to try and prevent English settlers adopting the Irish language
1394–95	King Richard II's first expedition to Ireland.
1414–47	Continual feud between political groupings of James Butler, Fourth Earl of Ormond and John Talbot, Earl of Shrewsbury, for control of Royal Government of Ireland.
1494	In the wake of Anglo-Irish support for Perkin Warbeck, Henry VII dismisses Kildare in 1492. Lord Deputy, Sir Edward Poynings, establishes 'Poynings' Law' making all English parliamentary legislation applicable to Ireland.
1496	Kildare reappointed.
1504	Battle of Knockadoe. Kildare victorious.
1509	Accession of Henry VIII.
1515	Anarchy sweeps Ireland.
1534	Kildare Rebellion leads to his arrest and death. Lord Offaly (Silken Thomas) takes leadership of revolt.
1536	Fall of Maynooth Castle – arrest of Lord Offaly and five uncles (all brought to England).
1536–37	Meeting of the Irish Reformation Parliament.
1540	Sir Anthony St Leger becomes Governor of Ireland.
1541	A Parliamentary meeting declares Henry VIII King of Ireland. The establishing of the 'Surrender and Re-grant' programme.
1558	Accession of Elizabeth I following the death of Mary I. The state-supported Reformation unpopular in Ireland.
1565–71	Sir Henry Sidney Governor of Ireland.
1569–71	Parliament declares the Lordship of Tyrone under the power of the Crown. Revolts in Munster, Leinster and Connacht against the policy.
1571–75	Sir William FitzWilliam Governor of Ireland.
1573	Private Colonisation ventures continue in Ulster.
1576	Reappointed Sidney launches conciliatory policy halting any further private colonisation.
1579–80	Rebellion in Munster. Exacerbated by a second revolt in Leinster led by James Eustace, Viscount Baltinglass and Feagh Mac Hugh O'Byrne. Support from discontented Palesmen. Arthur Lord Grey de Wilton is given the position of Governor to deal with the 'dual revolt'. Defeated at Glenmalure in Wicklow but successful at Smerwick.

1582–83	The suppression of both revolts in Munster and Leinster culminates in the killing of Earl of Desmond.
1595	Rebellion of Hugh O'Neill, Earl of Tyrone.
1598	O'Neill victorious at Yellow Ford, Ulster.
1601	O'Donnell, O'Neill and Spaniards defeated by Mountjoy at the Battle of Kinsale.
1603	The accession of James I leads to the enforcement of English law in Ireland, especially Ulster. Hugh O'Donnell and Earl of Tyrone surrender.
1607	The 'Flight of the Earls': O'Neill, Earl of Tyrone, O'Donnell, Earl of Tyrconnell.
1608	Plantation of Derry (City of London). Six other confiscated counties planned.
1641	Great Catholic-Gaelic rebellion for return of lands. Ireland thrown into chaos.
1642	Irish suppression hoped for by English Parliament with the 'Adventurers Act'. Robert Munro and army land in Ulster in April. Civil War in England. Catholic Confederation assembles at Kilkenny.
1649	Execution of Charles I. Cromwell's arrival in Ireland leads to capture of Drogheda, Wexford, New Ross. There follows a Cromwellian conquest and subsequent implementation of plantations.
1658	Death of Cromwell.
1660	Restoration period – accession of Charles II. Uphold Cromwellian conquest but restore property to 'innocent papists'.
1665	'Act of Explanation' obliges grantees of Cromwell to surrender one third of their lands to 'innocents'.
1685	Accession of James II.
1686–87	The newly appointed Earl of Tyrconnell, Richard Talbot, replaces Protestant officials with Catholics.
1688	Deposition of James II in England. Gates of Derry closed to James' troops.
1690	William of Orange defeats Jacobites at Boyne.
1695	Fourteen per cent of Irish land held by Catholics. Rights of Catholics restricted in education, arms-bearing and horse owning, and the Catholic clergy banished.
1699	Acts restricting Irish woollen exports.
1704	Catholics' presence restricted in landholding and public offices.
1713	Jonathan Swift becomes Dean of St Patrick's.
1728	Act removing franchise from Catholics.
1741	First performance of Handel's *Messiah* in Fishamble Street Music Hall.
1775	Henry Grattan leader of Patriot opposition in Irish Parliament.
1782	Irish Parliament successful in gaining 'legislative independence' from British.
1791	Wolfe Tone's *Argument on Behalf of the Catholics of Ireland*. Leads to foundation of Society of United Irishmen.
1792	Relief Act allows Catholics to practise law.
1796–98	United Irishmen plotting rebellion. Rebellion in Wexford in Mat 1798. Humbert lands in Killala in August. Tone arrested and dies in November.
1800	Act of Union – Ireland governed henceforth by Westminster.
1803	Robert Emmet's rising, trial and execution.
1822	Irish Constabulary Act (establishing county police forces and a salaried magistracy).
1823	Catholic Association founded, led by Daniel O'Connell.
1828	O'Connell elected for County Clare.

1829	Catholic Emancipation passed.
1837	Accession of Queen Victoria.
1840	O'Connell's Repeal Association founded.
1842	*The Nation* newspaper founded by Thomas Davis.
1843	O'Connell's 'Monster Meetings' for Repeal of the Union.
1845	Blight in the potato harvest. Beginning of Great Famine (1845–49).
1846	Repeal of Corn Laws. August sees Public Works started but stopped due to expectation of new harvest. Total failure of potato harvest. Public Works restarted. October sees first deaths from starvation.
1847	Foundation of Irish Confederation. Free rations first handed out from Government soup kitchens.
1848–49	Worst years of Great Famine. Rebellion by Young Ireland movement. Battle of the Widow McCormack's Cabbage Garden at Ballingarry.
1858	After James Stephens returns from France he establishes the Irish Republican Brotherhood. Fenian Brotherhood founded in the USA.
1861	Beginning of American Civil War.
1866	Archbishop Paul Cullen becomes the first Irish Cardinal.
1867	Attempted Fenian rising.
1869	Disestablishment of the Church of Ireland by W.E. Gladstone's government.
1870	Gladstone's first Land Act recognising tenant's right (August) and the foundation of Home Government Association by Isaac Butt (September).
1875	Charles Stewart Parnell elected MP for County Meath.
1879	Threat of famine in Ireland. Irish National Land League founded, instigated by Michael Davitt, widespread evictions.
1879–82	Land War.
1881	Gladstone's second Land Act.
1891	Parnell marries Katherine O'Shea (June), dies at Brighton (October).
1893	Second Home Rule Bill. Gaelic League founded.
1898	United Irish League founded.
1900	John Redmond elected chairman of Irish Parliamentary Party and United Irish League.
1907	Dockers' strike and riots in Belfast.
1914	Illegal importation of arms by Ulster Volunteers and Irish Volunteers. Buckingham Palace conference collapses just before outbreak of World War I.
1915	Reorganisation of the Irish Republican Brotherhood and formation of military council (December).
1916	Irish Republic proclaimed in Dublin (24 April). There follows martial law, rebel surrender, imprisonments and 15 executions. The Ulster Division also loses significant numbers in the Battle of the Somme.
1917	The Irish Convention ineffectual and Sinn Féin and Irish Volunteers reorganise.
1918	The General Election sees Republican success and the formation of Dáil Éireann in following January.
1920	The Government of Ireland Act introduces partition between two Home Rule states. Dublin's 'Bloody Sunday'.
1921	IRA setback. King opens Northern Ireland Parliament in Belfast. Sir James Craig Prime Minister in Northern Ireland. A truce is called. December witnesses Anglo-Irish Treaty.
1922	Convention of Anti-Treaty IRA. 'Special' powers given to Northern Ireland police. National Army given emergency powers after murder of Collins. Irish Free State established, Northern Ireland excluded.

1923	End of Civil War – IRA 'dump arms'. Free State admitted to League of Nations.
1924	National Army re-organisation, cutbacks and mutiny.
1925	Partition confirmed by tripartite agreement.
1926	De Valera founds Fianna Fáil. General election in Free State.
1929	Proportional representation abolished in Northern Ireland.
1930	Irish Labour Party and TU Congress separate.
1931	Banning of the IRA in Free State.
1932	In the general election Fianna Fáil prove successful.
1933	National Guard (Blueshirts) formed. United Ireland Party (Fine Gael) formed under O'Duffy (Blueshirts leader).
1934	Cosgrave reinstated as O'Duffy resigns.
1935	Importation and sale of contraceptives banned in Free State.
1936	Free State Senate abolished.
1937	Constitution of Éire replaces Free State.
1938	UK agree to subsidise Northern Ireland Social Welfare payments to UK standards.
1939	IRA bombing campaign on Great Britain in World War II. Éire neutral.
1940	Death of IRA hunger strikers in Éire. Anglo-Irish military consultations. Economic sanctions imposed on Éire.
1941	The most destructive German air raids on Belfast and Dublin. Death of James Joyce.
1945	Congress of Irish Unions formed after split in Trade Union Congress. Churchill's and de Valera's radio speeches post-World War II.
1946	Northern Ireland National Insurance aligned with Great Britain.
1948	NHS introduced in Northern Ireland — Irish Republic enacted after Costello's repeal of External Relations Act. Fianna Fáil lose election, de Valera out of office after 16 years.
1949	Ireland Act, agreement that partition will be perpetuated.
1954	IRA attacks in Armagh.
1955	Republic admitted to UNO.
1956–62	Border campaign initiated by IRA.
1958	First programme for economic growth in the Republic.
1961	Republic unsuccessful in joining EEC.
1964	Lemass-O'Neill talks held on reconciliation.
1966	Anglo-Irish Free Trade Agreement.
1967	NI Civil Rights Association founded.
1968	First Civil Rights march. Clash in Derry between CRA and police. O'Neill's programme for the removal of discrimination against Catholics in local government, housing and franchise.
1969	People's Democracy march from Belfast to Derry in January. There follows a series of explosions. Chichester Clark becomes Prime Minister. British troops sent in.
1970	Dublin Arms Trial. Splits in Sinn Féin and IRA lead to provisional factions setting up.
1971	Paisley's Democratic Unionist Party founded. Re-introduction of internment. First British soldier killed by IRA in Belfast.
1972	Following Derry's Bloody Sunday in January, Direct Rule is imposed.
1973	Republic, UK and NI join EEC. Proportional representation restored in NI (December). Sunningdale Agreement.

1974	Multiple deaths in Dublin bombing. Guildford and Birmingham pub bombings in November and December.
1975	NI internment suspended.
1976	British ambassador in Dublin killed. Republic's Emergency Powers Bill referred to Supreme Court by President.
1978	Twelve killed by Provisionals' fire bombs in a Co. Down restaurant.
1979	Earl Mountbatten and relations killed in Co. Sligo. Eighteen soldiers killed at Warrenpoint, Co. Down. Relaxation of Republic's ban on contraceptives.
1979	Visit of Pope John Paul II.
1981	Following the death of Republican hunger-strikers, the Provisionals' strategy of 'H-block' protests collapses.
1982	Mass killings of soldiers at Knightsbridge (July) and Ballykelly, Co. Derry, (December).
1983	Referendum bans abortion in Republic.
1985	Bitter Protestant disagreement over Anglo-Irish Agreement at Hillsborough.
1986	Confirmation of Republic's ban on divorce.
1987	Eleven killed by IRA before Enniskillen service on Remembrance Sunday.
1989	Fianna Fáil form coalition government for the first time in their history following general election. Their partners are the Progressive Democrats. Charles Haughey remains Taoiseach.
1990	Republic of Ireland reach quarter-finals of the soccer world cup in Italy under the management of Jack Charlton.
1990	Mary Robinson elected seventh President of Ireland, the first woman to hold the office.
1992	Dr Eamon Casey, Bishop of Galway, flees country after it was revealed that he had fathered a child in the course of an affair nearly 20 years previously. The first of a succession of sexual scandals that eroded the authority of the Catholic Church in the course of the decade.
1994	IRA and Loyalist paramilitary groups announce ceasefire.
1996	In the Republic of Ireland, a constitutional referendum to permit civil divorce and re-marriage is carried narrowly.
1996	Canary Wharf bombing marks end of IRA ceasefire.
1997	Following Labour victory in British general election, Dr Marjorie (Mo) Mowlam appointed first woman Secretary of State for Northern Ireland.
1997	Fianna Fáil-PD coalition under Bertie Ahern replaces Rainbow coalition (Fine Gael, Labour, Democratic Left) following general election in the Republic.
1997	IRA declare a resumption of the 1994 ceasefire (July).
Autumn 1997–Spring 1998	Former US Senator, George Mitchell, chairs negotiations at Stormont.
10 April 1998	Good Friday Agreement signed by all parties except DUP.
2 May 1998	Agreement ratified by large majorities throughout Ireland.
15 August 1998	Omagh bombing kills 31 and dashes euphoria.
2 December 1999	After several failed attempts, new devolved power-sharing government meets for first time.
11 February 2000	Northern Executive suspended because of Unionist insistence on IRA decommissioning.
1 June 2000	Executive restored after IRA commitment 'to put arms beyond use'.

BIBLIOGRAPHY

Aalen, F.H.A., Kevin Whelan & Matthew Stout (eds), *Atlas of the Irish Rural Landscape,* Cork University Press, 1997.

Andrews, J.H., *Ireland in Maps,* Dolmen Press, 1961.

Bagwell, Richard, *Ireland Under the Tudors,* Longman, 1885–90. *Ireland Under the Suarts,* Longman, 1909–16.

Bardon, Jonathan, *A History of Ulster,* Blackstaff, 1992.

Barnard, T.C., *Cromwellian Ireland: English Government and Reform in Ireland, 1649–60,* Clarendon Press, 1975.

Bartlett, Thomas, *The Fall and Rise of the Irish Nation: The Catholic Question, 1690–1830,* Gill & Macmillan, 1992.

Beckett, J.C., *Protestant Dissent in Ireland, 1625–42,* London, 1966.

Bell, J. Bowyer, *The Secret Army: History of the Irish Republican Army, 1916–79,* Gill & Macmillan, 1979.

Bew, Paul, *Land and the National Question in Ireland, 1858–82,* Gill & Macmillan, 1979.

Bowman, John, *De Valera and the Ulster Question, 1917–79,* Oxford, 1972.

Boyce, D. George, *Nineteenth-Century Ireland: The Search for Stability,* Gill & Macmillan, 1990.

Boylan, Henry, *Wolfe Tone,* Gill & Macmillan, 1981.

Bradshaw, Brendan, *The Irish Constitutional Revolution of the Sixteenth Century,* Cambridge University Press, 1979.

Brown, Terence, *Ireland: A Social and Cultural History, 1922–79,* Fontana, 1981.

Buckland, Patrick, *A History of Northern Ireland,* Gill & Macmillan, 1981.

Byrne, F.J., *Irish Kings and High-Kings,* Batsford, 1973.

Canny, Nicholas P., *The Elizabethan Conquest of Ireland: A Pattern Established, 1565–76,* Harvester Press, 1976.

Clarke, Aidan, *The Old English in Ireland, 1625–42,* London, 1966.

Comerford, R.V., *The Fenians in Context: Irish Politics and Society, 1848–82,* Wolfhound, 1985.

Connolly, S.J., *Priests and People in Pre-Famine Ireland, 1780–1845,* Gill & Macmillan, 1982.

Corish, P.J., *A History of Irish Catholicism, 28 fascs in 16,* Gill & Macmillan, 1967–72.

Cosgrove, Art (ed.), *Dublin through the Ages*, Irish Academic Press, 1988.

Cullen, L.M., *An Economic History of Ireland Since 1600*, Batsford, 1976. *The Emergence of Modern Ireland, 1600–1900*, Gill & Macmillan, 1983.

Curtis, Edmund, *A History of Medieval Ireland*, Barnes and Noble, 1983.

Daly, Mary E., *The Famine in Ireland*, Dundalk, 1986.

de Paor, Máire and Liam, *Early Christian Ireland*, Thames & Hudson, 1978.

Dickson, David, Dáire Keogh and Kevin Whelan (eds.), *The United Irishmen: Republicanism, Radicalism and Rebellion*, Lilliput, 1993.

Duffy, Seán, *Ireland in the Middle Ages,* Gill & Macmillan, 1997.

Dwyer, T. Ryle, *De Valera: The Man and the Myths*, Poolbeg, 1991.

Edwards, Nancy, *The Archaeology of Early Medieval Ireland*, Batsford, 1990.

Elliott, Marianne, *Wolfe Tone: Prophet of Irish Independence*, London, 1989.

Ellis, Steven G., *Tudor Ireland: Crown, Community and the Conflict of Cultures, 1470–1603*, Longman, 1985.

Fitpatrick, David, *Politics and Irish Life, 1913–21: Provincial Experience of War and Revolution*, Dublin, 1977.

Flanagan, Marie Therese, *Irish Society, Anglo-Norman Settlers, Angevin Kingship: Interactions in Ireland in the Late Twelfth Century*, Clarendon Press, 1989.

Foster, R.F., *Modern Ireland, 1600–1972*, Penguin, 1988. (ed.) *The Oxford Illustrated History of Ireland*, Oxford University Press, 1989.

Frame, Robin, *Colonial Ireland, 1169–1369*, Helicon, 1981.

Gillespie, Raymond, *Colonial Ulster: The Settlement of East Ulster, 1600–1641*, Cork University Press, 1985.

Graham, B.J. and L.J. Proudfoot (eds), *An Historical Geography of Ireland*, Academic Press, 1993.

Greaves, C.D., *The Life and Times of James Connelly*, London, 1961.

Harbison, Peter, *Pre-Christian Ireland*, Thames & Hudson, 1988. (ed.) *The Shell Guide to Ireland*, Gill & Macmillan, 1989.

Hopkinson, Michael, *Green Against Green: The Irish Civil War*, Gill & Macmillan, 1988.

Hoppen, K.T., *Ireland Since 1800: Conflict and Conformity*, Essex, 1989.

Kelly, Fergus, *A Guide to Early Irish Law*, Dublin Institute for Advanced Studies, 1988.

Kelly, James, *Prelude to Union: Anglo-Irish Politics in the 1780s*, Cork University Press, 1992.

Keogh, Dermot, *Ireland and the Vatican: The Politics of Church-state Relations, 1922–60*, Cork University Press, 1995.

Kinealy, Christine, *This Great Calamity, The Irish Famine, 1845–52*, Gill & Macmillan, 1994.

Laffan, Michael, *The Partition of Ireland, 1911–25*, Dundalk, 1983.

Lee, J.J., *Ireland 1912–75*, Cambridge, 1980.

Lee, Joseph, *Ireland, 1912–85*, Cork University Press, 1989.

Lecky, W.E.H., *Ireland in the Eighteenth Century*, 5 volumes, London, 1892.

Lennon, Colm, *Sixteenth-Century Ireland*, Gill & Macmillan, 1994.

Lydon, James, *The Lordship of Ireland in the Middle Ages*, Gill & Macmillan, 1972. *The Making of Ireland*, Routledge, 1998.

Lyons, F.S.L. (ed.), *Ireland Since the Famine*, Fontana, 1973. *Charles Stewart Parnell*, Fontana, 1978.

Mac Niocaill, Gearóid, *Ireland Before the Vikings*, Gill & Macmillan, 1972.

Meehan, Bernard, *The Book of Kells*, Thames & Hudson, 1994.

Nicholls, Kenneth, *Gaelic and Gaelicised Ireland in the Middle Ages*, Gill & Macmillan, 1972.

MacDonagh, Oliver, *The Hereditary Bondsmam: Daniel O'Connell, 1775–1829*, London, 1988. *The Emancipist: Daniel O'Connell, 1830–49*, London, 1989.

Mansergh, Nicholas, *The Irish Question, 1840–1921*, London, 1965.

Mitchell, Frank, *The Shell Guide to Reading the Irish Landscape*, Country House, 1986.

Mokyr, Joel, *Why Ireland Starved*, Allen & Unwin, 1983.

Moody, T.W., *Davitt and Irish Revolution, 1846–82*, Oxford, 1981.

Moody, T.W. and J.C. Beckett (eds), *Ulster Since 1800: A Political and Economic Survey*, London, 1957.

Moody, T.W., F.X. Martin and J.F. Byrne (eds), *A New History of Ireland*, 9 vols, Clarendon Press, 1976–.

Murphy, Brian P., *Patrick Pearse and the Lost Republican Ideal*, Dublin, 1991.

Norman, E.R., *The Catholic Church and Ireland in the Age of Rebellion, 1859–73*, London, 1965.

Nowlan, K.B. (ed.), *The Making of 1916: Studies in the History of the Rising*, Dublin, 1969.

Ó Corráin, Donncha, *Ireland before the Normans*, Gill & Macmillan, 1972.

Ó Cróinín, Dáibhí, *Early Medieval Ireland 400–1200*, Longman, 1995.

O'Ferrall, Fergus, *Daniel O'Connell*, Gill & Macmillan, 1981.

Ó Gráda, Cormac, *A New Economic History, 1780–1939*, Oxford, 1994.

O'Kelly, M.J., *Early Ireland*, Cambridge University Press, 1989.

O'Neill, Timothy, *Merchants and Mariners in Medieval Ireland*, Irish Academic Press, 1987).

Orpen, G.H., *Ireland under the Normans*, 4 vols, Oxford University Press, 1912–20.

O'Ríordáin, S.P., *Antiquities of the Irish Countryside*, Methuen, 1979.

Otway-Ruthven, A.J., *A History of Medieval Ireland*, Ernest Benn, 1968, 1980.

Pakenham, Thomas, *The Year of Liberty: The Great Irish Rebellion of 1798*, Dublin, 1969.

Richardson, H.G. and G.O. Sayles, *The Irish Parliament in the MiddleAges*, Philadelphia: University of Pennsylvania Press, 1952.

Seymour, St. J. D., *Anglo-Irish Literature, 1200–1582*, Cambridge University Press, 1929.

Simms, J.G., *The Williamite Confiscation in Ireland, 1690–1703*, London, 1958.

Simms, Katharine, *From Kings to Warlords: The Changing Political Structure of Gaelic Ireland in the Later Middle Ages*, Boydell & Brewer, 1987.

Smith, Jim, *The Men of No Property: Irish Radicals and Popular Politics in the Late Eighteenth Century*, Dublin, 1992.

Smyth, Alfred P., *Celtic Leinster: Towards a Historical Geography of Early Irish Civilisation, AD 500-1600*, Irish Academic Press, 1982.

Stalley, Roger, *The Cistercian Monasteries of Ireland*, Yale University Press, 1987.

Taylor, Rex, *Michael Collins*, London, 1958.

Vaughan, W.E., *Landlords and Tenants in mid-Victorian Ireland*, Oxford, 1994.

Watt, John A., *The Church and the Two Nations in Medieval Ireland* Cambridge University Press, 1970.

Whyte, J.H., *Church and State in Modern Ireland, 1923–79*, Gill & Macmillan, 1984.

Woodham-Smith, Cecil, *The Great Hunger*, Hamish Hamilton, 1987.

Younger, Calton, *Ireland's Civil War*, London, 1968.

INDEX

References in this index in **bold** face are maps and in *italic* face are illustrations. References to monarchs denote Kings/Queens of England/Britain unless otherwise specified.

ACKNOWLEDGEMENTS

The publishers would like to thank the following:

Linzi Simpson   11, 26, 35, 41, 54, 62, 73, 95, 97, 98, 123, 124, 125, 163, 173, 220, 208, 216, 220, 223, 237, 239
The Ulster Museum   12, 155
Office of Public Works, Dublin   15, 19
A. Purcell   18
National Gallery of Ireland   22, 146, 150
Liam Blake   27
National Museum of Ireland, Dublin   28, 29, 61, 57, 131, 189 (bottom)
Margaret Keane and Conor McDermott   30
Department of the Environment, Northern Ireland   33, 105
The Dublin Institute of Advanced Studies   41
Con Brogan   46
Trinity College, Dublin   52
Private Collection   74, 183, 218
Public Record Office, London   76
Trustees of the British Museum   81, 114, 119
Commissioners of Public Works in Ireland   84
Fiona Gunn   85
National Library of Ireland, Dublin   88, 102, 136, 138, 140, 145, 166, 169, 178, 180, 186, 199, 202, 204–205, 206, 209
Peter Newark Historical Pictures   93, 100, 132, 137
Roger Stalley   94
National Picture Gallery   108
British Library   120
Leeds City Art Gallery   135
The Illustrated London News   157, 161, 164
St Patrick's College, Drumcondra   165
Hulton Picture Library   168, 192, 193
Kilmainham Gaol   174, 187, 189 (top), 190
Irish Life   181
Municipal Gallery of Modern Art, Dublin   185
Lafayette   194
Trustees of the Imperial War Museum   197
The Illustrated London News and *Sketch Ltd*   201
Oldham Art Gallery, Lancashire   207
Military Archives, Dublin   210
Irish Tourist Board   212
Crawford Municipal Art Gallery, Cork   214
Industrial Development Agency of Ireland   221
Belfast Telegraph   225, 229
Camera Press   226, 227
Public Relations Section, Defence Forces Headquarters   232
National Museum Photo Library   233
Army Information Service   234

Illustrations: Peter A.B. Smith

Cartography and Design: Peter Gamble, Isabelle Lewis, Jeanne Radford, Malcolm Swanston and Jonathan Young for Arcadia Editions Limited, England